As I Was Burying
Comrade Stalin

As I Was Burying Comrade Stalin

My Life Becoming a Jewish Dissident

ARKADY POLISHCHUK

McFarland & Company, Inc., Publishers

Jefferson, North Carolina

Library of Congress Cataloguing-in-Publication Data

Names: Polishchuk, Arkady, 1930– author.
Title: As I was burying comrade Stalin : my life becoming a Jewish dissident / Arkady Polishchuk.
Description: Jefferson, North Carolina : McFarland & Company, Inc., Publishers, 2020 | Includes index.
Identifiers: LCCN 2020006946 | ISBN 9781476680200 (paperback : acid free paper) ∞
ISBN 9781476638171 (ebook)
Subjects: LCSH: Polishchuk, Arkady, 1930—Childhood and youth. | Polishchuk, Arkady, 1930- | Dissenters—Soviet Union—Biography. | Jews—Soviet Union—Biography. | Jews, Russian—United States—Biography. | Jewish journalists—Soviet Union—Biography. | Journalists—Russia—Biography. | Mascow (Russia)—Biography
Classification: LCC PN5276.P635 A3 2020 | DDC 070.4/3092 [B]—dc23
LC record available at https://lccn.loc.gov/2020006946

British Library cataloguing data are available

ISBN (print) 978-1-4766-8020-0
ISBN (ebook) 978-1-4766-3817-1

Front cover image: Red Square in Moscow © 2020 Taiga/Shutterstock

Printed in the United States of America

McFarland & Company, Inc., Publishers
Box 611, Jefferson, North Carolina 28640
www.mcfarlandpub.com

The longer you can look back, the farther you can look forward.—Winston Churchill

Table of Contents

Preface

This memoir is about growing up and coming of age in Stalinist Russia in turbulent times that began before World War II, went on during the war years, and continued after the dictator's death in 1953. The book starts in 1930, with the day of my birth, and encompasses 28 years of my life. One-third of the book is written through a child's eyes. Being born into captivity made me unable to understand that I worshiped my slaveholder. Later, despite resentment and injustice this Jewish urchin experienced, my love for Stalin persisted until I realized that Stalin had been preparing the country for the next Holocaust. Nonetheless, communism still was my religion, and I believed in the building of the egalitarian Heaven on Earth. Culturally Russian, this assimilated Moscow Jew considers my Jewish identity exclusively as my ethnicity.

In 1956, I began working at a provincial newspaper and discovered that the vast majority of Stalinists did not lose their high positions. During my extensive travels, often in hard to reach places, I met with destitute plowmen, teenage milkmaids, and yesterday's prisoners, now tipsy woodcutters. Attempts of the Party elite to put an end to my journalistic career led to the collapse of this young reporter's ideological and political illusions.

My human rights activities have been covered by American and European media. In 1977, I was stripped of Soviet citizenship. For years, I worked as a Radio Liberty correspondent in Washington, Munich, and Prague.

I hope that this memoir by a rare eyewitness and participant of long-past but still relevant events will attract a wide variety of readers interested in the firsthand tale of a brainwashed non-religious young Jew, in the unfolding drama of my life, and those who are concerned about present-day attempts to revive Russia as a superpower. Scholars and students in the fields of American and Russian politics, human rights, sociology, history, Slavic, Jewish and religious studies, philosophy, and the Holocaust should all be part of my audience.

This book is the prequel to *Dancing on Thin Ice,* published in 2018.

A Cow in My Room and Other Well-Established Facts of My Life

I could not foresee that my arrival at a new, revolutionary type of dwelling from a maternity hospital would have political consequences for my entire life. Newborns usually stay away from politics. Carefully unwrapped from my thick quilt and a sheet underneath, I settled into the communal apartment of a two-story house overlooking the frozen Moscow River. By that early March in 1930, apartment ownership in the Soviet Union had been abrogated, and, according to Russian Marxists, the coexistence of several families in one apartment strengthened the worldwide proletarian fraternity.

There is something disturbing in the inability to remember your first adventures, as a toddler I clearly remember there was a cow who lived in our room and kept staring at me, her enormous horned head often hanging over my little body. Eight days later, during a time when my father, Papa, proudly paraded on his lapel the membership badge of the Godless Atheists' Union, I was secretly circumcised. Innocent, uninformed, and an integral part of Mama's being, I was busy suckling her milk, oblivious to my involvement in this political controversy. When she was somewhere else, our childless neighbor Nina Timofeevna comforted me with her aging milk-less breast. The woman laughed when I shrilly protested against her attempt to extract her Orthodox cross out of my mouth. "Should we ask some rabbi what would happen to our circumcised baby if he swallowed a cross?" Papa said then. "A split personality?"

One spring day a drayman, the husband of Nina Timofeevna, raised this baby to the muzzle of his carthorse, Venera (Venus). She studied me, dilating her nostrils, and was very happy; since then intelligent Venera often paid attention to my growing presence in her world.

3

It was scary, although I knew this mammoth was a friend. My only protection from this head, half the size of my bed, was a thin horizontal bar. I did not know then that cows could not live on the second floor, and later, as a mature five-year-old, I asked Papa for her name. The adult population of our apartment urgently discussed this matter of the big cow. All three families were good friends, in their thirties. Papa, known for his sharp tongue, made up all kinds of silly adult explanations, but nobody wanted to share the real story with me. That was unfair; I had already taught Nina Timofeevna how to read. Finally, Papa disclosed a secret: it was not a cow. I was sick with measles and had a high fever, with a rash covering my face and body. In those years, the disease could be crippling or deadly. We had a German shepherd and, though young and lighthearted, she expressed her concern about my health through deafening barking. Papa and Mama felt uneasy about that and gave the dog to a friend.

I also remembered Comrade Stalin and, as a three-year-old, did not like him. Papa and our neighbor Uncle Israel mentioned this comrade every day after looking at a big sheet of paper they called a newspaper. Once, when I flatly refused to sleep, Papa covered his ear with a porcelain cup, tapped it with a magic spoon he called "phone" or "phony" and joined up with this Comrade Stalin and his friend Comrade Kremlin. He invited them to come to us to bring me to my senses. But they did not come, probably because I fell asleep.

At the age of five, I read Pushkin's tale about a cheapskate priest to the pious Nina Timofeevna. She called the poet a cruel pagan but my aging eleven-year-old sister Maria and I already knew that God did not exist. From Pushkin, we moved to the priceless primer I inherited from Maria. On its first page, there was a picture "Lenin and children" and an introduction by Nadezhda Krupskaya, the famous wife of this very famous founder of our great country. After Nina Timofeevna heard that "Lenin passionately wanted to see children growing up as staunch communists," she smiled wryly and exclaimed, "Sure, who else!" When I ecstatically read the question of Krupskaya, "You'll be a communist, won't you?" my student said, "Only God knows what will happen tomorrow." To teach her a lesson, I asked if God knew the words "collectivization," "industrialization," and "Soviet passport."

"It's better not to know them," she said.

I had borrowed those words from Papa and Uncle Israel's conversations. My luck, Nina Timofeevna did not ask me for their meaning.

One day the drayman and his horse got tired of delivering heavy loads and found an occupation more appropriate for the advanced century of airships, portable gramophones, and enormous wooden radio sets. They began selling kerosene from a light cistern. They were making stops to fill the cans of Muscovites, and his aging lady wife could rest. To discuss these technological advances, I rode up to her on my horse, which had a stick instead of a trunk and legs, but its head was a replica of Venus's head. She nodded approvingly several times.

❖ ❖ ❖

In that wooden house near the river, I had two girlfriends, both much younger than I was. The first time I arrested them, Rita was four years old, her little sister Paulina was three, and both enjoyed the detention. I had everything needed for taking these foreign spies into custody: a tin pistol, a piercing tin whistle, and a firefighter's cardboard helmet. With this red helmet, I looked almost like a real militiaman; the difference in shape and color did not matter to us. We knew that the spies were very nasty people. There was only one bad thing about this game. At times, in the middle of a marvelous arrest, the girls' father, Uncle Israel, would grab me, lift me high in the air, keep me there kicking it for a while, and then put me on his vast lap and begin pinching my cheeks. This old man, twice my dad in all directions, loved pinching my cheeks! Sometimes it was okay, but this time it was especially untimely, annoying, and out of place. He just ignored the deadly weapon in my hand and my loud protests. Fortunately, the spies, as I ordered from that dizzy height, stayed facing a wall adamantly waiting for my release. Being girls and young, they were unable to understand how embarrassing this whole situation was—a law-and-order man treated like an unarmed baby.

My pistol—called a *poogutch*, a frightener, a popgun—looked like a real silver revolver, though small and with nothing inside. It did have one beautiful feature—a bullet called a *probka*, a cork, which wasn't really a cork or a bullet. One could insert it into the open end of the barrel, and after that, you could aim at somebody and pull the trigger and, with the sound of a real shot, this thing would fly and hit the enemy, say a cat or a spy. I begged Papa to buy me at least one cork from the Chinese; they visited all Moscow courtyards with sacks of valuables, but he told me about a boy whose eye such a bullet burned out, and the boy was unable to join the Red Army and fight our despicable enemies. I was determined to confront them one day. Papa didn't want me to miss a chance of joining our Red Army.

The neighborhood urchins looked down on me. They had the corks. It was especially humiliating when in the twilight, real fire and smoke were coming out of their barrels, and to add to this insult, all of a sudden, Mama would appear in the window tactlessly demanding, "Alik, it's time to go to bed!"

At this tragic moment, I pretended that my popgun was full of murderous corks, I mean bullets, and, while retreating in the direction of my bed, I yelled from a creaky wooden balustrade that in the evening my many corks were turning into tracer bullets. Those boys could use only one cork at a time.

◆ ◆ ◆

Our communal kitchen served as a club, theater, political forum, and circus where we sang patriotic songs, danced, and played games—cards, checkers, lotto, hide-and-seek, and noisy dominoes. I pounded these bony blocks on the table much louder than other participants of this game of chance did. Papa and Uncle Israel preferred chess, but they were busy working and played on rare occasions. When I borrowed their wooden chess horses for better use in my war games, they couldn't play their boring game, and our kitchen turned into a courtroom again. The hardened old offender pledged to never again steal the lousy horses, never experiment with the meat grinder, Mama's sewing machine, and never use expensive coal for writing on walls and on girls' faces. I also promised not to touch a kerosene stove. Yes, the kitchen and I smelled like this slow cooker for a couple of days, but to kindle it was the only way to figure out how its wick drew fuel from the flat tank to the burner. I also promised nevermore to release a mouse from the mousetrap, not on my life leave the yard, and never ever play near the river. I repented with heartfelt tears, but soon, under the influence of subconscious impulses, broke the law again.

In quieter days, I enjoyed sitting on a footstool in front of the kitchen stove and looking at the red-hot coals building unpredictable mountains in the dead ashes or at the dancing flames of crackling firewood, shooting erratic sparks. Lately, the two sisters had been irritating and kept trying to close the cast iron door of the stove. When I used my muscle power to resist, the tattletales, interrupting each other, complained to our moms, Nina Timofeevna, and my sister Maria. They tried to convince me that if just one spark would miss the square iron sheet nailed to the floor, then all of us, and Venera down there in her stall, would die in the fire. That was ridiculous. But I didn't want to upset them; after all, I loved them and didn't argue with them too much, keeping in mind what Uncle Israel had told me as man to man about women: girls didn't always appreciate the real pleasures of life. I asked Papa, who left so many burn marks outside that iron sheet. He kissed my curls and said, "There was a little boy who lived here. He loved to stare at the fire. Just like you."

Only many years after my childhood, when I had almost grown into an adult, Papa told me that a year before I had entered this world, my seven-year-old brother Jacob had drowned in the Moscow River, close to home. They never talked about him. However, on rare occasions, even years after I got married, Mama would call me by his nickname—*Yashenka*. A fear-filled invocation in Yiddish always followed this slip of the tongue; she never interpreted its meaning.

◈ ◈ ◈

When I was approaching six, we moved to a house made of brick. It was a high-rise in the center of Moscow, at Tverskoy Yamskoy Lane, and, with a sinking heart, I looked at the distant land from the dizzy height of our top fifth floor. We didn't need coal or firewood anymore. For some stupid reason, the paunchy radiators of central heating were half-hidden under both windowsills, and it made it impossible to turn them into a reconnaissance aircraft, although I drew on them our red five-pointed stars and stuck out there our world-famous red flag.

One troublesome feature of this modern building made it worse than the old house. It had an attic. The wooden house also had something that passed as an attic, but there were no stairs or a door leading there. Sometimes rain dripped through the rusted roof, leaving wet stains on our ceiling and our neighbors were bringing to us their pots and troughs. Two brave uncles in the soldiers' shirts were putting silvery patches on our roof, and it was fun to watch them working with a sliding wooden ladder and learning their thought-provoking words loosely related to their mothers and some parts of human bodies. Once one of them called his partner a Jew-boy and a Half-Dick. This half-of-Dick became, I didn't know why, very angry and threatened to throw his partner from the roof.

In our new dwelling, while in bed in the evening, I heard rustles and muffled steps in the attic above our room. It was scary. While climbing to our top floor, I was all ears beginning on the third floor and panicky by the fourth, right in front of my buddy Shurik Khazainov's apartment. I envied my Aunt Riva (Rebecca)—her place had a dozen doorbells, each with an electrical cord leading along the corridor walls to every neighbor. If our new apartment had four doorbells, I would have needed to push this button only once instead of three times. A split second was of vital importance. Occasionally, during the daytime, Shurik and I would overcome fear and walk up the two short staircases; together, we would push open the attic's stubborn iron-plated door and enter a gloomy world in which we felt like we were inside the ghastly still skeleton of a gigantic fairy-tale animal. It was a long way from our entrance #1 to the farthest entrance #4. We were slowly advancing under the long wooden ridge—the backbone of this pale creature, between the unfriendly wooden ribs of the carcass; they supported the sloping sides of the iron sheet roof. Dusty daylight was penetrating small, dirty windows. With every step we made, the floor was breathing like a living beast. The large coarse grains and crushed stones were releasing dark puffs toward our noses. We were sneezing.

Once, after the endless journey to the entrance #4 through three more landings, after opening several iron-plated doors, we walked to the last roof window, stepped onto a wooden platform under it, considering and reconsidering climbing out on the slippery roof. A sunbeam filled with dancing dust hit Shurik in his eyes and he closed them tight; they remained squeezed when the sun disappeared behind clouds. I said, "Open your eyes."

Shurik didn't. Maybe he was waiting for the sunbeam to strike his face again and I said, "The clouds are getting thick."

"I have a *papa*," he said in his squeaky voice.

"What?" I said.

"I have a *papa*," he squeaked again.

"Good," I said. "Open your eyes."

Now he looked at me with his big eyes wide open and drawlingly whispered, "I ha-a-ve a *Pa-a-a-pa*."

"So? Everybody has one."

"Mama told me that I have a *papa*." Vigorous nodding and shaking of his head accompanied his every word. "I didn't know."

"So, good, now you know. It's good to have a dad."

"But Mama told me not to tell you, not to tell in the kindergarten, not to tell when I go to school, when I go to the Red Army. Nobody in the world should know that I have a dad."

"Maybe she doesn't like him anymore."

"She loves him and me, and Papa loves us, too. Everybody loved him and now his friends turned their heads away when they saw Mama," he panted, "in the street."

"Maybe he killed someone," I suggested.

"Swear that you'll never tell anybody about him," said Shurik.

"Sure thing," I said. "Don't worry."

"No-no! You swear!"

"May my tongue and hand wither and drop off," I said.

"No-no! It's not good enough!" He banged his fist on a wooden beam.

Then I bulged out my chest and said, "I salute all our leaders and swear by their hallowed names!"

That was the paramount solemn oath of all Soviet boys and girls. I would never dare to break this oath. It would be like telling a lie to Comrade Stalin himself. I could lie to Mama and Papa, but not to Comrade Stalin.

"She cried," Shurik said. "We think he's far away from Moscow."

"Yes," I said with conviction. "To keep the state secrets, his chiefs forbade him to visit you."

"Recently many spies were arrested in Moscow," said Shurik.

"I know," I said. "I read Papa's paper. Some uncle pretended to be a good Communist and even traveled to fight Fascists in Spain, but turned out to be a traitor helping foreign spies."

It was getting murky; the skeleton was beginning to return to life. What recently looked like a dirty window now turned into a glassy eye; it was quickly darkening. We hurriedly stepped from the platform back on the deceptive floor, opened the last plated door, stepped on the last landing, and ran down the stairs, laughing with relief. We were rushing to get out on the cobblestoned yard through entrance #4.

By the color of my face, dusty shirt, and dirty hands, Mama instantly determined that we had been surveying the attic again. She was nuts about cleanliness. My parents boiled water on a primus and a *kerosinka* in the kitchen and forced me to sit in a tin washtub in the center of our room. They mixed hot water with cold, poured it upon my head and body, and kept schlepping pots and kettles back and forth. I kept yelling, "It's too hot! It's too cold!" but, my luck, I continued to grow and once the water overflowed the banks of the tub. Papa began taking me once a week, sometimes every ten days, to a luxury place called a municipal public bathhouse, just 25 minutes away, including 10 minutes' walk to a streetcar stop. It was quite a show to see a hundred naked men and boys carrying galvanized tubs with hot water around a huge hall filled with steam. We were better off than others, and, for a fee, a philosophically minded attendant took care of my father's corns and toenails, while Papa, wrapped in a thin sheet, discussed with him political matters of different importance. Once they debated an article in *Pravda*. Class enemies tried to blow up our railways, poison our wells and ruin our crops. I asked if they also could spoil our weather.

"Quite possibly," the attendant said and looked at me approvingly. Papa explained that class enemies were greedy peasants called *kulaki*, illiterate priests, corrupt intelligentsia, and enemies of socialism. I pretended to understand all this rubbish.

There Is No God, but the Devil Frightens Me Every Day

Shurik's mother was coming home late and did not have time for cooking or for washing him in their baby-size washtub. My parents pitied him, and when we played with tin soldiers for too long in his apartment, Mama was bringing hot lunch for both of us. One day she came down with two pieces of gefilte fish. Shurik sniffed his piece and asked, "What is this?"

"Jewish fish," I said.

"A Jew-fish?"

"No, a fish for Jews."

"Can a Russian eat it?"

"I'm a Jew," I said.

"I know, the boys in the yard told me."

"What did they say?"

"That Jews are stingy and tricky cowards."

"And what did you tell them?"

"That you aren't a Jew."

"Why?"

"Because you aren't tricky and stingy and you're brave."

"And what did they say?"

"That you're okay, but all other Jews are no good. They also said that Jews, when a child is born, cut off a huge part of the baby's penis and that is why a Jewish penis is much shorter than the Russian one. Show me yours."

I unbuttoned my pants and pulled the thing out.

"Yours is short and thick," Shurik jabbed his finger at my penis.

"Oh!" I yelled. "Sharp nails!"

He shook his head in sympathy, "That's why it's so short."

"Ask your mom to cut your nails," I said. "Show me yours."

After studying his penis, I jabbed my finger at it and concluded, "Yours is like a long worm. Mine is better. You know what? Tomorrow we'll recheck everything. Papa promised your mom to take you to the public bath."

Our neighbors suspected us of peeing in our communal kitchen taps. They were wrong. We risked bringing our world to the brink of war only when we became taller. We did it if the toilet was occupied for too long or for the sake of thrills. The neighbors used the small sink with a cold-water tap for washing dishes, pots, hands, and faces.

Not everybody in the public bathhouse liked our field research. The evidence was inconclusive anyway. We were splashing hot water from our round tubs into each other when a large man approached our long stone bench and said that we insolently studied his member. Papa demanded an explanation, and I had to admit that we were looking for an adult Jew whose parents cut his penis in half when he was a baby.

"Why did you take me for a Jew?" the man asked.

"You have curly hair," Shurik said cautiously.

"On the head and your chest," I specified.

"Just like Alik," my friend clarified.

"I have it only on my head," I said.

They laughed like mad and Papa explained that Jews cut out a tiny piece of skin from the tip of their babies' penises. "This tradition is thousands-years-old," he said.

"Did you do that to me?" I asked, with a lot of pain in my voice. "Why?"

"To avoid certain illnesses. We'll discuss it at home," he said.

"Boys, you're lucky," the big man guffawed again, "my best friend is Jewish, and he doesn't have curls. Anywhere."

After that incident, it has become crystal clear that my Jewishness had little to do with what was hidden in my pants; it had much more to do with the shape of my nose, with Mama's gefilte fish, and with my grandfather's visits. Sometimes, always in the spring, he would bring from Ukraine a wooden trunk full with gifts for me and my sister Maria (Manechka); he would place it on our floor next to my parents' bed and, on his knees, extract from it unshelled walnuts, raisins, and these mysterious squares called matzo. He talked about a certain Pesach and preferred the language my parents called Yiddish. They sometimes used it to hide something from their children; in fact, Mama wrapped in Yiddish endings Russian and Ukrainian words and this amused us. For the parents, there was no other way out but to join us with laughter. Once, before grandfather's arrival, Papa took from his lapel the badge of the Godless Atheists' Union and said that for years Grandpa was giving to his synagogue one-tenth of his meager income. Mama used matzo on gefilte fish stuffing only when he was in town; otherwise, she would not waste it and used the regular white bread instead. Grandpa was a vendor, an ancient occupation of adventurous man, traveling with needles, buttons, ribbons, and other valuable merchandise on his back, with unpredictable consequences for a bearded Jew in a long black coat in Ukrainian villages. Luckily for him, Grandpa died from stomach cancer before the war, in 1940 and did not witness the torturous death of his wife and daughter the next summer, after the Germans occupied Kiev.

◈ ◈ ◈

I was about seven years old when our family was staying in Kiev, the capital of Ukraine. We were sitting at the table, and Grandma was walking around it, approaching only the men with an unhappy chicken in her hands and praying in an unfamiliar language. When she was cruelly swinging the white bird three times around my head, I hoped that it would not drop on my head. My understanding of the happening was similar to that of the fowl. Only in America was I to find out that it was to die soon on the chopping block to become a kosher gift for some needy family. Kapparot, the mystical ritual of my ancestors, was about returning to G-d and repentance; we were readying for the Day of Atonement—Yom Kippur. Medieval Jewish sages called this tradition a foolish pagan custom. At seven, I would certainly agree with them.

We were very progressive. Fairy tales like *One Thousand and One Nights* were more exciting, and pictures in this thick book were far more beautiful than the painted on boards emaciated unsmiling people the know-nothings worshiped. Yet, my atheist father introduced me to a frightening religious event. He bought me a selection of Nikolai Gogol's works.

My parents went to Mama's sister Aunt Riva. I was alone in the entire apartment. In the hope that the new good read would divert me from this disturbing fact, I lay on my tummy on a sofa, my bed and reading quarters, and picked "Viy" for its strange title. In the beginning, it was a funny fairy tale, but soon, for the first time in my life, I was reading a horror story about a real event in a strange part of old Russia called Ukraine. Here's how it went:

At a queer farmstead, a student of theology, Khoma Brut, was half-asleep in a sheep's stall when a witch with flashing eyes, wrapped in sheepskin, sprang like a cat onto his shoulders; striking Khoma with a besom, she forced him to gallop like a horse all over the countryside. Since that moment, I had to pay attention to both her riding of this seminarian and to the rustling in the attic above me. To my delight, after chanting prayers, the witch couldn't stand, Khoma managed to jump in turn on her back while beating her with a stick. She collapsed and turned into a dying beauty with long eyelashes. It didn't surprise me; I already knew about a frog turning into a princess and felt now a bit better, but not for long. Khoma had to read psalms over her coffin for three days and nights in the wooden church, black with age. That would be ridiculous if it was not trustworthy and scary. I didn't like churches. All Moscow churches were closed because the priests did not like those who loved reading ungodly books. "How would those ignorant priests know what book is ungodly and what is godly?" Papa said. He read only newspapers.

This student of theology was afraid of darkness just like me; that is why he lit so many candles in that abandoned church. The first day and the first night the witch, sitting upright in her black coffin, was flying around the church, walking close by him gnashing her teeth and unable to get him because he had drawn a charmed circle around himself. The next night winged demons with flaming eyes and claws joined her, but Khoma was invisible to them. On the third night they brought terrible iron-faced *Viy* into the church, drew up his closed enormous eyelids, and he pointed at Khoma with his iron finger. Now the creatures leaped upon him, and he dropped dead from horror.

With all the lights on, I waited for my parents to return home. Khoma believed in the power of prayer, in God, and the devil. In the daylight, I knew that such things didn't exist, but for years, in the dark, I believed in the evil forces in the attic and never thought of using prayer as a defense against them. My quick legs were more reliable.

Amid playing war in our courtyard, I often was caught by the arrival of twilight. We soldiers were running between all eight apartment houses of our large housing complex while returning fire, hiding under staircases, taking prisoners and arresting unhappy foreign spies. It was too late. I had to climb the ten landings in the dusky dark. Only half of them, floor landings, had a dim bulb and the last one was on my floor. The stairs to the attic had no light. Up there, in the pitch darkness, diffused shadows of zombies were readying to attack me. My heart was pumping. Often it was even worse: the bulbs were broken or burnt out or unscrewed, or maybe those monsters from the attic had fused the plug. What could I do? This was unbearable. I rushed to the bell, pressed it three times, as rapidly as I could, and after a sec, did it again, and waited and waited and waited for Mama or my sister to come to the rescue.

The School of Life
and Russian Blood
in Jewish Cookies

Our friend Oleg had awesome soldiers, in various colorful uniforms, and a self-propelled tank. It moved from wall to wall, overcoming all the obstacles we erected in its path while the turret with strange letters on it was noisily shooting and turning from side to side. His father was not afraid to travel to the countries preparing to attack us and brought these toys from a city called Paris. For the first time in our lives, Shurik and I saw such a brave man, and I asked his wife if Nikita Nikolayevich was a top-secret Red Army commander.

"Oh no," she laughed, "Milovidov"—she always called him by the last name—"is an outstanding engineer and took part in the construction of the Soviet Pavilion at the Paris World Fair in 1937; now he's been building the Palace of Soviets, the tallest building in the world."

The whole country already celebrated this project; the American Empire State Building would look like a dwarf in comparison with our Palace. Comrade Stalin asked to put on its top a gigantic monument to Vladimir Ilyich Lenin, and Oleg, Shurik and I were very thankful to him for this bright idea. In the end, we concluded that being a builder of the Palace was almost as good as being a commander in the Red Army or a brave border guard or a Soviet secret service man fighting spies and saboteurs.

I shared my new knowledge of the existence of Paris with Lev Junior, the 20-year-old son of my favorite neighbor Alevtina Petrovna, and he pulled from his bookcase a heavy scholarly volume about Napoleon Bonaparte. He had books about theater, history, and wars; I was interested mainly in wars, of course. The very process of reading was sweet and absorbing, though sometimes it was like reading in a language you never knew. Never before had I heard of this little French emperor in a

14

three-cornered hat. I enjoyed the detailed descriptions of his victories, but the maps in that book created an unpleasant problem—the names of places and countries Napoleon conquered were new to me. I wondered how many months it could take for our Red Army to cover on horseback the territories, which my palm could hide in a split second, on this map. The second heavy volume from that shelf was used in Soviet military academies; unfolding and folding its maps made me feel like a participant in those World War I battles. Skipping some dreadful pages, diagrams, and some difficult-to-unfold maps did not affect my military successes.

Impressed by my in-depth knowledge of France, Oleg's parents helped my folks to overcome the persistence of the nasty school principal unimpressed by my reading and counting. He kept stressing my age of seven and a half. Nonetheless, probably out of respect for the builder of the famous Palace of Soviets, he allowed this violation of the law, and I became a first-grader. The school quickly bored me. In several days I didn't hear anything new, they were learning what I had known for years. I was moving restlessly, pinching Oleg, looking around, and hitting my desk with the stupid primer. Lubov Vasilievna looked at me with a critical eye and once asked me to read something in the primer. I began reading with the speed of the seminarian Khoma Brut chanting prayers, but she stopped me and said, "No-no, sound it out!"

"I've been reading since the age of four," I said with dignity.

"I know," she said, "but please sound it out. That's the way we're learning here."

It was ridiculous, I had spent half of my life reading books, counting beyond one thousand, and studying military maps and she wanted me to begin my life anew. One of those dreary days, I couldn't stand it anymore, so I got up and started quietly strolling between school desks.

"Sit down, Alik," said Lubov Vasilievna softly.

"No. I'm taking a walk. I'm tired," I said.

She rose from her chair and began moving toward me. I walked away from her but the wall stopped my advance. The angry teacher was coming at me. I had no choice but to climb on a rear desk shared by a freckled girl with large pink bows on her pigtails and a fellow who sometimes played war with us. The girl began screeching like a fool. At this, Lenya Sharupich seized my leg with both hands; to make the grip stronger, he pressed his cheeky face and bony shoulder to my shin and slobbered right at my pants. Why had he tried to help the teacher? It was treason. I had no choice and several times hit him over the head with my fist, using it like a jackhammer. He began crying and let go of my leg. Now, I was jumping from desk to desk like a mountain goat, and nobody dared to touch me anymore. Lubov Vasilievna was running between the rows, back and forth, reaching out with both hands, trying to catch me. All of a sudden she stopped and went back to her desk. "Children," she said, "let's ignore him."

The lesson continued. When a cute girl called Ella Ivanov, holding her textbook next to my shoe, began reading aloud disyllabic words, I moved my leg to give her more space and, after she finished reading, I jumped to the floor, returned to my desk, and sat quietly next to softly giggling Oleg in anticipation of the upcoming storm.

When Mama came to pick me up, the teacher had a long conversation with her and Sharupich's mother in the empty classroom. Lenya approached me in the corridor to say, "You're a fool. They'll expel you from school, and you'll stay illiterate for the rest of your life."

"Well, I don't care," I said. "I can read, you—can't."

"Anyway, you're a fool." Sharupich sounded like a nice guy.

After ten minutes, I refused to apologize in front of the class but agreed to write a letter asking for forgiveness. It was a victory of a sort; I was the only student capable of writing full sentences, though in block letters.

The school could not interfere with my favorite activity. It continued throughout our first school year in 1938 and when the second school year began. We played war against capitalist bloodsuckers. The commander Minka appointed me as his deputy. I climbed fences faster than others and jumped without hesitation from the roof of a dilapidated single-story barrack right into a snowdrift in the alley behind Building #4. It was not easy; we were armed to the teeth with sticks, rifles cut out of boards, toy pistols, and pockets filled with stones for grenades. For years, Minka, the tallest and oldest member of the neighborhood army, had kept his paramount post. When two dozen soldiers were drilling or marching behind him, I advanced or ran at a jog-trot by the side of the file and loudly repeated commander's orders like "forward!" or "quick march!" or "on the double!"

Lately he, already thirteen, began telling us that all Jews were rich, tricky, and stingy cowards, and once added, "Alik isn't like a Jew, he's bold and can read military maps."

I did not like this and said, "You're brave because your fists are the biggest."

He immediately tried to hit me, but I jumped behind a pale soldier who had recently moved to that dilapidated barrack with a low ceiling, bedbugs, and many out-of-town workers. We called him *Kolkhoznik*; for us townsfolk this official word for a member of a collective farm meant an ignorant villager. He shouted, "Ugh, kike," and hit me in the face. I hit him back, and we began swinging. He fought ferociously. Soon we both had bloodied faces. Minka stopped us and ordered his army to retreat from the front yard to a wasteland behind Building #3. With the wooden barrel of his rifle, he drew a circle in the dirt next to the stinky refuse boxes and said in a businesslike manner, "Let's continue." We stepped into the ring with bits of broken brick and glass, and the fight continued. Everybody knew the rule: if you are a coward, you could step or crawl out of the circle, and this way admit your defeat. After a while, I said, "Listen, *Kolkhoznik*, let's continue tomorrow."

To everyone's surprise, he agreed. The commander considered this turn of events as a mutiny and said, "You're dismissed, not my deputy anymore. Maybe you're a French spy."

I shrugged off his decision and said, "Let's attack rats!" To Minka's dismay, the whole army began throwing stones at innocent rats darting in and out of the tall refuse boxes.

The next day *Kolkhoznik* called me a kike again, a rich kike, and the war stopped to give us a chance to fight. Minka drew a ring in that waste again; we stepped into it and began beating each other. The fight lasted forever. Blood was everywhere—in my mouth, on our shirts, even on our shoes and the ground. I could not breathe. *Kolkhoznik's* eyelids swelled, and for some funny reason, he kept glancing at his shirt. We walked, stumbling, circling each other, waiting for the exhausted enemy to drop his fists. The rank and file excitement began fading away; they stopped yelling and just looked at the two staggering fighters. Oleg Milovidov swore, "*Kolkhoznik*, you're a stupid fuckin' fool."

The commander was critically observing the battlefield. The moment had arrived. He could use his authority. "Stop fighting!" he ordered and I trudged home thinking that now it would be impossible to deceive Mama. It was beginning to look like a hopeless impasse. The next day *Kolkhoznik* called me a kike again, and again we fought. Then all of a sudden, I had a break—for three days my enemy did not come to the yard. However, Minka did not stop hating Jews. I still wanted to prove that the Jews were brave and not stingy, and good friends. I was stealing Mama's cookies; when she didn't bake them, I asked her to make an open sandwich, a piece of white bread with a thick layer of butter covered with plenty of granulated sugar. I ran with that bread to the yard, she never stopped me, and every boy, in turn, took a bite from the piece in my hand. I was also picking change from the coats of Papa, Mama, and Maria and distributing it among the boys. Sister complained, but not the parents.

When *Kolkhoznik* came back, his eyes burned with hatred. His mother could not wash out the blood from his shirt, and his father beat him up. For some unclear reason, I didn't enjoy the news. I would not hate him if only he could shut up, but he couldn't. He came to Moscow from some stupid place where they left his little sister with Grandpa who told him that Jews were spying for Germans, French, and Japanese in past wars; 1,940 years ago, Jews killed the son of a Russian god, and since then they used Russian children's blood for their cooking.

"I'm going to beat up this kike," he said. So all of us again walked to that wasteland, but before signaling the beginning of the fight, Minka rather hesitated. He patted the big self-made red star sewn on his chest and said, "Wait!" More than a dozen boys were waiting. "I have an announcement to make." His leaden eyes looked at me. "Yesterday," he said, "we caught in our kitchen a neighbor pouring Russian blood into Jewish cookies. Jews love Russian blood."

Everybody looked at me. I was lost. I did not know what to do. I stepped up to Minka and hit his potato-like nose. A tiny red stripe began slowly moving out of his nostril down to his lips. I knew that I would never win this fight. I was lucky and lost consciousness instantly when he kicked me right in the gut and fully regained it only after Oleg and a strong fellow nicknamed Mug dragged me to my fifth floor. Mama put me on my sofa, washed my face with a wet towel, put some iodine on the scratches from the broken bricks' shards, and after that gave homemade cookies to my hushed friends. I took the towel from my forehead and asked, still grimacing from the burning iodine, "Aren't you afraid that there is some Russian blood in these cookies?"

"Very tasty blood," Oleg blurted out.

Mug began neighing like a stallion, without stopping his chewing. He was not taking his eyes from three shameful stains on my reputation—oil paintings in golden frames adorning our room.

"Why do they call you a Mug?" I asked him and noticed a motionless old woman with a fixed face sitting in the corner, near a painting and our parents' bed. She had recently come from Ukraine, was my mother's mother, and she annoyed me. I did not consider her as my second grandmother and did not want to know her. She smelled terrible and had nowhere to live. The previous night, I heard an angry whisper of my parents in their bed. After the death of Uncle Misha, Aunt Riva lived alone and wanted to have, as Mama said, a personal life. She had a spacious room with a large window but did not want her mother to live with her. I could not imagine where we could put this ruin with a petrified face to sleep—under the table?

Mug returned me to a more important problem—methods of identifying Jews. "Maybe my round face and round eyes," he said thoughtfully and asked, "Why do they call you a kike?"

"The long nose and curly hair," I guessed.

"You don't have a long nose," Oleg said. "You have a loose tongue."

Mama interrupted us. I saw the tension in her face. "When I was like you boys, in my hometown a Jew, Mendel Beilis, was accused of murdering a Russian boy of your age to use his blood in a matzo." Her voice trembled. "I don't want to talk about it anymore," and she went to the kitchen. A shadow passed over the old woman's face in the corner. My friends did not seem to see her.

"What is matzo?" asked Mug. "A saucer?"

"Jewish cookies," Oleg explained.

That evening, Papa came with good news. He found a tiny room on the outskirts of Moscow for his mother-in-law. She did not thank him, opened her toothless mouth and mumbled, "On your street, a goy called me an old kike."

Papa frowned, pushed his newspaper aside, and grunted something about the Party leaders sentenced to death after they admitted that they were enemies of the people.

"Probably, Comrade Stalin unmasked them," I stepped in.

Papa looked at me gravely, "Do they call you a kike?"

"How d' you know?" I was surprised. "Mama didn't have time to tell you."

"I've known it for two thousand years." He hugged me. "They will never stop saying this; so you have a choice—either to be a proud mensch and fight them for the rest of your life, and, one day, you may be beaten to death, or not to be so proud and learn how to live with this. Keep in mind, they don't know any better."

"Did you learn?" I asked.

"Yes, I did," he said and turned his eyes to the sea in a painting.

"He had to feed his precious children," Mama said.

"During the revolution," Papa said, "we believed that soon all the peoples would become like brothers."

"And now?"

"Now I think it might take fifty more years."

"So I'll be then an old man like you," I did some counting. "In 1988."

"Yes. But you'll be a happy old man," said Papa.

"I told him," the old woman broke her silence again and muttered, disfiguring the Russian words, "I'm proud of it."

I remembered for years how my father turned his eyes from me, glanced at her, and said, "Keep in mind, they don't know any better."

✧ ✧ ✧

The last time we fought, *Kolkhoznik* ran at me holding a stick over his head, and this was against our rules. One could do this only to outsiders invading our territory. Mug tripped him up; he fell on the ground, quickly got up, and looked at his pants, torn to shreds, probably by broken glass. The tough *Kolkhoznik* began crying, "Father will kill me! I don't want to go home! He'll kill me!"

I knew how to help, but would not dare to say. Mama had an old sewing machine called Singer. We never saw *Kolkhoznik* again. Probably his parents could not get a new permit to continue work in this town of rich Jews. I hated Minka more than this hayseed, though. Minka knew that I was a brave soldier; he took my change with a smile and did not miss a chance to eat Mama's cookies and sugary sandwiches. *Kolkhoznik's* disappearance did not solve my problems. Some boys made no secret of their contempt for the Jews, but they tolerated my presence in our yard. A couple of them could easily beat me up but never did it. That was an achievement in itself. Everybody knew that the wealthy Jews worked in grocery stores and ready-made clothes shops and were always trying to steal money or cheat in weighing. When Papa told me that he was the manager of a department store, I felt bad.

"That's why we are so rich?" I asked with pain in my voice.

"To be a thief," he said, "you don't need to be a tradesman."

To cover up this disgrace, I found ways to make my new pants and boots to look worn. To demonstrate the Jewish generosity, I began to "forget" in our communal kitchen our soap after washing my hands in the sink. My attempts to look cool and manly led to new trouble, though sometimes of a noble nature. Until recently, we had been unaware of the very existence of Lithuania, Latvia, and Estonia. In 1940, these nearby Baltic dwarfs finally understood the danger of living near the Western imperialists and cheerfully joined the Soviet Union. Everybody in my neighborhood was happy. From now on, boys could smoke Latvian cigarettes. The Latvian beauty was longer and thinner than the cigarettes stolen from Ducat factory where hundreds of my neighbors worked. They had a similar cardboard holder, but neither had a filter. We were unaware of the very existence of such a sophisticated device.

One summer day, two boys gave me a graceful "Latvian." At once, I squeezed it between my teeth pretending that I was born with this thing sticking out of my mouth; the blond Grizzly with worn-out appearance struck a match, I bent fearlessly over the tiny flame and patiently waited for my cigarette to begin burning. Only one side of the thing caught fire.

"You don't know how to smoke," said Grizzly condescendingly.

"I d-do," I said through my clenched teeth, and energetically wheezed in a huge portion of smoke. My well-wishers began laughing, I began coughing, and the cigarette dropped on the cobblestone, still emitting the smoke. They couldn't stop laughing. I couldn't stop coughing, and torn formations of smoke were emerging from my mouth. The blood rushed to my face, and noisy vomiting now accompanied the coughing. "You know what," Grizzly said magnanimously, "lay down on this bench and relax. When you stop puking, we'll teach you how to smoke in style."

I forced out an "o-k-a-a-y," my spiteful stomach turning inside out.

The dudes were waiting. Gracious smoke rings were melting in the air. They enjoyed life. I promised to pass the stern school of life some other day and was lying on that courtyard bench for a long time. However, this day did not materialize. Less than a year later, the graceful Latvian cigarettes disappeared from our yard. The war began.

Papa Goes to
Fight Germans;
I Go to Weed Tobacco

The door of our carriage compartment opened with a bang and a porter with an argent badge on his sackcloth apron rattled, "The Germans have bombed Kiev!"

It was June 22, 1941. Our train made a stop in Kharkov, a large city in the middle of Ukraine.

"Oh, my God!" Mama said, "Your sister is in Kiev, with Grandma. She had to join us in Dnepropetrovsk."

My new friend, a Red Army commander with three enameled rectangles on his collar exclaimed, "It's a lie! They are our friends! This is a provocation!"

We still heard that narrow-shouldered porter, already at the end of the car, for the fourth or fifth time banging the doors and yelling with Ukrainian accent, "Hitler has bombed Kiev!"

"Sonny, we have to..." Mama almost lost her voice, "...return home at once." Now she was thinking out loud, "We have to get your sister back to Moscow.... Aunt Fanya will bribe a railroad cashier in Kiev..." For the first time in my life I understood the meaning of the word "bribe." "Papa should talk with Grandma from the Central Telegraph ... but she has to come to the city call center ... she's fragile ..." Probably my face reflected bewilderment, and she explained, "He'll send her a wire."

The commander was chain-smoking in the corridor, looking absently out the window all the long way from Kharkov to Dnepropetrovsk. Soon after our departure from Moscow, he allowed me to touch a medal over his chest pocket. I shared with him my newly acquired knowledge and explained that watermelons of this southern city were impossible to lift or embrace and I intended to attack watermelons with a knife and a sharpened spoon right in the field. The commander and Mama laughed. Mama was the source of my expertise, and I could not understand why she continued laughing when I bragged about extracting huge black jackets with sweet seeds from sunflowers taller than I was.

Late in the evening, two unfamiliar men waited for us on the train platform in Dnepropetrovsk. They kissed me, the older relative pinching my cheek just as Uncle Israel did when I was a little kid, and got off the train with our luggage. When Mama and I, with the rest of the load, were leaving the sleeper, I gazed up at the commander, "I want to fight the Germans, too!"

He stroked my curls and said gloomily, "They captured Paris exactly a year ago, today."

Mama did not sleep our only night in Dnepropetrovsk. She and a young woman were emptying our suitcases, trunks, and bags of their cargo of sunflower oil, semolina, pearl, buckwheat, fine-ground barley, oatmeal, laundry soap, and candies, tons of sugar for making jam, utensils, and gifts for the little ones. Early in the morning, this woman, now pale, said to my mother, "Raya, we'll keep intact all your food. Next summer, don't bring anything. Just the children and Abram."

"No-no, please, eat it all," Mama said in a tired voice. "After the war, come to us. I'll show you good stores, the Kremlin, Lenin's Mausoleum, and the All-Union Agricultural Exhibition." She smiled, "Alik will take you to the Palace of the Soviets, the tallest in the world. He's an expert on this building."

Their kids were still asleep when we left the house. The same two men brought us to the station, managed to put us inside the jammed-full train, hugged and kissed us, and stepped back on the platform. Mama gave a deep sigh, pulled down the sleeper's window, and said with a crooked, fabricated smile, "Maybe you should also leave, I don't know…. Remember the Civil War?"

"No, this is our home," the older man said and kissed his hand to me. I waved mine.

"This is Ukraine," Mama said. "Just twenty years ago, everybody—the Whites, bandits, anarchists, even the Reds—were killing the Jews first…. Centuries-old fun…"

Never before had I heard such talk from her. The car clanked to life, starting like the horse Venera, and the train began its slow move forward. My mother kept her head turned, following our relatives as we passed. The passengers, glued to the windows, were eying the gentle sky, maybe thinking of how to jump the train if necessary. These June nights were the shortest of the year.

❖ ❖ ❖

My parents never talked about my Ukrainian relatives again. In that June of 1941, eighty thousand Jews had lived in Dnepropetrovsk. Three days after the Nazis conquered the city, they shot the first group—eleven thousand Jews. Only fifteen men, women, and children survived to the end of the war. I never saw green islands with white beaches and lush meadows in the shady oak woods stretched along the bend of the Dnieper River.

Upon our return home, Papa announced that he was going to join the Red Army. Mama began sobbing. I did not hide my joy. Sixteen-year-old Maria looked scared. Aunt Fanya failed to buy a ticket to Moscow, even for a bribe, and some man, when the train started, pulled my crying sis, by the hand, right from the platform into the car.

The district military commissar told Papa that he was too old to join the military; however, he suggested enigmatically that my father drop by in a week. The colonel himself did not know much about the near future. This time Mama was cheerful, I almost cried, and Papa was disappointed. To our surprise, the next day the city military commissar summoned him. Two senior officers from the People's Commissariat of Internal Affairs (NKVD) called three dozen men in the room the best general managers of Moscow department stores. They were to be in command of military-technical logistics of construction regiments in the front-line area. I knew that Soviet border guards were NKVD soldiers and our secret service men and women, under assumed names risking their lives in the capitalist hell, were NKVD officers. This knowledge made me proud of Papa; I assumed that he knew a thing or two about martial arts, the Morse code, and could jump out of a plane with a parachute.

The first of July 1941 we got up early—right after breakfast he would go to war. So far, one thing worried him more than anything else; Papa pointed at the black speaker that had been hanging on our wall for almost a week and said, "I hope Comrade Stalin isn't ill. After nine days of war, he hadn't addressed the nation on the radio."

From now on, we citizens had only this ten-inch, papier-mache dish, connected to the one and only radio station, to give us news. "Maybe this thing doesn't work well," I guessed.

We had already taken our heavy radio sets to the nearest post office; Papa questioned the military need of the tunable radio receivers' parts. In his opinion, this step protected the population from Fascist propaganda and from spies transmitting coded radio messages. We did not know that our plants were producing radio sets capable of receiving the signal of Soviet radio stations only.

Mama crowded Papa's backpack with food, winter underwear, warm socks, and two of my brand new exercise books for letters. Papa just looked at her silently. He was dressed like Comrade Stalin—in a soldier's green tunic, riding breeches, and shining high boots. He didn't allow Maria and me to go with him. On his way out, Papa stopped, touched the doorframe with his fingertips, and quickly kissed them. I had seen him doing this thing before. It was some innocent habit, he said, that he learned in his childhood. It was just a good luck thing, a kind of little talisman buried in the doorpost. He caught my inquisitive eye and said, "Okay, you're now eleven years old, during the war children mature fast. I don't know when I'll return, nobody knows. I grooved here, in this frame, a right-angled hole, put into it a small roll of parchment in a metal case, and covered it with a layer of white paint; now nobody can see this roughness on the frame." My father faltered. "I don't want Jew-haters to see this mezuzah. The words on that parchment are from the Holy Book." To show that the topic was exhausted, he looked at his watch.

"But you don't believe in God." I was amazed.

"Sonny, all I can say now, for me it's not about the Almighty. It's a tradition."

It could be just a fluke, but recently Papa had taken off his lapel the Union of Godless Atheists' badge. The Union had asked the government to take the final step away from religious influence and to rename all months. Comrade Stalin rejected the idea as unworkable; we had to bow to the necessities of life on the planet shared with backward believers in God. In 1940, the USSR reverted from the revolutionary calendar with its six-day week to the old Gregorian calendar with its religious implications. Otherwise, the month of my birth, March, would be called Revolution and my sister's November would turn into Great Revolution.

In a couple of minutes, our parents were walking, arm-in-arm, across the cobbled yard. I yelled from the opened window, "Papa!" They skewed their heads, and he waved his hand until they turned the peeling corner of Building #3. I envied Papa and looked forward to our quick victory over Hitler.

Soon came my turn to contribute to the war. A tacky train with stiff-backed wooden benches took about a hundred fourth graders from my School #136 to Ryazan Region. We kept looking for shiny armored trains with smiling soldiers and heavy artillery on tidy platforms we used to see in the movies and magazines. The three teachers who traveled with us said that the majority of trains were mobilized for the war and the military moved by night. We were stopping unpredictably, I hoped, for top-secret reasons, but we used the opportunity to compensate for absent toilets. Everybody hurried to a blind spot behind the last car, although we preferred the privacy of trees and bushes, the solitude of deep ditches and abandoned ruins. The whistle of our steam engine signaled the termination of this daring procedure.

One teacher knew that the German railroad tracks were narrow and worried that the need to convert them could slow down the Red Army's offensive in Germany. Once near a big railroad hub, we saw soldiers with fixed three-sided bayonets guarding several faded cargo cars parked without a locomotive on a siding; behind tiny grated windows, we saw pale faces.

"Probably German spies," said a teacher.

In twelve hours, we covered a distance of 130 miles. Two dashing truck drivers smoking rough shag were waiting for us in front of the Ryazan railroad station. The dirt road with many potholes was dry and hard, the dim headlamps flatly refused to shine forth and preferred resting against the ground or the black sky. Sitting and bouncing on the wooden bed of the open truck, I thought of searchlights looking for enemy planes. In the total darkness, two shuttle trips brought us to a one-story school building, turned into a dormitory. To our delight, someone refused to unlock the local public bathhouse, but the teachers coerced us into using three wash-hand bowls hanging on nails driven into a powerful horizontal tree branch; the water flowed directly to the grass. It was such a pleasure to stretch out on sacks of hay, spread out on the floor. We hid our faces in the smaller bags with the same heavenly smelling hay—and fell asleep covered with dust, bruises, and scratches.

In the morning, we learned that the villagers were not impressed to have, instead of strong drafted men, a bunch of spoiled leeches from the fat city known for sucking the peasant masses' blood. After cowering and weeding by hoe and hand the tobacco fields only for four hours, many of us earned a headache. According to the locals, the best way to fight the smell was to learn how to smoke this rough *makhorka*. Every urchin and many women in this settlement had a rag or cloth pouch filled with this shag, homegrown or stolen from the collective-farm plantations, some embroidered by loving hands.

The next morning, I was carrying four warm loaves of sweet-smelling bread from a bakery to our improvised dormitory, about four hundred feet away. Oleg Milovidov and I got this job, and we did our best not to lose it. The shiny crust hung over the edges of aromatic loaves like the thatched roofs of white Ukrainian houses on my way to Dnepropetrovsk. We quickly learned how to break off this tiny outgrowth on the sides of a brown loaf so that the cook would not notice the damage. If you walked slowly, but not too slow, and managed to press a load, just with arms, to your chest, then, with relieved fingers, you could put this little tidbit in your mouth. If somebody was nearby, you hid it in your clasped fist and waited until an opportunity presented itself. We also put the crumbs into our pockets and excavated them with extreme meticulousness, without losing the smallest scrap. It didn't work when we carried five or six loaves. In three days, our home provisions had evaporated. We kept digging in our pockets, time and again, even knowing that today you were unable to steal that tiny bit.

"Yeah, it's not Parisian chocolates," mused Oleg. I'd heard this choc-olate story a couple of times already but didn't stop this gourmand when once again he mentioned the metal box with Paris on its cover. Oleg's father brought it from France years ago. I felt sorry for my buddy.

My arms were busy with bread when a skinny teen approached me, tried not to look at the bread, and asked if I wanted to try his "goat leg," a cigarette rolled in scrap torn out of a newspaper; its burning *makhorka* emanating dark-blue stinky smoke. This country fellow even began put-ting his dribbling mouthpiece in my half-open mouth. The scorching brim of the upper joint was devouring the paper's letters right in front of my eyes. To carry in your arms huge bricks of bread was not an easy task, and here he was in my way, this jerk with a colorless tobacco pouch hanging on a cord he used as a belt, trying to strike up an easy chat. Outraged, I shook my head. Since my experiment with the Latvian cigarettes, I hated smoking. I did not talk with him, just goggled disdainfully and continued walking toward the school building. Nonetheless, the next morning, he approached me again. I risked my career and, without a word exchanged, passed him a tiny bit of tender crust.

Ella knew that we were stealing those bits but never criticized us for this, though her father was an NKVD officer. When I had jumped on her school desk four years ago, Ella knew that I would never kick the primer in her hands. Now she was my friend despite the inconvenience of being a girl. For the last two years, we sat at the same desk, and nobody dared to question the nature of our friendship after one boy called us "the groom and the bride." Ella sunk his face in a dirty snowdrift—with my active as-sistance, of course—and we kept his face there for a while.

On Sunday, we had a day off. After the usual breakfast, Oleg, Ella, and I left the dormitory. The "goat leg" was already waiting next to the wash-hand bowls.

"I'm Ivan," he said while vigorously shaking my hand. Ella asked him not to blow smoke in her face. He turned red, frantically spat several times on his fingers, and began squeezing the upper part of his "goat leg" until the fire was extinguished. I began suspecting that he liked Ella though she was much younger than he was.

"Alik," Ivan said, "I know you think I'm hungry."

He certainly wouldn't mind having our boiled pearl barley with a drop of melted butter in a dent in the middle, a glass of fresh milk, and a piece of bread.

"Would you all come to my house? I don't want my neighbors to see me here. If you don't...," Ivan shook his tousled head towards the forest. "We might even pick some wild strawberries."

The glutton Oleg and Ella wished to pick berries. "They will still be there tomorrow," I said.

◈ ◈ ◈

From a distance, his gray cabin looked like the rest of them, but soon we saw the coarse tow sticking out from between cracked logs and weeds growing between three rotten steps, all broken. There were no bunches of tobacco leaves hanging and drying on the barn beams and on the rusted nails driven into the cabins' logs. Inside, we sat on two benches on criss-crossed legs on both sides of the dusty table made of thick planks. Nothing else, except a faceted greenish glass in the middle of this table and a *pjec*h, a tall brick stove, was in the house.

"For five years I've been coming here," Ivan said.

"Why?" I asked.

"They deported my father to Siberia."

"Why?" Oleg's voice broke. He turned pale.

"He didn't want to give his horse to the collective farm. They called him antisocial element."

"I don't understand," I interrupted him. "Why not give the horse to your own *kolkhoz*?"

"Father loved Speck. He didn't want to let some lazy drunk mistreat her."

"Where's your mother?" asked Oleg.

"She and Nastya, a toddler, went with him. It wasn't a prison, you know ... they left me here with Aunt Vera. She has no children. She's good."

"Are you in touch with them?" Oleg asked.

"Father wrote two times. He felled trees. In the taiga, north of Lake Baikal. Never in his life had he seen such swarms of stinging gnats. The third letter was from Mother; Dad was arrested and sent to a camp further north, I think, in the tundra."

"Where is she now?" Oleg kept asking. I have never seen my light-hearted friend so gloomy.

"They wanted to live somewhere near the camp."

We sat in silence on a bench polished by human butts, looking at his fingers distributing shredded *makhorka* on an old newspaper scrap and rolling up another goat leg. I asked him if he knew how to build a *pjech*. Ivan shook his head, said, "They never wrote again," and began to lick the narrow edge of the paper sticking out along the entire length of the cigarette.

Ella said, "You could cut your tongue."

Ivan politely smiled, pressed this now wet strip tight to the cigarette's body, bent the thing in half, and said that he asked the farm's chairman to find his father. The man yelled that he didn't want to help the people's enemy and turned Ivan out of his office. "I tried to talk to him several times," said the boy. "He threatened to send me to Siberia, too."

"He can't," I said.

"A *kolkhoz* chair is a god and a tsar. Recently he called me to his office. Drunk. 'Listen, Ivan,' he said, 'don't make my life difficult. You're lucky—all your letters end up on my desk, not in the NKVD. Stop writing!'"

"Why the NKVD?" I interrupted him. "It fights with spies and traitors. My father is now with NKVD, fighting Germans."

Ivan frowned, shrugged, and continued, "He poured me some vodka and said, 'I have my own children. Nobody will help you, son.'"

"Did you drink it?" asked Ella.

"Yes," he looked puzzled.

"Was it a big glass?" she asked.

"No. Normal, like this one," he said, flicking the dusty glass.

"Wow!" Oleg said.

"My dad is a senior lieutenant of the NKVD," Ella said thoughtfully. "He thinks that a lot of prisoners will be sent to the front. Your dad may be fighting right now."

Ivan shrugged again, blushed, and asked, "Are they kind?"

"Our fathers?" I said. "Of course," and repeated the phrase I read in the children's newspaper, "The NKVD officers have a clear conscience, a warm heart, and a cold head."

It looked as if he never knew of our books, movies, and magazines.

"I'll talk about you with my dad," said Ella. Her eyes were watery.

"Where's your horse now?" asked Oleg.

"Dead."

I looked around again, discovered a rusty bucket and a handmade broom, worn out up to the long stick, and asked, "What do you want us to do?"

"Write about me to Comrade Stalin."

"Why don't you write yourself?" teary Ella asked.

"They will again stop my letter at the post office."

"Do you have his portrait?" I asked.

"Aunt Vera has his photograph with a girl in his arms."

"Yeah, we know the picture. Comrade Stalin loves children," I said.

"We know it," Oleg said grimly.

"She cut it out of a Moscow magazine," Ivan said.

I pointed at the flat part of the *pjech*, far above the cooking opening, "I know what it is. It's a kind of a brick bed, I read about it in folk tales."

"Yes, it's a hookup of a stove, a fireplace, and a bed." Amused, Ivan began acting like a tour guide. "In the winter, we sleep there together or just loaf around, playing cards."

"Aren't you scared to sleep on the hot stove?" asked Ella.

He rolled with laughter like a little boy.

"Don't worry," I said, "he's too bony and won't turn into a pork roast."

When we calmed down, Ivan continued his lecture, "Yeah, we also dry wet clothes and *valenki* there. Do they know in Moscow what it is—*valenki*?"

"Sure we do," said Ella, "I have my own, matted of white wool and very warm."

"Fancy," said Ivan. "Ours are dirty gray. They say a Muscovite can't distinguish between a hen and a rooster."

"It's silly, everybody knows," Oleg said.

"But, if I pull out his tail feathers, could you?" insisted Ivan. He hemmed, "Have you ever seen a headless rooster running like mad in a yard? It's unfair, we, hayseeds, chop their heads off for you."

"The trees don't grow there," said Oleg at the door. "Nothing grows there." He probably meant the tundra.

Nobody else invited us to see their cabin.

◆ ◆ ◆

We were working in the tobacco field when a man in semi-military outfit rolled up in a two-wheeled carriage, and still holding the reins, yelled at the top of his lungs, "Ella Ivanova! Alik Polishchuk! Oleg Milovidov! Come here! Quickly!"

He looked very important in his green tunic, belted by a soldier's belt, and ordered us to show up tomorrow at the District Party Committee at 11 a.m. sharp; somebody from the Moscow NKVD wanted to talk to us.

"Is it my Papa?" asked Ella.

"I don't know," he said arrogantly. "I don't ask questions."

On the way back to our hoes, I said, "A puffed up fool. It's your father. But what does it have to do with Oleg and me?"

◆ ◆ ◆

The main settlement of the district had two black rotary phones: one was on the First Secretary's desk, the other on the wall of his reception room for the district committee staffers and other senior officials, among them, the chairman of the Lenin collective farm, the largest in the district.

Ella cried on the phone, "Daddy, take us home! Nobody likes it here. We are hungry ... tired ... dirty."

The next day, he came in civilian clothes and had a lengthy conversation with the First Secretary behind closed doors. Oleg's and my mothers entrusted him to bring us back to Moscow, and the Party Secretary did not mind. On the train the senior lieutenant asked me, "Alik, do you understand why I couldn't take all of you with me?"

"No," I said. "You saw them crying."

"Your father and millions of others on the front line need your help here on the home front."

"So, are we deserters?" I asked.

"No, you're our children." He looked for a while out of the window and smiled wryly. "They highly respect the NKVD in Ryazan Region."

Ella talked about Ivan. He sighed and said, "We have to wait until the war is over."

Oleg asked him why our secret police kept changing its names. He laughed, "To confuse the enemy."

When later People's Commissariats changed it again, now—in ministries, the new word smelled with decaying capitalism and offended our revolutionary feelings. For years, we continued to call the neighboring luxury complex "the NKVD houses." The fights between their hated underage inhabitants and us had nothing to do with our admiration of their heroic fathers who remained indispensable.

Waiting for German Bombs on the Roof of My House

On the late afternoon of July 22, 1941, Maria and I were helping Mama to glue the crosswise paper stripes on our windows; they were cut from the important copies of *Pravda* Papa had collected. "They aren't that important anymore," Mama kept putting starch generously on the stripes, "just recently they've been too friendly toward the Germans."

These strips crisscrossed almost all windows in the city and could keep together the cracked and broken glass during bombings; at least that was the idea. In the evening, the windows in our neighborhood were painstakingly curtained. Militia, Tatar street-and-yard cleaners, and activists with red bands on their sleeves were looking for the forbidden signs of lights. About midnight our pitch-dark papier-mache radio and street loudspeakers woke us up—"This is Moscow. Attention! Air raid warning!" Through the howling of the sirens, the announcer asked citizens to proceed in an orderly manner to the nearest shelters. To the sounds of distant explosions and the anti-aircraft gunners, we walked to the Mayakovski subway station. The luminous columns of the searchlights were relentlessly crisscrossing each other's beams on their way to the treacherous torn clouds. At the doors of the subway, people looked gloomy but not panicky; many held bags and suitcases. My old wish to scrutinize the tunnels came true: they were lit. People were settling on boards covering the rails, some talked, some ate, and some tried to read. We looked for a smoother board when my neighbor Adik Ivanovsky from the apartment opposite to ours pinched my butt. "It's a goodbye thing," he said. In a few hours, Adik and his mother would be going somewhere with other families of the Soviet Artists' Union. They sat next to us and my friend asked, "How spies with their small flashlights can compete with our powerful searchlights?" Rumors were afloat that these spies would direct German pilots from the Moscow rooftops.

"They're here now, right?" I said.

"Yes, they're everywhere and speak Russian just like us."

"We just have to be on guard all the time."

"Yeah," he said, "maybe their children were your school buddies."

"I don't think so. Maybe you had such friends in your School #126."

Adik shrugged off my suggestion. "What if your neighbor is a spy?"

"I doubt if you're a spy," I said, and we began laughing like crazy.

"I'm freckled like a red-haired Fritz," complained my buddy. "I don't like it."

"Neither do I." We giggled again.

When at dawn, after the all-clear signal sounded, we emerged from the metro, the air was fresh, and the city looked confident. Adik advised me to take a last look at the unfinished portrait of our Great Leader waiting for his father's return from the war. The fumes of white zinc or lead, the smell of paint thinners, and the stink of boiling carpenter's glue stopped filling their only room. Ivan Vasilyevich had been making his living by painting Comrade Stalin. Adik was losing his morning privilege, still half-naked, to greet Stalin in his brand-new marshal uniform. When leaving for school with the red Pioneer tie on his neck, my buddy would sometimes even salute him. Now, he looked thoughtfully at the portrait and said, "When I grow up, I will grow a mustache like Comrade Stalin's."

"And if he shaves it off by then?" I assumed.

Adik shook his head reproachfully.

◈ ◈ ◈

My favorite neighbor, Alevtina Petrovna, worked in the Theater of Satire and had friends everywhere. They told her that a direct hit had demolished the famous Vakhtangov Theater. With a bunch of boys, I rushed to see the ruins. Underage street experts informed us that Hitler used 2,000-kg bombs to destroy the Academy of Science building. (In fact, the Fascists usually used 500-kg bombs.) One fellow gloated that his multi-story house near a central railway station cracked when a half a mile away they destroyed a military train loaded with ammunition.

The first bombardments lasted three nights. According to our black dish radio, Moscow was almost unscathed, and every night our anti-aircraft gunners were shooting down enemy bombers. The German Luftwaffe reported that during the first raid it had dropped on our capital 100 tons of explosives—15 on the Kremlin—and 45,000 incendiary bombs—300 on the Kremlin. This resulted in 1,900 fires. We still do not know how many people died. The absence of disturbing information helped for three months to maintain the calm, tranquility, and trust of the city's population, and even convinced many to stop hiding in shelters. It is a blessing to be misinformed.

The last day of July, when all three apartments of my fifth floor were already empty, a massive pre-revolutionary apartment house at Mayakovski Square was bombed. For our boys, it was sworn enemy territory, but we knew the building well, a five-minute run from us; we did not know its inhabitants, but judging by the silence of our radio-dish, all of them survived. Dead and wounded did not belong in our world. The same night fiery bombs burned to the ground two old houses near the Ducat Tobacco Factory. We still didn't think of killed and crippled. It never came to my mind that we lived right in between those three ruined buildings, only two or three seconds' flight from them. Our neighborhood passed the war test.

◈ ◈ ◈

One bright early September day, the blue-eyed Grizzly, smartly holding a cigarette in the corner of his mouth, as always, brandished under my nose several molten pieces of silvery metal. "Firebomb fragments," he said with majesty in his husky voice. "My mother and I were throwing the burning bombs on the ground."

"From where?"

"Don't be stupid, from the roof."

I was impressed but asked him to show me the burns on his hands.

"You're a stupid fool," His Majesty said. "We used thick gloves, shovels, brooms..." he caught my cynical eye, "and ... a stick. I even kicked one bomb; it was hissing and jerking like a wounded rat from our garbage dump."

I remained cautious and asked in a business-like manner if they used the buckets, sand, and water.

"What sand?" Grizzly was lost. "On the sloping roof? Water on the roof? You're crazy! You read too much! You just have to push 'em from the roof."

"Sure! But how did you get the melted pieces if you had been throwing the incendiaries on the ground?" I was cruel, envied him, and, more importantly, was determined to find out how he managed to acquire the priceless shiny splinters. "What if you had ruined your neighbor's hairdo with the bomb?"

Objectively speaking, the feeble Grizzly already had good reasons to look down on me. Several months younger than me, he already masterfully smoked and drank vodka, but now he began losing ground. "Don't remember.... We were drunk ... oh yeah ... we threw 'em down and ran to the yard ... and there they were ... on the cobblestones..."

My irony shielded my gratitude: it was such a smart idea to climb on the roof during a German raid! Besides, Grizzly made this great discovery: when the incendiary bomb hits the ground, it breaks into small innocent pieces.

The next night sirens were blaring again, and I said drowsily, "Mama, I don't want to go to the tunnel. I'm too bony to sleep on the boards. Let's stay home."

Mama and Maria were already half-asleep, we did not hear any shooting, and they agreed, to my delight. They slept like happy babies while I built a semblance of myself from a half-dozen books and three sofa pillows and covered this construction with my blanket. I grabbed my clothes, checked if the piece of bread destined for Shurik was in my pocket, cautiously closed the door behind me, and ran two flights down to the fourth floor. He was already at the open door. I hurriedly put on my pants, shirt, and sneakers.

The attic was dark as a pit, but this time no infernal creature could scare us. The slippery roof was on our mind. Soon we were sitting on it in darkness, clutching at the window frame, and waiting for the bombs. And oh, boy! Did they come! We were surrounded by explosions, the pale ghosts of searchlights were dancing in the sky, the anti-aircraft guns were deafening; they were nearby, probably on the flat roof of Tchaikovsky Concert Hall, right over the subway entrance. Our strained eyes and ears were trying to overcome this hellish roar and flash so we would not miss the moment when some nasty Fritz would aim his entire arsenal directly at us. To our relief, no bomb hit our roof. We sat there shivering until the all-clear signal; now we felt like real heroes, only our hands were numb after prolonged wrestling with the attic's window frame.

"What a pity!" I said while passing the smashed bread to Shurik. "No bomb hit our roof."

"But we were there, ready to fight," he, with a mouthful, exulted. "Next time they will hit without fail for sure."

Mama and the sister were asleep when I whisked under my blanket and pushed the books aside.

Late in the morning, I found on the cobblestones under a bench two small melted fragments and a piece that looked like a warped bomb fin tail. I showed this treasure to the trustful Grizzly, presented him my version of throwing bombs on the ground, and did not mention the exact location of my find, just in case he found his glory under the same bench. However, he knew what Shurik, Oleg, Mug, and I did not know—from then on Hitler's pilots would not be able to find the Kremlin. Grizzly saw the gigantic camouflage in the center of Moscow with false parks and buildings. The green plywood sheets fixed on barges covered even the Moscow River near the

Kremlin. We worried that the spies could discover this huge paint in the daytime, and Grizzly took us to Pushkin Square, where four soldiers were guarding a camouflage. They ignored our advice to cover it. We traveled the whole day and couldn't find more soldiers. Instead of rows of anti-tank obstacles welded, as I concluded, out of bristled up railroad rails, there were some ridiculous sacks with sand on some street corners. Nobody worked. Looters were attacking stores, factories, stalls, and even a state institution; uniformed guards didn't shoot, they pretended not to be there.

◈ ◈ ◈

On October 15, 1941, almost four months after the beginning of the war, our gang saw two German tanks near the river port Khimki, some twelve kilometers from our neighborhood. They did not shoot at us, turned around and went back along the river. They were a reconnaissance unit, we guessed.

"They could go by the Leningrad Motor Road and Gorki Street, like the trolley we took here," Mug said grimly. "No anti-tank obstacles at all."

"By Gorki Street, they could go right to the Red Square, to the Kremlin," Oleg said, "and shoot at Lenin's Mausoleum."

In our courtyard, we told my white-bearded buddy Abdullah about the tanks. Leaning on his long broom, he said in broken Russian, "Don't worry, boys, Comrade Lenin already out of the Mausoleum." The wise Abdullah knew what he was talking about; almost all Moscow street cleaners were Tatar villagers. "You boys better go home and pack quickly. Subway doors are locked."

It was frightening. The main shelter stopped working. We concluded that Moscow served as bait, luring Germans into a trap.

"Where is Comrade Stalin?" Shurik asked.

At that moment, Grizzly approached us and boasted, "I saw him today!"

"Too many people saw Comrade Stalin today and yesterday," Abdullah snorted.

"Near the wine store on the corner of Pushkin Square," Grizzly ignored the irony. "He looked at the broken shop window, on the bunch of alcoholics, kicked torn placards on the asphalt and a broken bottle, got into a big black car with security, and left."

"You boys talk too much. Be careful." The irritated Abdullah looked around. "None of my relatives have seen a Red Army man in town for more than a month, since early September." He grabbed my shoulder, took me away from my friends, and whispered, "All the big bosses are already in my Tatarstan, 700 kilometers from here. Stalin ordered to set up a committee for sabotage under Hitler."

Mug apparently heard this loud whisper. "At my dad's plant," he said, "they've been laying explosives for a week already."

"Stalin will go to Tatarstan tomorrow." Abdullah did not whisper anymore. "Three American planes will guard his train. The NKVD and the Central Committee have been burning documents, day and night."

Yesterday, our quartet had already seen this black, acrid smoke billowing from the chimneys of these important buildings. All day.

Grizzly drew a deep smoke, blew a long stream into the sky and completed his story. "I neared these dirty placards on the ground—these were his portraits."

Flight from Moscow

The next day, gray October 16, 1941, we were loading our homemade backpacks when someone banged on our door. Mama hesitated and said with conviction, "Marauders." Then we heard Papa's angry voice, "Well, open up at last."

Here he was, thin as a rake, hollow cheeks, shadows under sunken eyes. Behind him stood an unshaven soldier, for some reason in a helmet and with a rifle on his back. Instead of kissing us, Papa ordered very loudly, "Collect some winter clothing, *valenki*, warm socks, and some food. Hurry up! Tomorrow, German tanks may be in this yard." After that, he kissed us—Papa reeked of something rotten. "Nikolai will help," he nodded at the soldier.

"It's cold today," Mama said, without emotion, as if Papa had never left home. She gave them glasses of hot sweet tea that had been just prepared for my sister and me and extracted from her backpack two slices of dark rye bread, covered with some lightly salted goose fat.

"Don't drink," Papa yelled to Nikolai, put his bread on top of his glass, and passed this structure to me. The soldier did the same, whispered, "Your father has been shell-shocked," and picked up two bulky suitcases we intended to leave at home. Mama nodded, and he hurried downstairs. In the yard, I placed their glasses on the warm hood of a colorless three-ton-truck, stepped on the lower part of a wheel, then on the top of it, grabbed the sideboard, and climbed into the shabby wooden body. A silent woman with two scared girls of my age sat there on their belongings behind the driver's cab. Trying to unbolt, open, and lower the backboard for Mama and Maria, I painfully groaned, grunted, and made faces. The soldier and Papa smiled but did not help. I asked, "Why helmet?"

"To scare the crowd," the soldier explained gloomily.

We settled ourselves on our belongings, Nikolai deftly returned the board to its place, our three-ton GAZ moved to the wide-open cast iron gates, turned right on the cobbles, and in three minutes stopped at the corner of Gorki Street. This main city artery now became a one-way street. As far as the eye could see, people were moving toward the Leningrad Motor Road, a couple of kilometers away from this intersection. Our soldier kept honking, trying to enter this endless monolithic body, but it ignored him. People hated us, comfortably seated on our bags and suitcases.

"Why are we moving toward German tanks?" I asked Mama. "We saw them yesterday in Khimki."

"Why are we?" she said and concluded, "It's a madhouse."

At the opposite corner of the Gorki street several men and women, one of them my pal, Abdullah's son, were stealing shabby sacks from the bakery, probably with the dried crust, or dried rolls, or dried buns. Just yesterday, I realized, it was my custom to buy long white loaves and bricks of rye bread there. From the wide-open door of our neighborhood pharmacy, anxious people carried out cardboard boxes, breaking them down on the move and shoving drugs in their pockets. All of a sudden, out of nowhere in front of us there was a woman in a man's winter coat down to her toes, with a baby carriage and two determined boys a bit older than I was, both with backpacks produced from faded draperies. In seconds, the older boy was standing next to me on the body platform and ordering angrily, "Help me! Help!" On the ground, the woman and the younger boy were lifting the carriage, which was dangerously tilted to one side. Maria and I were helping. Finally, we managed to bring it in, and their mother climbed up like a lioness to join her cubs. Mama approached the carriage, looked inside and said, "Oh, I thought you had a baby here."

"Where're you going?" asked the woman.

"Beats me," Mama sounded carefree.

"Is it a secret?" the woman asked.

Mama looked back at the silent mother with two daughters. By now, they had slid to the bed of the truck. The woman shrugged off the question.

"Neither of us knows," stated Mama.

"Do they know?" asked the older boy and nodded to the cab.

"They do, but they didn't tell us," said Mama.

"D'you know them? Did you pay them?" pattered his mother. "What if they are bandits?" She sighed, "I don't care anymore."

"It's my husband," said Mama.

"Oh!" she said softly and touched the fur collar of her coat, "My husband is fighting."

Her sons hated us.

"I don't care," she sighed and shook her disheveled hair. "We're going with you. Wherever they take you."

After a hopeless wait at the intersection, our truck began backing up, almost hit a lonely three-horned anti-tank obstacle and made a U-turn. Soon we entered a narrow street running parallel to Gorki Street and were able to reach, though slowly, the Belorussian Railway Station. Here we again came up against the same panic-stricken human tsunami entering the bridge to the Leningrad Motor Road. By this time, Nikolai had learned to demonstrate his readiness to crash into anyone who would try to stop us. It worked, except several youngsters on the steps of the automobile were screaming and bashing on the flat cab's top. Nikolai and Papa swiped them off, howling, by opening the truck's doors. Never in my life had I heard so many insults and threats, never saw so many fists hitting the lurching truck. The knock-down-drag-out did not happen; the crowd had only asphalt under its feet, not stones. The resolute woman in her husband's coat, to my delight, had a talent for the trash talk and yelled to the swearing crowd, "They will shoot you like stinky dogs!"

Papa twice came down at the cab's step to ask her to leave the truck. She refused. "Don't yell at me!" Her head was shaking, "My husband is fighting! You're here, fighting with children!"

"You just can't go with us!" Papa yelled back, and we continued moving.

"He doesn't yell," I said, hating that woman with steely eyes, "he was shell-shocked."

She looked at me, held back, and said quietly, "You're his son. You look like him. He's drained."

Her older son said, "Where?"

"Under Smolensk, some two or three hundred kilometers from here, he didn't say."

The woman moved closer to me, "Ask your father to take us with you. He'll listen, he loves you."

Mama covered her face with her hands.

We picked up two more officer families and at dusk stopped at a gate in a narrow lane somewhere near the Airport subway station. Papa passed a piece of paper with a large round stamp to a sentry. The soldier opened the metal gate and raised a striped bar. The truck did not move. Papa opened the door again and said to that woman, almost apologizing, "They won't let you in. I really don't know what I can do for you."

"Do something," she said hoarsely.

"What's your occupation?" he asked.

"Accountant.... I'm a good cook ... can clean up barracks." She began weeping.

"I will talk to the commander," Papa said. "I don't think he can help you. This is a special unit. Come to this gate in the morning, sharp at nine. If I'm not here, wait." He pointed at an unlit apartment house on the other side of the lane. "D'you see that bonfire next to the dumped piano? I'm sure you can find an abandoned room over there."

The flame flared up, illuminating red leather book covers.

"Bastards!" Papa said. "Burning Lenin and Stalin. Waiting for Hitler."

✦ ✦ ✦

In the barracks, the four families settled together in an incredibly long room; it could accommodate at least a hundred soldiers. In its farthest part, Papa picked four single metal beds with battered mattresses, rough gray blankets, and no bedding; he kissed Maria and me good night, sat on Mama's squeaky bed and tried to whisper. I was sleepy but wanted to listen and thought, life is funny, Papa cannot whisper, so I can hear. Mama kept muttering, "Hush! Quiet!" He tried hard, but it was a difficult task. At one point, she stopped interrupting him and I heard: "... forty-year-old rifles ... hungry youngsters ... scratch German Panzers with bayonets? ... they were crushing them ... crying ..."

I wasn't sleepy anymore. I was listening. Papa saw worker's battalions, some on foot, not all had rifles, "... moving to their death...." Suddenly there was a silence. I opened my eyes; in the dark Mama's white hand was covering his mouth. Shaken, I said loudly, "I've heard every word!"

They rushed to me.

"Papa," I said, "how many Germans did you kill?"

"None," he said.

✦ ✦ ✦

Every morning Papa and three other officers would go somewhere and return in the evening. I asked him if he helped that woman with two sons. He said, "I don't know." The next day when I asked him again, he grew angry and yelled, "Even Comrade Stalin can't help her!"

When Papa said that he was going to build defensive lines to the east of Moscow, Mama asked, "Why not to the west?"

"You don't know why?" he yelled. "Do you know why the state of siege has been declared only today in Moscow? Not a week ago? Why are we sitting in this barracks for four days doing nothing?"

That morning an NKVD officer with a pistol on his side came up to him and said, "Abram, we have to talk." He embraced Papa like only good friends can do, and they went somewhere outside of our room. Mama shouted after them, "At least, we could go home and pick up some more belongings!"

It was written across her face that she did not care about our belongings; she just wanted to say to them, to all of them, that something was dead wrong. In half an hour Papa came back. "We ran together from a tank," he said, "twenty meters away from the pine trees. We heard it rumbling through an opening in the forest and miscalculated; he didn't even care to shoot, was just having a good time," he paused, and all of a sudden grinned crookedly, "Pavel begged me to keep my mouth shut."

The next day, we finally headed east. That woman and her boys joined us on the very spot where we had left them four days earlier. Against the background of the raised black fur collar, her face was as white as that of a corpse. The commander allowed them to travel with us, but no more than 50 kilometers. The temperature suddenly began plummeting; our winter clothes could not protect us from the piercing wind, and innocent snowflakes turned into prickly icy sand. Like a flock of sheep in a merciless storm, five women and ten children sat huddled together on the open wooden bed of a three-ton-truck. The tin shutters with a narrow slit now covered its lights. Overnight, the impassable mud of the bruised highway shoulders turned into a hard crust. The wind was drawing and right away wiping off odd white figures from its unpredictable path.

The flight from Moscow had been going on for eight days already. Families, or what remained of them, small and larger groups, lone persons—all were trudging east, away from the capital. In silence. The howling of the wind broke it. Overcrowded trucks were occasionally passing by. A lone old woman, a boy who looked like a first-grader with a brand new school backpack, a limping old man with a cane, and many others begged us to let them in.

"Mama, look!" I yelled. "The meat is also walking!"

A small herd of drained cows did not want to walk anymore. Two boys and a woman in sheepskin coats were beating them with sticks. A heavily loaded cart with two horses in harness moved before the herd. On the trunk sat a gray-haired man in a fur hat with a whip in his hand.

"A family of a collective farm president," Mama guessed.

A column of vocational school students in black greatcoats looked like a funeral procession of hunched elderly women—dark uniform shirts covered their backpacks and black peaked caps, long sleeves tied under their chins. Some had their soles fastened to tattered shoes with ropes and rags. We stopped about three hundred yards ahead of the column, and Papa ran back toward them. He and its middle-aged leader, probably a teacher, began swinging their arms as if they were going to strike each other. The teens, no more than three years older than me, had ceased plodding. I wondered again why Papa didn't have a pistol when they went together along the column selecting some boys. A Moscow ambulance, a city bus with a white sign showing its Moscow route, a fire truck without firefighters, a cargo van with the sign "Bread" passed by us before Papa brought a dozen boys to the truck. He yelled, "These fellows will travel with us to Noginsk. They can't walk anymore." He looked at that stubborn woman with two sons, yelled, "I didn't follow the orders!" and added, "I suggest you leave us in Noginsk. We go through villages from there, they don't have jobs." He nodded at the skinny teens slowly settling in the truck, "Wait with them for their group. They might need a cook or just another adult."

She nodded. Now their backpacks looked more like the coarse potato bags. I wondered why none of them took those bags off.

◈ ◈ ◈

We stopped at the dark outskirts of Noginsk covered by the first snow. Papa ordered, "Everybody leave the truck! All of you, with no exception! Dance and jump until further orders!"

After that, he and Nikolai began knocking at the doors. Dogs were raging behind the high fences, Papa and the soldier shouted threateningly. Only in the fourth house, a hunched woman with a gray shawl on her shoulder, stepped outside, closed the door behind herself, and soon, in a sheepskin coat and *valenki* in thick gumshoes, she led Papa and the driver somewhere. We kept looking in that direction and continued stomping on the whitish road under the indifferent pale moon. The dogs, now joined by many other dogs, were barking unceasingly. A couple of the teens could not move anymore. The women shook them, but they remained withdrawn. My little Mama was shaking this long fellow with his sleeves tied under his chin, his fragile body and backpack almost did not move, he was only bending a little, his head trembling.

It seemed an eternity since Papa and Nikolai had left us on the road. When they returned, we all climbed back in the truck, some boys with great difficulty. Nikolai was helping them. After a short ride, we disembarked and entered a big house where two women were busy cooking something beautiful. A unique aroma emanated from two massive cast iron kettles sitting deep inside the *pjech*, next to blazing logs. Papa called them *kazans*.

"It's a mutton soup," Papa said proudly, as if he did the cooking. "Through the night, they will stew for us some barley *kasha* in this *kazan*. It's the best pot for *kasha*."

"They're good aunties," I said slowly. Since his return to Moscow, Papa had continually been closely watching the lips of speakers.

"They're also good with money," he said.

"I saw such stoves in a Ryazan village," I said.

"Do you know why the bottoms of these big-bellied pots are small?" he asked.

I guessed, "Otherwise, they could be too heavy."

"No," he said. "It makes it easy to put a large *kazan* deep into a *pjech* and remove it with these oven tongs on a long handle."

It wasn't difficult to feed some thirty people. The teens, many still with their impromptu scarves made out of their shirts, were asleep upon arrival; they lay on the floor, using their potato sacks for pillows, the luckiest ones close to the *pjech*. We were stepping over them; several raw potatoes rolled out of a dirty backpack. Mama said, "Frozen potato tastes like diluted sugar."

After we finished eating, it was not easy to wake them up. They had slept for two hours and opened their eyes only when their noses discovered the magnetic powers of the mutton soup. The heat of aluminum bowls and spoons was unable to slow the boys down. Some faces writhed, probably from a burn, but they still preferred swallowing to chewing. They kept their faces close to the aromatic-breathing bowls and stared in one direction.

After the teens finished, the younger auntie took them to an extension of the house under the same roof with a few small windows that looked like gun ports cut through the logs. In the past, many cows and horses had lived there; now it accommodated a melancholic cud-chewing cow, two sheep who looked like twins, and several speckled hens. The rooster pretended to be the boss and ignored the boys. The woman quickly covered the ground of two empty stalls with layers of straw, brought in some rough sacks, and, without saying a word, returned to the house.

⟐ ⟐ ⟐

In the morning, we left this warmest house of my life. Papa put me on his lap, scratched me with his stubble, and almost barked, "Let's shout a little."

I yelled, "Why not yesterday?"

"I didn't want to irritate the people on the road," he tried not to yell. "If you'd been inside the cab, they would think that we weren't military."

"Why don't you have a pistol?"

"We aren't the military; we are the NKVD construction troops."

"I don't understand," I said.

The soldier smiled, "People's Commissariat of Internal Affairs."

"I know," I said. "Are you an NKVD soldier?"

"Yes, I'm a sergeant. See the two triangles on my lapels."

"Where is your rifle?"

"Right here, in this green cover behind my seat," Nikolai kept smiling.

"In the NKVD," Papa said, "there are all kinds of people."

"Even dogs," put in the sergeant without taking his eyes off the road.

"Yes, at the border," I said. I took his helmet from a hook next to the rifle and put it on my head. It covered my eyes and rested on my nose.

"Not necessarily so," said the sergeant.

Papa ignored our chatter, helped me to take the helmet from my head, and continued, "For the construction of fortifications we need shovels and bread, not pistols."

"And prisoners," said the sergeant.

"Nikolai!" bellowed Papa. "Can't you just shut up?"

"Why?" I said.

After a minute of silence, Papa explained that all men under fifty had been fighting. For the construction of defenses, the NKVD mobilized older people, among them imprisoned criminals.

"But criminals could be dangerous." I was surprised.

"It's a war; we need the unskilled laborers. They will live under a garrison-like regime."

"Will soldiers guard them?"

"Yes."

"Isn't it better to use those soldiers?" I asked. "They are younger."

"Don't get smart, my boy!" Papa said.

"Some of those 'unskilled' have university diplomas and speak foreign languages," Nikolai grunted.

Blood rushed to Papa's face. He hit the dashboard, "Never talk this way to the child! Never! Ever! If you wish, keep bringing trouble upon yourself!"

Nikolai changed in the face and punched the wheel. "I'm so sorry, Abram Davidovich! It's all my tongue! I wanted to help you to protect Alik." He hesitated, but said, "In that village, there will be some stool pigeons.... Today we'll pick up such an investigator. You know, I'm thankful to you for the rest of my life."

My father was still panting.

"Papa," I said, "you saved his life?"

"Kind of, sonny," he said and resolutely changed the subject of the conversation. "Forests and the ground near the cities of Vladimir and Shuya give everything you need for bunkers, observation posts, and pill-boxes."

Papa put his hand on Nikolai's shoulder and Nikolai sighed with relief. "I was telling jokes; it's all my big mouth!" He sighed again. "One snooper reported that I was telling anti–Soviet jokes. They arrested me, kicked me and started to beat me with rifle butts. Abram Davidovich yelled at that major from *SMERSH,* and they released me in four hours."

"What is *SMERSH*?"

"Death to Spies—counterintelligence directorate," Papa said.

"Personally subordinate to Stalin," Nikolai said. "No one returns from them alive."

"How do you know?" Now Papa sighed.

"Your father is a fearless man."

"Just was lucky for a change. For the first time in my life I saw a hatchet smiling," said Papa and changed the subject again. "Alik, you're getting heavy. Please go back to the body."

The truck moved to the roadside and stopped.

"What is an investigator?" I asked while opening the cab door.

"An inquisitive person," said Papa.

"A snooper?" I continued.

"Another inquisitive," said Papa.

"So it's like a diligent schoolboy," I said.

"Exactly," giggled Nikolai.

"A stool pigeon?"

"A nasty wingless bird in a chair," said Nikolai. Papa burst out laughing and told me in the back that no outsider could see the construction sites. I wasn't an exception.

We found this man in a room called the village council, with a portrait of Stalin. Under an open blue police overcoat, he had a heavy turtleneck sweater; his soldier's winter hat with hanging earflaps had a Red Army star. For the first time in my life, I saw tall brown boots.

"I've been waiting here for three days," he said with a slight accent.

"We got stuck in Moscow," Papa said. "We're delivering four families to Mikhailovskoe; one of them is the regimental commander's. This little investigator is my son."

When we climbed into the truck, I asked this man, "What languages do you know?"

"Latvian and Polish," he said. "Why?"

"And German?" I asked.

"No, I don't need German. I have enough trouble with Poles and Balts in our battalions."

"Have you ever seen wingless pigeons?"

"What? Only in a skillet. Yummy. You are a really inquisitive boy."

My Favorite
Horse Groom

In Mikhailovskoe, we settled in the groom's house. It stood by itself next to a recently frozen pond, a bit off an earthen road, which I called the street; the villagers referred to it as "The Road." Deep ditches flanked it and ran along endless rows of unpainted log houses on both sides of this only route to the outside world. The stableman, I called him *Dedushka* (Grandpa), lived with *Babushka* (Grandma), their almost 17-year-old son who was to be drafted soon, a daughter-in-law, and a cute one-year-old baby boy named Ilia. His father, the only teacher of the now padlocked school, was already fighting and they did not have letters from him. The very fact that we came 300 kilometers northeast of Moscow to construct defenses near this snow-covered village proved to me that Hitler wanted to conquer the entire world.

The first thing that caught my eye in the stableman's house was a large old photograph in a drab wooden frame on the bare log wall. In my dreaming eyes, everything shone on this faded black-and-white picture. Studying this cavalryman on a rearing up charger became my daily ritual. The sharp ends of his dyed black mustache curled up, a long saber lifted over his helmet. Tight trousers with the side stripes tucked into the shiny leather boots, covering the soldier's knees; his feet rest against the stirrups, the steady hand in a high bulky glove pulls the reins. The broad-shouldered warrior and the stallion appear confident in their strength and courage.

"It's me," said *Dedushka*, who was passing by without slowing down his pace. I was lost in time looking at the medals on his chest, the shoulder straps, belts, and badges, twisted, definitely multicolored, cords hanging from his shoulder, and the powerful horse in a smart décor. I could hardly wait until the evening. When *Dedushka* came back, I rushed into the cold annex where he was pulling off his clothes that smelled of stables.

"Why is he so big?" I asked.

"I was a horse-guardsman. Only the biggest and smartest animals were selected for my regiment," quietly said the groom. Horse Guards, he explained, were guarding the Empress Catherine the Second, Alexander the First, and other tsars.

"And soldiers?" I asked.

"It wasn't enough for a soldier to be big; he had to be literate and adroit."

"Why does the eagle on your helmet have two heads?"

"We called them 'doves.'"

That was very funny. Double-headed silvery "doves" with strong wings almost spread out, ready to take off. He did not want to talk anymore and even turned his back to me, so I asked his back, "Did you fight in 1917, during the revolution?"

He turned to me, stroked my head and said, "The most difficult year of my life."

"I know," I said. "In that year we overthrew the tsar."

"No, he left the throne before you boys seized power," *Dedushka* said.

❖ ❖ ❖

Two days later he said, "Do you want to go with me?"

My voice quavered, "To the horses?" Instead of saying yes, I nodded many times, lickety-split.

Dedushka said, "Get dressed!"

Without saying a word, I pulled on my fur hat, *valenki*, coat and mittens and stepped toward the door.

"Don't worry," he said. "I talked with your mother."

In a minute, I stood benumbed, afraid to approach a small mare harnessed to a sleigh—just for two riders. She was busy lunching out of a bag of hay attached to her brown-reddish muzzle, but *Dedushka* unceremoniously took away this bag of hay, put it under the seat box, and now was untying the reins from a tree trunk. He glanced at my desperate face and said, "Touch her," while making himself comfortable on the box, holding the reins loosely in one hand.

Without removing the mitten, I barely touched her round belly.

"She likes it when kids stroke her. Stroke!" ordered the old man. "Isn't it true, Chestnut?"

She moved her ears—I was astounded! Grandpa looked at me and chuckled, I didn't understand why. I pulled the mitten off and stroked her warm stomach several times. Her side gave a start, and a dark eye squinted at me.

"And now stroke her muzzle," ordered the horse-guard.

I did it, but not exactly at the white stripe between the eyes where I wanted to do this. What if she bites? Those huge yellowish teeth looked threatening.

I sat in the sleigh next to *Dedushka*, he barely moved the reins, and we started down the trail. Chestnut effortlessly overcame the snowed up ditch, we emerged onto the Road, crossed it, dived into the second ditch and entered an immense field. On one edge of this glaring carpet, the forest showed deep blue, and on the opposite side of it stood a big gray stable.

"Come on, let's give a good ride to the overseas guest," the groom said, hardly raising his voice, and the horse went into a trot.

"She understands!" I gasped.

"A horse is like a human," he said, "can be stupid, can be smart." A shadow flashed across his face. "Only, they're kinder."

All the way across the field, *Dedushka* did not utter a word. I couldn't tear myself away from the magnificent view—I was studying the equine croup. It was rhythmically moving from side to side, as if in a dance. The tail was occasionally, though reluctantly, stroking Chestnut's flanks. The hooves were strumming a monotonous tune in the soft snow. The runners were whispering this ancient song.

◈ ◈ ◈

The next day I skillfully put fragrant hay into a manger and mixed it with some clover. Despite my short stature, I took a collar from a hook—but to put it on a horse was a challenge. Fortunately, there always was a dry stump somewhere nearby. Once, out of desperation, I put a ladder against this stubborn, stupid animal, but she stepped aside and looked at me lying on the ground next to her hooves with disgust. More than that, she joined the groom and his son in their burst of laughter.

It was easy to put a harness saddle on the horse but to tighten the saddle's girth underneath her tummy wasn't. *Dedushka* allowed me to handle this most dangerous task—to remain between four unfriendly legs while her cast-iron hooves moved menacingly up and down, up and down; alas, it was the only way to thread and tighten the bellyband under Chestnut's belly. To tighten up a collar and this bellyband, the so-called girth, the stableman and his son brusquely rested their feet right on the horse's flank and pulled the strap with all their might. I tried to copy my dear friends but was able to lift my leg not much higher than the mare's knee; when I attempted to use the old stump again, the son pushed it away with his foot and said that not to look ridiculous, I should grow a bit more.

Every day was bringing me new knowledge, new joy, and new troubles. We traveled to the haystacks in a broad sleigh called *rozvalni* (collapse) with the sides diverging apart, right from the front end. It did not have seats, and Grandpa was standing on his knees, reins in hand.

It was a pleasure trip until I, sitting behind him, began worrying that a snow-covered stone could cut through the low bottom of the *rozvalni* and scratch my bottom. We reached a high haystack covered by old rags, cloth, and pieces of tarpaper, and the old man began gathering mountains of hay on a pitchfork and depositing them into flat layers on the sled. My fork was no good; it was able to get only a handful of hay and flatly refused to make layers out of it. We unloaded the bundle in the stable and were returning to the haystacks, when *Dedushka* passed the reins to me. "Just don't pull, she knows the route."

Holding the divine reins, I thought of the boys from my Moscow yard and my enemy Minka. If only they could see me! Nonetheless, my main concerns were, "What if Chestnut wouldn't obey?" "What if she stops?" "What if I drop the reins?"

And it happened.

No muscle moved in Grandpa's face. He treated with indifference my timid attempt to pull the reins from under her hooves relentlessly heaving toward my face. He ignored my perilous bending down below the horse's tail. He and the horse remained unconcerned when I, in despair, jumped out of the sleigh and, trying to catch the reins, ran in the fluffy snow next to her. Somehow, I managed to do it and said humbly, "Probably, I should cry 'Whoa!'" Grandpa grinned vaguely but did not say a word. Probably they both saw such a show for the first time.

The next day, after two runs to another haystack, under sheds on four wobbly uprights, I was rewarded for my foolhardiness and allowed to take the hay to the stable. "I'm gonna rest here a little. Remember, Chestnut knows this neighborhood inside out. Just don't bother her when you reach the ditch."

I touched her with the reins, yelled heroically, "Gee up!" and everything was just beautiful. We, the horse and I, were in love. Until we reached the damn ditch. When the time to cross this Rubicon arrived, I discovered that I was sitting high on the top of the dangerously shifting load; it could easily slide into this bottomless hole. Why did my hands pull the reins? Chestnut didn't anticipate such an abrupt turn in our love affair and, caught by surprise, she dashed off to the side. In a second, a part of the bundle, myself included, was in the hellish ditch, the rest of the hay was still traveling with the horse, though on one runner and under a critical angle. The acrobatics ended when twisted wooden shafts leveled out after the rest of the hay fell out on the Road. After partitioning it, the horse mercifully stopped, patiently waiting for my return on all fours out of the terribly slippery ditch. At first, I was schlepping innumerable armfuls of hay back to the sleigh. For some reason, now there was too much of it. So I started to rake up the remnants of the hay in one huge pile on the edge of the road and put some of it before the horse to atone for my guilt and to keep her busy with stimulating activity. Usually, the road was empty for hours, but the real life was always here—kids and dogs alike would noisily greet every passing truck and horse pulling a cart or a sled. My luck, one of my newfound friends witnessed my embarrassing incident from his log house and came to the rescue. He felt a strong connection with me since we met; he bragged about electrical street lamps in the downtown of Shuya City, some eight miles away. He also saw over there two lamps lit up the monument to Lenin all night long.

While delivering to the stable what we put back in the sleigh, so foresightedly called *"rozvalni"* (collapse), my thoughts concentrated on freezing *Dedushka*. I knew for sure, he hadn't been feeling well in the icy breeze around the haystacks. Ten minutes later, his snoring at first scared me but quickly made me feel better—he slept in the stack surrounded from all sides with layers of hay. I felt the blood rush to my cheeks, woke him up, and told him about my failure.

"You raked the hay, well done," he said, "it won't grow damp. Don't worry, you townsfolk know a lot about things you never saw, but in real life, you even can't chop wood."

Tricky was *Dedushka*, he already taught me to chop wood using, in turn, a light ax and a massive splitter with a blunt blade.

One day, I did it by the pond, when several boys approached me. They suggested I join them in fun-running on the young ice. The chaste snow in the boundless fields and distant blue forests bored them. Usually, they ignored the pigpen, the cowshed, the chicken run, and even the stable, too. This time our interests coincided. Only three of us dared to do rushing and skimming. I crossed the sagging pond first and victoriously started to jump at the edge of the ice. It cracked, and the happy victor, I, went to the shallow bottom. Only my earflaps remained dry. Accompanied by cheers and crunching ice, I dragged myself to the bank in the suddenly heavy *valenki*, splashed out of them the icy water and, holding them in my hands, walked to the porch. There I threw off everything but underpants. The boys shouted, "Come back Snow Maiden, with skates!"

My plan to change clothes without being noticed did not work; the groom's wife came out and caught me turning blue, "What are you, dear? Out of your mind?"

"Yes! Yes!" the boys shouted.

"Oh, those Muscovites!" *Babushka* clasped her hands, hustled me inside, unceremoniously pulled my underpants down, and began rubbing me with a thin kitchen towel. After that, she drove me on the hot brick bed of the *pjech*, slapped me on the butt, and covered me with a homespun quilt. At this moment Mama appeared. Lips trembling, swallowing tears, with my wet clothes in her hands. Never before had I seen her like this. She kissed me, tucked in the blanket, and went for the dry stuff. Only years later, as an adult, in America, separated from her forever, I understood what she had been thinking about on that porch. Her seven-year-old son Yasha had drowned right near our Moscow wooden house.

❖ ❖ ❖

One evening *Babushka* was trying to lull her grandson to sleep in her arms. I liked to be near her. The little Ilia had the blues and kept studying everybody, his unblinking eyes wide open. The old woman was getting tired and raised her voice. "Go to sleep! Or a kike will come to get you!"

I slid toward her along the bench and whispered, "*Babushka*, I'm a kike."

Grandma looked at me in disbelief, "Come on, Alik, you're a good boy!"

"I'm a kike," I said vindictively. "And all of us are kikes!"

She put the unhappy Ilia in a wooden rocking bed, pulled me with both hands toward herself, and, stroking my curls, said, "No-no, my dear boy! You don't have horns! You're like a grandson to us. We love you all."

"And all my relatives are kikes," I repeated vengefully.

That winter evening we both made a great discovery. She found out that not all Jews had horns, and some of "them" could be nice. I discovered that not all Jew-haters were bad people. I even felt for the old woman; I stabbed her innocent heart. I am sure *Babushka* shared her new, fascinating knowledge with her family. I did not share mine with my family. Horns or no horns, we already knew how bad we were, and I did not want my parents to feel bad about Grandma and Grandpa. Papa remained an authority for their family in all vital matters. They appreciated the very fact that such a big shot with his armed driver was so simple and kindhearted, never missed a chance to make a joke and was bringing home bread, salted pork fat, lump sugar, and kerosene for our lamps. To get a sliver of a sugar loaf hard like a rock, Mama and *Babushka* laughed when one of them held a chisel, and the other one used a hammer. This family treated us with potatoes from their cellar and beets, dried on the brick bed. Papa even suggested renaming their farm from "Red Banner" into "Red Beet."

What could they learn about Jews, eating with us our cured slabs of fatback and washing it down with tea prepared of herbs from nearby fields, while, for the first time in many years, holding in the mouth a tough sliver of sugar? They knew about my horns but, just like me, were unaware of the Jewish taboo of eating pork. Years later, I learned why Michelangelo's Moses had horns. The Jewish horns at that time were a well-established fact. Who knows, maybe the first followers of Jesus just miraculously shed them? I am not eager to elaborate on the subject of His appearance; just keep in mind, sent into the world of horned humans, He looked like one of them.

◈ ◈ ◈

Once *Dedushka* said, "Tomorrow we're gonna break Prince, the big fella. We have to be smart tomorrow. And remember, you must do as I say, and quickly."

I lay in bed and thought of these reddish-brown giants held separately from the rest of the horses. They did not like me. I approached their stalls with caution and never trusted the thick logs of the partitions. They were turning their backs to me, clearly implying that they could blow to smithereens this pathetic fence and all that was near it.

Early morning, when the most stubborn stars were still hanging in the sky, we entered the stable. Well, I was relieved when *Dedushka* ordered me to wait outside, at the wide-open gate. I did not see how they put the bridle on the three-year-old bay, the first time in his life, how he was trying to take a firm stand using all his mighty legs, but I heard his attempt to step back from the feeding trough. It was too late, the iron mouthpiece was already in his mouth, and I imagined the groom pulling the bridle rein while backing away in front of the resisting giant. I was listening to the approaching battle sounds, to the soothing voices of the two men and the indignant snort and broken tramp and thud. I felt the horse's pain and tried to reason with him in a friendly way, "Stop resisting, don't you see? The pain diminishes if we move with *Dedushka*; he never did any harm to you." I knew the charger was listening, "He fed, watered, soaped you, cleaned your hooves, brushed, combed, and let you into the corral to run and play."

The son, moving backward, was the first to reach me. Grandpa and Prince, his eyes rolling from pain and resentment, were advancing right behind him, to my surprise, side by side. Grandpa was trying hard to push the stallion to the wall with his tiny shoulder set against the powerful chest, holding the reins right next to the mouthpiece—next to the horse's open mouth. Prince was trying to shake it off, to push out the iron struts with his tongue; he bared his teeth, I was sure, in an attempt to bite *Dedushka*. He also talked to the bay, "Don't dance ... all is well ... the mouthpiece isn't strict ... we're almost there ..."

No matter how menacingly the stallion trampled the ground, he was led forward to a tiny sled and carefully spaced shafts waiting for him on the snow. *Dedushka* forced Prince to turn his broad croup toward the sled with a seat for two, and the horse began jibbing between the shafts, not keen to do this. The rest happened quickly. The son put the collar on him, threw the harness saddle on his back, attached the shafts to the bow, and grabbed the bridle at the point where his father's hand still was, next to the mouthpiece. In a second, his father was in the twitching sled, holding the reins tightly and shouting to me, "In you go! Quick!"

This daredevil raced past the side opening and started to climb over the back of the seat, the part of the sled most remote from the horse. Grandpa caught sight of my *valenki* timidly passing by his shoulder to the bottom of the sled and roared, "Sit down, really!" We were already moving forward in spurts, rather, in all unpredictable directions. Prince was trying to strike the fragile sleigh with both hooves at once, missing the target only because he hopped from side to side like a jumbo baby goat. The enormous hooves were flying right before my nose. Lumps of dirty snow flew in my face. It was clear, the charger chose me as the primary target. He couldn't blame for his troubles the old man who smelled of the mother-horse.

"D'you like it?" asked *Dedushka* in the middle of the battle.

Nobody could hear my whispering, "Scary." Finally, we moved forward and entered the boundless field.

"Now, you're free, dear," the groom loosened the reins. This horse was listening! We began racing through the unsullied snow at breakneck speed.

"Oh a-a-awesome!" I yelled.

"Hold on!" shouted the groom, "Now he'll try to dump you!"

The horse heard the message; at full gallop, he suddenly stopped with vengeful neighing. If I hadn't caught hold of the seat a second before, he would propel me off like a stone from a slingshot, and my life could've ended under his hooves or on his back. Yet, joy and love—for the horse, the vast white space under the pale-blue morning sky, and for this grand old man—seized me. I had nothing to fear. Survivors of a hurricane probably experience similar feelings.

"Run, kiddy!" the horse-guardsman ordered.

And we began running. No, we were flying. No racer could keep up with this carthorse! The legs with white markings above the hooves gently carried the body that no longer seemed massive and broad. It was a long trot, free, non-stop, and perpetual. Prince was simultaneously moving forward the front right and the rear left leg. Then his front left leg and the rear right one did the same. We sailed with the wind over the immense field without touching it. The iron bits in his mouth didn't bother him anymore.

"He likes it!" I yelled.

"You better ask him," suggested Grandpa, "and please ask why he refused to sniff the harness."

So I did. The horse released an extensive jet of steam from his mouth and said nothing.

"Talk to him when he rests," advised Grandpa. "Now he has no time for chattering."

"But then why did you tell Prince..." I began, but looked at Grandpa and stopped short. He smiled like a naughty boy. His eyes were gleaming.

We ran toward the distant forest and away from that forest, along its edge and around the white field, across the field, toward the village, and back to the infinite field. We saw less and less of kicking, shaking of the head, and hitting the air with the tail. Prince began to reconcile himself to his lot.

All three of us were returning home like good friends after a pleasant outing. When I, feeling like a victorious gladiator, was unhurriedly disembarking from my war chariot, now through the side opening, the groom put his arm on the back of the sleigh and said, "Well done! You put up a good show!"

When I was already standing in front of the stable with both feet on the trampled snow, he pointed at the sled back and asked, "By the way, how did you overcome this insurmountable obstacle?"

"I don't know," I said. "Probably in a hurry."

◈ ◈ ◈

In March of 1942, the construction of trenches, bunkers, and pill-boxes for machine guns was completed, and our battalions moved closer to Shuya. That day my parents stayed in Mikhailovskoe, and I sat in the cab next to Papa's driver Nikolai. In parting, *Dedushka* adjusted my earflaps and said, "Alik, after the war come to us in the summertime. Pasture grass keeps horses calmer."

"Come to us, too," I said. "I'll show you Moscow."

He began laughing, "Members of collective farms have no right to travel. We don't have passports."

"I don't understand," I said. "Come to see us anyway."

He did not say a word, only scowled.

On the short way to Shuya, Nikolai frowned and sighed, "When we were fleeing from Hitler, day and night, we saw a military transport, a string of carts with harnessed horses. They just stood there."

"Just stood there?"

"Yes. The soldiers ran away and left them behind."

"Were the horses hungry?"

"How would I know? We were running for our lives."

"*Dedushka* wouldn't leave his horses."

"It's so good to be young," Nikolai said.

Offended, I said, "He doesn't drink vodka and doesn't swear."

"A good soldier has to drink a lot," he said.

"Why?"

"Ask Comrade Stalin," Nikolai said.

"It's not true, Comrade Stalin doesn't drink vodka. Don't talk this way about him."

"You're just like your father," he said. "Stalin recently ordered to issue vodka to all soldiers at the front line. And it was a wise order: vodka saves lives."

"Remember what Grandpa said?" I asked.

"Yes, that in summer meadow grass keeps horses calmer. It was a hot July. The dirt road was like a stone. Dust burned the eyes. Even *Dedushka* couldn't do anything there." He looked at my darkened face. "He's brave, your *Dedushka*. After the revolution, he could be put up next to this portrait and shot."

"The portrait?" I was surprised.

"Yes, the evidence of his service to the last tsar. The Horse-Guard fought against the Reds."

Soon after the war, in 1946, I heard a radio announcement of another Soviet achievement. Collective farms in the Mikhailovskoe area raised the best strains of Vladimir Region Heavy-Duty breed. So, our old guardsman did something good for entire Russia famous for its lack of good roads. In the 21st century, strong horses are still more reliable than trucks in many regions of the country. The current rulers celebrated the bicentennial of the Horse-Guard Regiment. Wouldn't it be better for Russia to commemorate the life of the groom whose name I never knew?

Our new house stood on the hilly edge of Shuya. Our new mistress, Marfa, lived alone and for hours collected fallen branches and twigs, often hidden in the snow, in the nearby forest. Sometimes I accompanied her; one of us was pulling the sled while the other enjoyed the ride. To stack firewood in their sheds, her neighbors greased palms with a piglet, or a goose, or a demijohn of moonshine. Marfa could not cut trees at night as they did; demons and witches congregated next to her chimney and could harm her at night because she had icons hidden in her attics. Those demons and Red Pioneers with red neckerchiefs laughed at her tears when they were building a bonfire of icons and bibles, beating the drums and singing patriotic songs. Why did I like this tiny woman with wrinkles on the young face and weird beliefs? We heard her prayers every day. "Why do you pray to the wooden images," I asked, "not to God himself?"

She just crossed me. "Muscovites pray to their red icons. I pray for my husband and sons, they are at the front. An archangel instructed me to trust your family. You chose Christian names—your grandfather was David, your father is Abram, and your sister was named after Virgin Mary."

The archangels were supposed to know that we were Jews and I said, "I don't have a Christian name. I'm Alik, and when I grow up, I'll be Arkady." At this moment Mama entered the room. "We almost named him Aaron, after his late granduncle," Mama said, "but decided not to ruin the boy's life. Arkady was the closest to Aaron."

"I know what you mean," said Marfa.

When Nikolai brought a truckload of chopped wood, her joy had no bounds. I thought of prisoners and said, "I know who split the wood."

"Then don't use it," he became angry. "When Marfa stokes, just walk out of the house."

In the evening, I asked Papa who split the wood. "Nikolai," he said. "He loves it, just like you."

To prevent the escape of warmth from the house, after the firewood was burnt out, Marfa usually hurried to push the sliding iron damper, black with soot, deeper back into the slit at the top of the brick furnace. Once, she closed it too early; the coals had not yet burned through. I inhaled too much carbon dioxide and, unconscious, dropped to the floor. When I opened my eyes, I was lying under a couple of sheep-coats, on a rug placed in snow. "Mama, what are we doing here?" I asked. "Are we crazy?"

"You're right," she said. "Let's go inside."

That evening I asked Marfa, "If I died, would you speak with my spirit?" We already knew about her relations with the spirit of Alexander Pushkin. She crossed herself and me. An hour later, all three staunch atheists, Mama, Maria (turned Marina), and I—in the teeth of all rules of our all-conquering ideology—communicated with the poet's spirit. We wanted to know when Stalin would defeat Hitler. Marfa served as an intermediary between the dead and the living. She was forgiving, discounted our ignorance and giggling, and only warned us to be respectful. Otherwise, the hot-tempered poet could decline from the encounter and could even maim us. I asked if my reading of his poems by heart could please the spirit. Marfa looked at me reproachfully. She probably never read Pushkin.

We sat around the table covered with a sheet made of several exercise book pages with a circle of alphabet letters and numbers from zero to nine. In the center of the ring, she placed face down a chipped porcelain saucer with an arrow drawn on the verso. We put our fingertips, very lightly, on the rim and intensely thought of the poet's spirit. What if d'Anthès hadn't killed Pushkin? I thought, what if Pushkin had killed d'Anthès instead? That was a duel, after all.

Marfa's calling stopped my train of thought. "Dear Alexander Sergeevich, dear Alexander Sergeevich, dear Alexander Sergeevich!" Wrinkles grew on her forehead. "In the name of loving God, please tell us who will win this war?"

We kept our fingertips on the brim. Why Pushkin, I thought, why not Lenin? He knew more about wars. Pushkin did not even know how to shoot properly. My sister was puffing. My fingers began sweating. All of a sudden, we felt a tremble, and the thing started moving! Marina-Maria looked nervous. The hesitating saucer kept toddling, and then the arrow pointed at the letter "S"! It was a bit scary. What if something pale like that Gogol's witch, only with Pushkin's dark curly hair, side-whiskers, and red-eyed, sitting in an open black coffin, flew over us? When Mama reassuringly smiled at me, the saucer moved a little again. With every new letter, it was gaining speed. After saying, "Stalin will win," Pushkin stopped, probably became thoughtful. The saucer trembled again, the spirit-rapping continued, and the tense Marfa whispered, "When? When? Please, tell us when!" Not only Pushkin, even we knew the meaning of her question. This time the answer came quickly: "In May of 1943." The great poet knew a lot—the war did end in May, though in 1945. We, humans, are very forgiving when it comes to spirits.

◈ ◈ ◈

Since mid–January 1942, my sister had been working as a secretary at the regimental headquarters. I kept asking, "What do you actually do there?"

Usually, her answer was, "I get a worker's ration card."

"For what?"

"For counting pens and pencils. Several officers' wives work there as office cleaners. Dependent's rations are too small."

"What do they actually do?"

"Flirting with your handsome friend when he isn't busy interrogating Polish and Latvian communists. This He-man is funny."

"Why interrogate communists?"

"He doesn't tell. Only once he said that they had joined the Party before Western Ukraine and Latvia joined the Soviet Union."

"So they're supposed to be decent and brave."

"Look," she said, "all I know is that they aren't young and no good for combat, but good enough for shovels and two-handled saws."

That evening I asked Papa, "Are there many old Poles in your battalion?"

He looked at me keenly, "Who told you about this suicide? Nikolai?"

"You," I said. "Right now."

Papa clearly let it slip, turned to Mama, and said that he got hold of one hundred brand-new *valenki*, and the colonel ordered to distribute them among the healthiest and the strongest.

My sister said, "I know about these boots."

"What do you know?" asked frowning Papa.

"When the chief of staff and you left the regiment commander's room, you held a pair of new valenki in your hands."

"Oh, you know a lot," Dad said and grinned wryly.

"The chief of staff tried to whisper," continued Maria, "but you couldn't hear him. And then he said, 'If the colonel followed your advice, all three of us would face a military court and could be put up against the wall.'"

I was amazed. I could not get it, "For what? For a bit of advice? To be shot?"

Papa blushed, waved his hand, hopelessly, and explained, "For advising to give half of this batch to the sick and old." He shouted at Maria, "Everything that happens at the headquarters is a military secret! Ask your charming friend what happens for disclosing military secrets!"

◆ ◆ ◆

The snow began to sink and melt when the battalions started moving south to continue erecting defense lines.

"Is the war over?" I asked Papa.

"No, sonny, the blitzkrieg is over," he said. "We pushed the Germans back from Moscow up to two hundred kilometers. They're stuck in the snow. I'm no good for fighting, decommissioned, and will work at an NKVD munition plant in Moscow."

"What if they attack Moscow again?" I wanted to fight them. Newspapers wrote about sons of regiments. "Can you talk to your top commander about me?"

"Don't be silly, Alik. I never saw my top commander. People's Commissar of State Security Sergei Kruglov has a million friends like me."

Later in the war, Kruglov was awarded the three-star rank of colonel general. "Can you imagine," Papa, with *Pravda* in his hand, said, "how many millions were erecting the defenses under his command?"

My Blitzkrieg
Against Germans

We were back home by mid–April 1942, half a year after the mass flight from Moscow. During that exodus Oleg Milovidov's mother, much to my surprise, refused to join the multitude of people walking out of the capital. She wasn't afraid of Germans, she told him. Now, the three of us celebrated his twelfth birthday with real tea. She did not allow inviting Shurik and Mug; she did not like, she joked, the ruling working class and would not have enough sugar for everyone. I put in my mouth a piece of rock-solid lump sugar, made a few sips of the fire-breathing tea while ascertaining that this sweet little stone didn't melt, and glanced at a cardboard box with French toys. My sidekick had lost interest in its treasures before the war, in the spring of 1941. I had no idea why this anomaly happened and pestered him with offers to play with those awesome soldiers and the self-propelled tank. He looked somewhat irritated and when his mother went into the kitchen, whispered, "Dad's not at the front."

I patted him approvingly on the shoulder and said, "It's good that he looks like a blue-eyed blond German. All three of you look like Aryans. Is he a good shooter?"

My buddy screwed up his eyes as if in pain and said, "Mom wants to share a very important secret with you."

It was apparent—his mother had asked Oleg to keep quiet about her husband's mission behind enemy lines while Nikita Nikolayevich was fighting somewhere in France, or rather, in Paris, which he knew inside out. At this moment, she returned from the kitchen and Oleg said, a little too cheerfully, "This little stove devoured our books and trees and benches from our courtyard, and attic floors."

He knew that I knew it. These *vremyanka* chimneys sticking out of windows and our courtyard without trees were the first things that caught my eye upon our return to Moscow. When Oleg's mother began talking about her secret, she turned from confident, even arrogant, lady into a nervous wreck. Two years ago, she said, in the spring of 1940, her husband had hidden a tin box under a tree root near their summer cabin. It was my job to dig up and bring the box to her. Milovidov's fate depended on it. She could not do this—the neighbors would recognize her. She smiled sadly when I recalled how her husband rewarded Oleg and me for completing our first academic year and took us to the enormous construction site of the Palace of Soviets. Workers were greeting him; he was helping us to put on shiny steel helmets and said, "Alas, foreign." For some reason, she remembered the stupid question I asked after we walked up to a wooden deck no higher than the fifth floor of our house, "When do you plan to finish the construction?" He replied, "I don't know. That's the very question the leadership of the country wants to have an answer to."

The next morning, she traveled to the railroad station to choose the right train so we would reach that tree in the twilight. The plan worked nicely. The neighbors' windows were dark; they were probably, like the host of other Muscovites, far away from the endangered capital. Oleg jumped out of the bushes and joined me in search for the right tree. With the find, instead of running to the station, we went deeper into the woods. There we extracted the metal French chocolate box out of a dirty bag. I recognized Paris on it. Oleg opened the box and we discovered moist photographs and a beautiful pocket pistol. I began aiming it at the moon and suspicious trees. He took the little pistol from me, put it back into the box, and started mumbling in a broken voice, "For a couple of months Dad would return from work in the morning. Tired and pale. They whispered."

In an empty carriage with the lights on, Oleg looked around and started to study the pictures, with the lights on.

"They're at the Eiffel Tower," he whispered.

"Funny tower, without walls," I said.

"This woman between my father and Peter is Vera Mukhina."

I had no idea who she was and said, "Very serious aunty, doesn't smile."

"She's a world-famous sculptor," he whispered. "I'll show you at the All-Union Exhibition her huge sculpture, of a man and a woman with a hammer and a sickle above their heads. Peter laughed when he posed with a hammer for Mukhina."

I said, "Stop whispering. Nobody is here. With this pistol we can fight the Germans."

"Good idea," Oleg continued whispering. "Once I overheard through the keyhole Mama asking, 'Did they beat you?' 'No,' Papa said and talked about some confrontation with the enemies of the people brought in some room before sunrise, and Peter couldn't straighten out and couldn't open his eyelids. Mom cried."

I could not imagine this proud woman crying. In Moscow, she was waiting for us at the station. At home, all of a sudden, she pressed the pictures to her chest, sobbing, moaning, and unable to calm down. Her son was hugging her, with tears in his eyes. She stammered, "Boys, why did you open the bag? If you tell anyone, we all will perish. Why did I, the old fool that I am, ask the children to do it?"

She began shredding the photos with scissors, "Probably all of them are long dead," she said in a cheerless voice. "And Vera, too."

"Who killed them?" I asked.

With a twisted smile, she left the room and returned with a kerosene can and a cast iron pan. She put in it the remnants of the photographs and let several drops of kerosene fall on them; her long fingers trembled as she held the burning match to the paper mound. She never said a word.

We convinced her to bury the pistol in the Moscow River. "In the morning," I said, "we'll go to Gorki Park. It's always empty, only some boys could be there playing soccer. At a convenient moment, we'll drop the bag in the river. It's easy."

In the morning, we took the bag to the attic of my building # 2. *Vremyankas* devoured its wooden floors, too, and we buried the pistol in the coarse grains and crushed stones. "Citizens have no right to have firearms," I said and shook the black dust off my hands. "But why it was necessary to burn those photos? Who's she afraid of?"

Oleg shrugged. Comrade Stalin was so right in warning us of provocateurs, spies, and saboteurs. Somebody tried to do harm to the most talented, the most needed for the country and the war efforts.

◈ ◈ ◈

A couple of days later, to Mama's surprise, I woke up before 6 a.m., prudently protected my ration cards from pickpockets by a safety pin, and soon was in the queue waiting for the bakery to open. In an hour, I was back home with our daily ration of bread. Mama called me a "good boy" and kissed me on the forehead. After 8 a.m., Oleg and I dropped identical letters in our door mailboxes saying that our parents and the country will be proud of us.

My knowledge of maps and traveling experience helped tremendously. All we needed was a couple of troop trains heading south toward the Caucasus Mountains, one and a half thousand kilometers from Moscow. In the Caucasus we would move further south along the Black Sea eastern shores, pass the resort town Gelendzhik (I knew it well. As a five-year-old, I learned how to swim there), turn left to the city of Batumi, and soon we would be able to cross the Iranian border with our cargo trains. They were heading to the southern Iranian ports to pick up American trucks, tanks, machinery, and canned pork stew we liked so much. After that, it wouldn't be complicated. American sailors would be glad to let us on board because we intended to help our allies on the African front to fight German General Rommel's panzer divisions in Sahara desert. If some ignorant member of the small crew refuses, we could have slipped during the night on this large cargo ship. While already in Africa, we would improvise and play our cards according to circumstances.

At 9 a.m., we were already taking a free ride on a commuter train and searching through a window for troop trains at sidetracks. The most worrisome thing was the ticket inspectors, though we knew that all of them were old women now and they couldn't run fast. We were fortuitous—after 40 minutes of travel we passed a cattle train parked on a siding. Soldiers were hanging out in the open sliding doors; next to every wooden car stood a guard with a fixed bayonet seemingly not to allow soldiers to jump to the ground. We weren't eager to vault from the step of our slow train and traveled, luckily, only five more minutes before the train made a stop. We rushed back about a mile along the rail bed.

"It's so good that you read newspapers," said my friend, gasping for breath.

We walked, huffing and puffing, along the train, waving hands and smiling at soldiers. They loudly greeted us. All of a sudden, we saw an officer running and shouting, "Into the cars!" The guards climbed back into their wagons. In a minute, the smelly pre-revolutionary steam engine, without a whistle, began lazily pulling the train. Two soldiers yelled, "Come on, boys! Join us! To fight the Fritz!"

That was my moment. I ran to the iron ladder still hanging at the wide-open sliding door, seized its sidebars and in seconds, to everybody's surprise, was on the nicked floor, right next to a *vremyanka*. The train was gaining speed; I looked back and saw my chum with an expression of relief on his face.

The soldiers began yelling at me.

"All right, guys," said a gray-haired soldier, "the boy wanted to fight. We'll put him on a train heading back to Moscow."

"Yes, I want to fight," I said. "I even have my own pistol."

"Show it," said the soldier.

I took off my backpack, stitched by Mama when we were preparing to run from Moscow, and extracted my weapon from it.

"Colt," he said. "Is it loaded?"

"No, all six bullets are here," I slapped my pocket.

"Show them," he said quietly.

I passed the bullets to him.

"Are you sure, this is all?" he asked.

I nodded and said, "If you put me on another train, I'll do it again. Even unarmed. Please, give me back my weapon, please."

"I can't," said the older soldier. "I have a son like you. Children shouldn't fight."

"How about the sons of regiments!" I was ready to cry. "Don't you know about them?"

"Yes, I do. I feel sorry for them. It's propaganda."

"No, it's not! They're real boys! They got medals! I saw their pictures."

"Yes-yes," said the soldier. "Where's your father?"

"He was wounded and has been in Moscow now."

"Where did you get this Colt?"

"Papa brought it from the war."

"You lie," the soldier frowned. "Don't tell such nonsense to anyone else, or your father may be in serious trouble."

"Why?" I said.

"Because," he said. "I must pass this toy to our lieutenant. Otherwise, I might get in trouble, too."

"I found it in a forest," I said.

"You lie again, but I'll give this bull to the lieutenant."

The soldiers laughed.

"Go back to your family. Without you, they'll cry their hearts out. Those poor boys lost their families in the war, they are orphans."

I came home after midnight. Nobody slept. Oleg with a guilty face and his mother were at the table.

"There is a right time for everything," said Papa.

Mama grabbed me with both hands, kissed the back of my head, and said, "It's time for him to go to bed."

"I meant," Papa said, "that we had a silly son and we're happy to see him in one piece."

I looked at Oleg's mother and said approvingly, "You also aren't afraid of Germans."

She turned pale and said, "Where did you get this?"

"Oleg said it when they approached Moscow."

Oleg flushed.

Her voice cracked, "Why Africa?"

"It's because the Soviet military doctrine," said Papa crookedly smiling, "has always been—to wage war only in enemy territory. Children's fantasy."

Exciting Activities
Outside of School Boredom

The war had some positive qualities that would have been unattainable in peacetime. Shurik Khazhainov's neighbors still did not return to Moscow, his mother worked twelve hours a day, never had days off, and not a soul bothered us in their communal kitchen. We dragged into the middle of it one of the five kitchen tables, put on it our three-foot-long "soccer field," drew all required lines on this invaluable sheet of plywood, two small goals, a center circle, and penalty boxes. We were bringing our soccer teams in our pockets and had noisy championships. Nine coat buttons made the team. A big button's edge pressed the sliding side of each player, and it made him move and kick the ball, the little fat button.

I had a great team, and just glancing at it, everybody knew that I was a rich Jew. Mama had a box with all kinds of buttons, from tiny white ones for Papa's winter drawers to big and colorful ones with ornate carvings—for female coats. Mug's lousy team made of buttons different in size and color was ending up with crushing defeats until one day he brought a winning team. I never saw Mug so happy. After that, he disappeared and didn't respond to my heart-rending screams under his window, "Mug! Mug! Mug! Nick!"

One day he came to Shurik's apartment with his old miserable team and revealed a secret of his transient glory: his winning squad was cut off from the coats of his father, mother, and sister. His mother flogged him with a belt and grounded him for ten days.

"It was unfair; I left enough buttons on every coat. I took the ones which served as decorations. Father doesn't need his coat, he's fighting," grumbled Mug. "Buttons are for buttoning. I only cut my sister's coat a little with a dull razor. Shit happens."

❖ ❖ ❖

65

On August 31, 1942, we had to say goodbye to our championships, at least, Oleg and I did. After a year of absolute freedom, we enrolled in the 5th-grade class. We envied Mug; German retreat did not stop the second wave of evacuation from the capital and his school remained closed. The first month of school, we dug potatoes, carrots, and beets at a collective farm near the Oka River. Its men, tractors, and horses were mobilized for the war efforts. I had only two confrontations. When the Senior Young Pioneers Leader of my new school who brought us there said how unpatriotic and cowardly the Jews were, one redhead denied that he was a Jew. I despised him and slapped him in the face. I felt bad; he didn't try to fight back. But this leader of ours, a good-looking ginger woman, at least 19, kept blaming Jews for everything. After the first shock, I began calling her a stupid fool and a Hitler *Jugend* leader. It wouldn't be difficult for me to beat her up if she were a man. After I said it, she pushed me and promised to kick me out of school. One of the local boys, with whom I drove horses on the thresher, warned me that she asked them to give me a good lesson, and in the fields, in the outhouse, in a bed that was really a floor, everywhere, I kept a club at hand. It hung on my back when I was holding a shovel or riding that old gelding with a swollen belly.

Once, late in the evening, three guys, with a front-line cry of "For the Motherland! For Stalin!" burst into the classroom that had three dozen sleeping boys on its floor. The absence of electricity can be a blessing. Oleg and I kept changing places and slept next to different walls. In the darkness, stepping over the bodies and swinging their long whips, they were looking for me in the wrong place. Oleg woke me up. I jumped to my feet, swinging my club and howling hysterically, "If you touch someone here, one of you will be dead!" Boys began screaming, and the stunned enemy retreated, triumphantly smacking the whips in the air. For three years, I saw how children of my new school #126 loved the ginger. It was her job to be loved.

❖ ❖ ❖

Upon our return from the farm, Shurik paraded in front of us like a Gestapo soldier in all black—a coat, a uniform, wide belt, and shoes of artificial leather. "They feed us at the vocational school," he bragged. "Four hundred grams of bread every day. Many run away, many come back—it's better than starving."

He worked in twelve-hour shifts, making pliers, wire cutters, hammers, bodies for hand grenades, and Finnish knives for scouts. Soon Shurik had his own beautiful knife. He praised his school principal who ordered them to make rubber shock absorbers after one girl fell asleep and had both hands mutilated. I could not get it and the irritated Shurik explained, "At the head level, so we wouldn't fall headfirst right into the lathes, planers, and milling machines. You're grown dull in your fucking school."

Oleg envied him. Shurik alone was receiving almost the same ration of bread, margarine, and soymilk as Oleg and his mother together were.

Often, boys and girls slept right in the shop and felt lucky. At other schools, they slept in the foundry, the rolling and assembly shops. At night, they were sent to the flat roof of the workshop—to throw firebombs to the ground. Usually everybody quickly fell asleep, breathing fresh air, and no German bomber could wake them up. Once Shurik slept next to a fellow who had recently worked with me on a farm. "You beat him up," my friend said.

I asked, "The redhead?"

"Yeah, a good fellow, Germans killed his family."

"I didn't beat him," I said. "I just slapped him once. I didn't know."

❖ ❖ ❖

As soon as the first snow covered the streets, we skated right in the carriageways. Mug, now a cut above me, stopped near the tobacco factory Ducat and said, "Don't go to school tomorrow and I'll teach you how to make money. Do you see how the trucks slide? They cannot pick up speed or slow down. And this is good for our business." Mug checked my thick skates Little Snow Maiden fastened with ropes to my *valenki*, and promised to make a sharp hook for me from an iron rod.

In the morning, half a dozen of us were leisurely skating near Ducat Factory. Just like everybody else, I proudly held a long rod. The iron gates flung open and two swearing workers with long sticks began chasing us; a three-ton-truck with thousands of cigarette packs in cardboard boxes was slowly taxiing onto the snow-covered cobblestone of our Tverskoy Yamskoy Lane. These men in colorless padded jackets were no match for our squadron. Like cavalry with lances, like pursuit fighter-planes, like motorized wasps, we easily left them behind and surrounded the truck from three sides. An unshaven smoking brute at the vertex of this golden mountain brandished a heavy club. The truck was skidding in an attempt to pick up speed. Its idly rolling wheels squealed noisily, turning the snow into good ice. Everybody was trying to angle the cardboard goldfish. The brute tried to hit our lances, hands in mittens, and heads. After a short chase, the three-ton-truck left us behind, but we weren't discouraged. The next one was slowly coming out of the Ducat gates. This time, after several attempts, to my surprise, my hook stuck in a box. A savage in the truck was holding the end of my rod with one hand while trying to reach me with his club. This tactic worked beautifully. While he was preoccupied with me, Mug pulled out a different box and yelled, "Let it go! Run, Alik, run!"

I yelled to the animal, "Keep it as a gift!"

With a box sliding behind him, Mug was rapidly skating toward our neighborhood; his earflaps were waving. It made no sense for the driver to stop. This was a fantastic and decent way of making a good living.

The same day, the boys were briskly selling cigarettes piecemeal at all eight corners of Mayakovski Square, near the metro, next to Moscow Movie Theater, at the entrance of Tishinsky Collective Farm Market, and even at the nearby Pushkin Square, under the poet's stone eyes given to reflection. I stood at the boarded-up Theater of Satire's doors with a bag of cigarettes and burned with shame. The whole world knew that Jews were rich merchants who made their living by charging an exorbitant price for the necessities of life. And there I was—a Jew selling cigarettes to poor people. The fact that they were stolen did not bother me; I would gladly to do it again. That was cool! The boys respected me. But selling goods? That was a cowardly Jewish way of robbing people. I kept repeating to myself a line from a popular song: "Ivan is fighting in a trench; Abram is trading in a shop." I just couldn't take them out, stick four cardboard holders between my fingers, and, swinging my arm, cheerfully yell, "Cigarettes! The best in the world! Favorite cigarettes of our Leader!" I was a Jewish hawker! The son of a Jewish trader! The grandson of a Jewish peddler! What shame!

Mug interrupted my sad reflections. Instead of lecturing me, he passed to me his bag, full of coins and single rubles, took mine and began yelling the line created by me, "No nicotine! Only carotene!" Thank God, a couple of older guys immediately tried to rob him, so I could prove again that I was a brave and reliable friend. The robbers just ignored my presence—this skinny shorty didn't count. So I stepped back, calculated the right angle and rammed the behind of one bastard; he fell on his partner, and the partner hit his shaven head against the broken asphalt. We ran away, but after a short while returned, this time reinforced by two more boys with iron rods. Mug still believed in me. "Next time we'll go to the Tishinka market," he said, "For butts, you can get there a lot of goodies— from bread to shoes. What do you want?"

I wanted a Finnish knife and candies.

"That's easy," he said. "People change their gold rings for frozen potatoes. For three packs of Ducat, I bought there a *vremyanka*."

I laughed, "To make up for the parents' buttons with an iron stove?"

We faced heavy competition from adults. Fortunately, the law was on our side. Under the Decree on Criminal Responsibility, petty theft carried only one year of jail time for a stolen pack of Ducat. My neighbors—children, women, and old folks—served that lenient term. Around 1947, many men came home from the war, and the Decree was logically toughened. Until Stalin's death in 1953, a pack's price fluctuated from seven to ten years behind bars.

◈ ◈ ◈

After being an excellent pupil during the four prewar years without breaking a sweat, now, after a yearlong suspension, I intended to continue the same goofing off in a relaxed half-assed manner. It was still possible to fool the history teacher by raising my hand when Constantine Fedorovich would ask someone to summarize today's topic. Only at the end of the school year did he dethrone this favorite of his by asking questions about trivial events and dates. In comparison with Oleg, my head was still above the water, as he was rapidly drowning in the muddy waters of cognition. He and Shurik, now a turner, were making things with material and instruments stolen from Shurik's factory. We were drifting apart.

Once, during a school break, Oleg complained, "She's trying to kick me out of school." I wanted to save our friendship, and we developed a brilliant military plan again. First, we had to steal a weapon. Every Moscow school had a military classroom filled with rifles, training grenades, rubber gas masks, and entrenchment tools. The guns were real, though 40 years old and with a hole drilled at the base of the barrel, but the deadly bayonets had no flaws. All sorts of charts and diagrams—uniforms, ranks, new insignia—it all looked real. When the lesson was over, the class stopped marching, and Oleg extracted our coats from a large pile on the floor. The military instructor nicknamed Deep-Shit was the only teacher who did not allow us to sit in our coats in the classroom when coal was not delivered to the school. When we complained, he explained, "A soldier must learn to live in shit." I hid behind the battered wardrobe. Deep-Shit switched off the lights and locked the room. I sat on the floor under the portraits of Stalin and Prince Yuri Dolgoruky in chain armor waiting for the onset of winter darkness and executing the command "Fix!" Only weeks ago we despised recently introduced shoulder straps for their tsarist past, but now we loved Stalin in gold epaulets. I also thought about the latest dictum of our military man—"When bombarded, the first to enter the shelter are pregnant citizens, for example, women." After nightfall, with the triangular bayonet in place, I switched the lights on and off twice, opened a window, and whistled. Oleg moved to my window and reached for the rifle I held by the bayonet. I threw my knapsack on the trampled snow, climbed out on the sill, shut the window, and jumped into his arms.

Every Moscow school building had an apartment designated for the principal. Almost every evening his assistant was visiting him. All the boys were convinced that she and Ivan Petrovich were lovers. His wife taught at the same school and lived in that apartment, but this could not shake our firm belief. The wife was fat; Vera Yakovlevna was good-looking and single. We never thought that her apartment was as cold as ours. It was getting bitter outside; we were getting shaking chills. She appeared at Ivan's brick porch after 10 p.m., shrugged her shoulders wrapped tightly in a shawl, and stepped cautiously in the narrow path in the deep snow. No lights, no people. Only Vera and us, our faces covered by filched gas masks with holes we made for breathing. I aimed the bayonet at her stomach and, instead of premeditated German "*Hende Hoch!*" croaked, I didn't know why, "Undress!"

"I have no money," her voice faltered, "no food," and extended her shabby briefcase toward me.

"Undress!" I ordered again.

She dropped her thick briefcase in the snow and began unwrapping the shawl and unbuttoning the long coat, strangely bending her knees as if trying to squat. It was hilarious. I drove the bayonet in a snowdrift, and we ran away, laughing. The operation was a great success.

"Just imagine," I said, "she, half-naked, rings at Ivan's door, he opens it, and Vera, with our rifle in her hand, mutters, 'They said,' and yells hysterically, 'Undress!'"

"Ivan drops his pants," Oleg said unemotionally.

"And his wife comes to the door," I said.

"And also undresses," said Oleg in the same colorless tone.

"And Vera kills her with the bayonet," I said.

"And they bury her in the snow," said Oleg in a businesslike manner.

"And in the morning, they said that a schoolboy killed her with a stolen rifle."

◈ ◈ ◈

I was approaching thirteen when finally I saw a Jew worthy of respect. A throng of boys, two and three years older than I, treated that baby-faced Jew like a celebrity. At first, this thief-in-law, a high-ranking criminal who strictly followed the Thieves' Code, showed us Stalin tattooed on his bony chest. After that he rolled up a sleeve on his, thin like a blade of grass, forearm. A tattoo covered its pale leading edge from shoulder to palm; a heavy-set muscular man with a long spear-like penis was etched between his elbow and the wrist. From the shoulder to the elbow lay a prone woman with huge breasts hanging on either side of his arm, her legs spread apart. When this boy, one of the rulers of the Russian underworld, bent and extended his arm at the elbow, the flexing muscle of the forearm caused the couple to engage in sex—as many times as it was demanded by the excited audience. It was great!

When he said that a digger was alternately entering and exiting his ass with a shovel as he walked, I poked my head between the big fellows and politely asked him to show us the hidden part of his body. I wanted to demonstrate that I was a part of the action, but this kingpin named Kid parted with his baby hands the broad-shouldered figures and kicked me in the hidden part of my body. I squirmed and, despite the sharp pain, forced myself to straighten and run away, limping, for the monster was already holding a stone, ready to bring it down on my head. Maybe he decided that I was too young for this mature man-to-man talk. At thirteen, I believed that in a camp for juvenile offenders, under cover of night, Kid cut throats of his sleeping enemies with a sharpened aluminum spoon. Much later, I understood that this braggart was a most common pickpocket and could only dream of the highest position in the underworld hierarchy.

In fact, I already deserved the honor of hanging around with older boys and had recently begun standing with them right outside of our cast iron gate. The approaching passers-by warily looked at us, but we were not looking for trouble, we wanted to show our close rapport with a Hero of the Soviet Union. When they saw this highest medal for bravery on the seventeen-year-old chest of Fyodor nicknamed Tatar, the passers-by admired this courageous daredevil. I bought the largest pin with Lenin in a red banner and opened my coat when people could decide that this was an order earned in the war. The time of our glory lasted until some cops stumbled upon Tatar sticking out his chest with the pure golden star. He got a prison term for snatching it with a razor from the chest of an army officer.

My Love Life
During the War
and After the Victory

Our armed assault on the assistant principal did not bring positive results. Her attempts to make Oleg learn something failed miserably. Soon, he entered a vocational school. From now on, I sat with Irka. This cool blonde had already turned thirteen and, oh boy, she was fun. Don't misread me, I wasn't interested in her thing, the part of her body that some eighth-graders looked at with mixed feelings and commented on. She had breasts. One fellow even tried to smell a tiny white rose embroidered on her blouse. She hit him with her knee where no well-bred girl would dare to touch. He could not straighten up for a long time. I liked her way of husky giggling, not because of her bouncing contraptions with their ups and downs, but merely as her ha-ha was infectious. As a result, the teacher drove us out of the classroom. If I wanted, Irka could do it for free in the boys' restroom, but this blondie was wise and didn't insist. I felt relieved when the assistant principal caught us discussing this matter.

I was the only person who knew about her trade. She was a prostitute. When I, without any ulterior motives, asked her if she had a bed for that job, Irka found it funny and laughed aloud. To demonstrate my trustworthiness, I shared with her a secret of my recent sexual experience. One running fella saw me hanging in our yard with nothing to do. He stopped and said with pride that nearby, in the half-flooded basement of a building, a wench was giving to all comers, so that the boys would return her snatched watch. He also wanted to sell me a dead foreign fly. One had to fling this tiny Spanish fly into a candy, offer it to a girl, and she would take off her underpants after the first bite. I pretended to be busy with some urgent matters, and he ran toward that basement left unfinished because of the war. I stood there and thought, this girl must be rich, as not too many adults could brandish such a treasure.

Irka wished every male would be as good as I was. In fact, long before Hitler attacked us, I already had sex in a way, similar to her recent proposition. I kept it a secret, though it was one hundred percent true. It had happened in a Black Sea resort called Gelendzhik. The girl was also a damned blonde and, another funny thing, we made love in a place comparable to Irka's offer; it was a wooden outhouse with jagged pieces of newspapers pinned on a rusty nail. On that red-hot day, all we both had on was identical red panties our mamas bought in a local shop. She turned her back to me and, facing a wooden hole in the ground, pulled her panties down to the ankles. I pulled down mine and pressed my body against her tanned back and rubbery pale buttocks, but not very hard. I worried that she might fall in that big hole. We stayed in this exciting position for a minute enjoying the secret and the danger of being caught.

I remembered a great deal about that encounter. The steep winding road in the Caucasus foothills led directly from the pebble beach to the white adobe house where we rented a tiny room. A big eagle and a small bear lived in cages behind our solid wooden fence, and we climbed up to the top of it to admire and talk with them; we despised the overbearing peacocks walking between cages who despised and ignored the bear, the eagle, and us. Together with our mothers, we slept next to each other in the garden on a huge wooden platform secured on the spreading branches of a mighty tree. Before falling asleep, I counted aloud the stars visible through the black leaves and was very happy.

If that girl had been telling me the truth, she, just like me, was five years old.

◆ ◆ ◆

Once, during a ten-minute break, I was hopping around in the classroom and jumping on the backs of other boys, yelling, "I'm a cavalryman! Attacking the German tanks with grenades!"

Irka kept snatching my arms and shoulders trying to ride me and shouted, "I'm a witch, carry me to hell!" That was unusual. Good girls do not ride boys. Then the four horses and Irka managed to grab my arms and legs and threw me toward a window. After a short flight, I banged my head against a heating battery's cast iron rib and, stunned, was unable to raise my head from the floor. Something sticky was oozing between my fingers. Everybody was yelling, "Get up! We'll do it again!"

I already was kneeling when all of a sudden someone's fingers began tickling the private parts between my legs. Only Irka could do such a daring escapade to make me rise. I did not react; then did she understood that something had gone dead wrong. In a second, I heard her terrified scream, "We've broken his head! Alik is bleeding!"

The horses and Irka carried me to a nurse on the ground floor. My fortitude and resolve not to miss the math lesson stunned her. Usually, I would use the opportunity to play soccer in our yard. This time, determined to comfort Irka, I was bent to return. In an hour, to everyone's surprise, I was back in the classroom. She kissed my bandaged head, in front of the entire class and the unsmiling math teacher. I was aghast again.

The next day she brought an open-faced sandwich for me, of a kind I used to take for boys in our yard before the war; only now, the bread was dark, a bit sticky, and the margarine, which replaced butter forever, was generously sprinkled with granulated sugar. It was delicious. She and her mom had plenty of bread, much more than this lousy war ration of 600 grams for two of them, and they had plenty of sugar.

"Is your father in the war?" I asked.

"It beats me," she said. "He left us for another woman before the war, and we haven't heard from him since. Now we have a much better life, the clients don't beat us, and they bring food and kerosene. He used to beat Mom for nothing."

Before the end of the school year, Irka disappeared. It upset me, and I began searching for her. She lived on the other side of the Great Sadovaya Street, somewhere in front of the apartment buildings for intelligence officers from NKVD and their cowardly sons. I walked in the courtyards of that neighborhood many times and even overcame shyness and asked a Tatar janitor about her. He told me that there were too many girls called Irina Smirnoff or simply Irka in this city. I was her only intimate friend; she did not like girls since they were becoming niminy-piminy long before they understood the true meaning of being a woman. Not for anything in my life would I have asked the assistant principal Vera Yakovlevna for her address.

◈ ◈ ◈

In August 1943, thousands of Muscovites rushed to the streets to enjoy the first artillery fireworks celebrating the liberation of the city of Orel. The crowd around the Mayakovski Square was looking at the fireworks in the night sky. I was looking for Irka. The completed school year was the last one when Moscow's girls and boys studied together and were able to teach each other how to survive in the world we were destined to share. My school #126 was to become a boys-only school. It made me sad. Even a year later, in 1944, I continued looking for Irka in the streets, subway, shops, and sometimes wandered in the yards of her neighborhood. The front line was slowly receding to the west and crowds admired hollow banging fireworks, their exotic flowers with falling away petals, and unpredictable sketches. The seventeenth of July 1944 was the day when I stopped looking for her. A unique event absorbed my attention. A column of 57,000 German prisoners was moving through Moscow's main streets. Some had their legs, chests, arms, and heads bound with filthy and bloody rags. When they stumbled or fell, leaving behind broken improvised crutches, ripped boots, and rags, the crowds cheered. Our soldiers with fixed bayonets, some on horses, were forcing the prisoners to get up and to continue this endless parade of misery.

The horses reminded me of my first war winter in a remote village, and I said to my father, "Maybe *Dedushka's* sons are now serving in the cavalry."

Papa, his voice grim, said, "I hope they avoided this meat grinder. We regularly threw the cavalry against German tanks and artillery."

"I thought we'd never have horses anymore," said a one-legged man in a field shirt. "The whole cavalry divisions were disbanded."

"Horses? These skunks killed my neighbor," a woman next to us said. "Their entire cavalry squadron was killed by Panzers."

"Now we have tanks," said Papa.

The one-legged veteran looked at my father's medal.

"Yes, it's a new one," Papa said grimly, "for the defense of Moscow. We fled from them through Moscow."

"I know what you mean," the man said.

I had read recently in *Pravda* that Comrade Stalin was the first who received this medal, but decided not to show off. At Mayakovski Square, the column turned from Gorki Street to Great Sadovaya Street, passed the corner where I used to sell cigarettes piecemeal, and soon was trudging and stumbling by Irka's neighborhood. They reached the Youth Library where Lev Junior had brought me before the war. The Germans killed him. I was full of hatred and satisfaction, and especially despised those wretches who were trying to keep their chins high to show their Aryan pride.

Close to us stood an old woman. I looked at her faded eyes, narrowed as if in pain, and thought, "She hates them so much, she can't even scream like others." Then everybody heard her cracked voice, "Poor people! I'm sorry for these poor men!"

The woman next to Papa howled, "An old fool! Out of your mind! These bastards came here to kill all of us!"

The old fool stood her ground, "Do we need such a show?"

The one-legged man lifted his crutch, "Do you want me to maim you right here?"

"I'm Russian." She instinctively raised a hand and hastily stepped back, a gray lock covering one of her eyes.

"Anti-Soviet fool! Stupid moron!" yelled another man.

Somebody said, "Off with you while you're safe, you, nitwit!"
The old woman walked away.

◈ ◈ ◈

Ten months later, in the middle of the night, my life drastically changed. At 4 a.m. on May 2, 1945, our black loudspeaker woke us up. Instead of an air alarm, we heard the agitated voice of Yuri Levitan. We defeated them! The war was over! The whole country knew this announcer— for four years he had been informing us of the Soviet army's victories. Half-naked Mama began ripping off the paper strips from our windows. Papa joined her. I switched on the lights. Neighbors were running out into the dark courtyard and the lights, one after another, shone in the windows! People wept and laughed. Before running downstairs, I paused to knock at the Ivanovskys' door, but it opened before I touched it. Adik and his mother hugged us.

The next day, boys and girls from our neighborhood hunted for the military on the streets; we picked them up and swayed. The adults were helping. Joyful madness resumed with renewed vigor on May 9, declared as a Victory holiday. Several boys from our class rushed to Red Square. A vast crowd in front of the American embassy blocked our way just a few hundred meters away from the Kremlin. People stood on tramway rails; trams stopped one after another and rang. No one paid attention. Everyone screamed. Hats flew into the air. Adik caught one and gallantly passed it back to the pretty owner. She kissed him on a cheek and threw it up again. An American general came out of the gate and spoke in Russian; our major broke through the crowd to him. They shook hands, embraced, and kissed. Americans, many in uniform, dangled from all windows and the balcony. They were catching Soviet badges, pencils, lighters, everything that Muscovites were throwing. American badges, cigarettes, and fountain pens flew down. Embassy gates opened, and a Russian maid carried out a tray with glasses of champagne. The lucky ones grabbed them. Wineglasses appeared on the balcony next to our red flag and the American, star-strewn. One Muscovite emptied his fancy tumbler and cracked it on the asphalt. Our allies in the windows looked puzzled; they did not know our custom to beat wine glasses as a token of triumph and joy. Soon they joined the Russians. Thousands shouted, "Hurray! We defeated them!" Adik yelled so hard that he lost his voice.

The next day my father, for the first time in my life, put a bottle of sugary liqueur on the table. The previous night the Muscovites had bought all the stocks of vodka, and today the wine shelves were empty.

◈ ◈ ◈

Most of that postwar summer I spent in a Young Pioneer camp. Three red stripes on my white shirt sleeve reflected my highest position in the squad—the entire body of Pioneers. This Chairman of the Squad Council was probably the oldest and most experienced, politically irreproachable, the best informed of internal and international matters, the best athlete, a chess champion who ran faster and farther, and leaped higher and farther than anybody else. During morning and evening ceremonies I was ordering, "All units for the raising (or lowering) of the flag, be ready!" The commanders of units declared their patriotic alacrity to me, and we smartly saluted with our right hands crossing our foreheads. After that, I reported the readiness of the entire squad to perform Pioneer duties (or to go to bed) to the 20-year-old Senior Pioneer Leader. Daily, we marched in formation and sang popular songs by the Pioneer campfire. We were unaware of American Boy Scouts' camps for canoeing, archery, mountain biking, horseback riding, kayaking, sailing, and even weight loss. Our parents wanted their skinny children to gain some weight.

On June 25 of 1945, staying next to the flagpole, I read for the entire squad *Pravda's* (The Truth) reports on celebrations of victory over Nazi Germany. After that, with a newspaper in my hands, I solemnly marched along the ranks, showing our Great Leader atop of Lenin's Mausoleum greeting soldiers throwing down 200 Nazi banners and standards. Three days later, our camp celebrated Stalin's new rank. Generalissimo! We never heard such a word, but we loved it.

My brilliant career lasted until I got mad and unpredictable—all in response to being rejected, dumped, and spurned in love. Naturally, she was a youngish blonde of fourteen. She ignored my superstar status and never looked kindly in my adoring eye. Her best and ugly girlfriend never missed a chance to show me a hideous squint whenever I wasn't able to take my eyes off the blonde or did something smart and brave. Once during the war games, my new devotee found a rotten phosphorescent stump in the woods. We broke a huge chunk off it and made two pistols. In the dusk, we violated one of the camp commandments: Under no circumstances could the boys enter the girls' dormitory—a room for all twenty girls of the First Unit. When they switched off the lights, we, yelling "hooray!" and waving glowing pistols, entered their room where everybody was still talking and laughing. We stopped in the middle of the room with no intentions, God forbid, to approach anybody's bed. Some girls began snickering and chuckling. Only the ugly one jumped like a lynx in front of me, swaying her paws and growling wickedly in my face, "Get out of here, you, hooligans!"

She kept her distorted face so close to mine that I had to wipe her spit off my cheeks and the weapon. She tried to push me, and I had to push aside her hand. She screamed, "He hit me!" and at this point, the Senior Pioneer Leader burst into this shrine. I categorically denied the attack and was ready to offer my remorse to each of the nineteen girls personally, but not to this one. Keeping in mind that only one day remained before the end of my vacation, in the morning, on the advice of the Senior Pioneer Leader, I went home.

❖ ❖ ❖

This true love did not prevent me from befriending three neighborhood girls of my age in the fall, but only one of them had a unique advantage. Irene Nikolskaya had her own room. From her window in Building #2, we could see German prisoners erecting the luxury Beijing Hotel and broad red banners in Russian and German appealing to them to build the communist society. The only guard who mingled with our boys asked us to stop throwing stones over the barbed wire around the construction site; those prisoners were the future leaders of future communist Germany. Irene and I were in complete agreement concerning the future of humanity, class struggle, and relations between sexes. Under the intoxicating influence of this particular subject, we decided to have sex. Glued to our seats in opposite corners of the room, we behaved like good-mannered UN negotiators debating a peace treaty after a millennial war of the sexes. In her policy statement, Irene announced that she was in 99 percent agreement with me. As a true gentleman, in my first statement, I demanded 100 percent surrender. She thoroughly reconsidered her position and announced the new one—98 percent. I respectfully disagreed with her and repeated my uncompromising demand. She proposed a new approach to the problem and reduced her percentage to 95. I firmly rejected her new proposal and deferentially repeated my precondition—no less than 100 percent. The negotiating process ended when she, gradually, reduced her conditions for surrender to 49 percent. The intercourse was over. We remained friends.

The second girl from my neighborhood undoubtedly flirted with me; she even touched my shoulder. Once we walked by Lenin's Mausoleum and the long line of visitors, many with reverential awe. Galina said, "I remember how you forgot the Mayakovski's poem about Lenin."

"How do you know?" I was embarrassed.

"I was the first to applaud when you ran from the scene."

"I didn't run," I said. "I walked away. Quickly."

To forget the important lines of the most important poem of the most important Soviet poet about the most important person in the world while performing at the most important Soviet holiday celebration! That was unbearable. For the rest of my life I will remember that evening in the tobacco plant Ducat's club and the refrain, "Lenin lived, Lenin is alive, Lenin will live forever!"

She put her palm on my shoulder, now for the second time, and said, "We, performers, sometimes forget…"

One day, a relaxed stranger about 20 years old ruined our upcoming intimacy. He approached me in our courtyard, asked if I knew where Galina lived, took crumpled panties out of his pocket and said, "She forgot her stuff at my place. I want to return it."

Devastated, I told him her apartment number. I did not want to see her anymore. Only a few years later, at 18 or 19, I understood what a vile trick it was. Probably he just wanted revenge for the rejection. The scoundrel hoped that the news would quickly spread among the neighborhood. All I had to do was to strike him hard, knock him down, and trample him until I got bored.

◈ ◈ ◈

By the time of my belated epiphany I was already in love with Lucy, do I even need to say, another blonde? It was springtime. Everybody in my class was preparing for finals and weighing their chances of making it into a college. Looking for hours at the motionless curtains of Lucy's inspiring window, I concentrated my energy on perfecting a love poem.

We sat on a yard bench. She read my first report called "The First Fight" in the youth newspaper *Moscovsky Komsomolets* and said that beating people for fun and glory was disgusting. My attempts to explain that boxing and ballet had a lot in common seemed ridiculous to her, and a long-drawn-out yawn contorted her pretty face. It became clear that my poem called "Lucy" should stay in my pocket for another day. She was too young, only 16, and, judging by her reaction to my report, was unable to appreciate poetry. That evening some future famous writer suggested to my classmate Boris Epstein and me that, before trying to write something, we should dig potatoes and work as steelworkers for at least three or four years. To drive the message home, the true writer asked me to describe the emblem of the Soviet Union.

"Crossed hammer and sickle," I said glumly.

"What else?" he said.

I didn't like him and said, "Nothing."

"You forgot a little thing," he said, "the planet Earth. They're placed against the globe, the entire globe. Think hard about that. It's written there…"

"Proletarians of all countries, unite!" this greenhorn interrupted despondently.

"Good," he said condescendingly.

"Who's the author?" I played the fool.

The herald of socialist realism didn't answer and looked offended.

"Were there co-authors?" I asked innocently.

Boris took his newly habitual pipe out of his mouth and said thoughtfully, "Karl and Marx."

With this brand new thing in his hand, he looked like a veteran writer. I couldn't resist the temptation and introduced the name and surname of the second founder of Marxism in the same frivolous manner, "No, Friedrich and Engels."

"Cynicism distorts the truth of life," the true writer said.

I offended him again. "Pushkin had serfs, never dug potatoes, and didn't know a thing about the working class. In his time, Russia didn't have it."

The next morning, I nervously handed to Lucy three notebook sheets folded into quarters. In the evening, she looked at me as Empress Cleopatra would look at her miserable slave and said didactically in her velvet voice, "You know what people do with paper."

After the initial shock, I grasped the vulgarity of her remark—we, the Soviet masses, did not have toilet paper. It was the crushing end of the romance and my literary career. I chose journalism instead but did not see the point in a five-year study of what I was already able to do. To widen my horizons, I needed Marxist philosophy. I had a month to prepare for entrance tests to Philosophy School of Moscow University, the best in the world.

How to Become
a Philosopher

Papa was blunt. "Moscow University isn't for Jews," he said, and threw *Pravda* on the table, "Don't you read it?" It was the end of June 1949. "We're lucky. They still need Jewish doctors. There is no competition for admission to medical schools and they accept Jews. Yes, physicians are poor, but people get sick today and will get sick tomorrow." He yelled, "Don't you know that we are traitors, disloyal bourgeois nationalists, and rootless cosmopolitans?" The blood rushed to his face. "Remember the defense lines far to the east of Moscow? He was scared and created the Jewish Anti-Fascist Committee to rally American support, to help him to survive."

"But you volunteered for the war!" I stuttered.

"Do you understand who killed Solomon Mikhoels, the most famous Soviet Jew?"

"It was a car accident!" now I yelled.

"Stop shouting," pleaded Mama. "The neighbors can hear you."

"Wake up, my boy!" Papa ignored her warning. "All members of that Committee were arrested."

"How do you know?"

"I know! Mikhoels was its president. I don't want you to be hurt; they won't let you study philosophy."

"Please stop yelling," Mama pleaded again.

However, we continued.

The next day I asked Papa to allow me to try my luck at the university. "If I fail in July, I'll still have the whole of August to pass the tests at the First Medical School."

Papa waved his hand, sighed, looked at Mama, and said, "I hope not every university professor is an anti–Semite."

"But they have families," she said, "and they want to save their bacon."

I successfully passed all five tests at the Philosophy School. In three subjects, I got a perfect score, and after that, I had a strange conversation with the literature examiner. He looked at my exam form and said, "I read your essay and don't think these questions would be difficult for you to answer."

"Yes, they're easy," I said.

The young professor pushed the form aside, and for a long time we chatted as equals about problems unrelated to what one could find in the school textbooks. While discussing the rules of syllabic-tonic versification, he asked my opinion of *Letter of the Rules of Russian Versification* written by Mikhail Lomonosov in 1739.

"I never heard of this work," I said.

"I'm not sure," the professor said, "that your teacher is aware of such work either, but if you read it, you'd have gotten the highest score for both—for today's exam and your essay."

The guy sent me a warning signal without endangering his slice of bacon. He lowered my grade for the essay written two weeks ago because I had not read an article unknown to anyone! However, I didn't worry—the passing score was 22 out of 25. I got 23. The next day I saw my score on the dean's bulletin board and rushed home to share the good news. The list of first-year-students had to be posted on this board on August 20.

"You deserve some rest." Papa hugged me and said, "You can stay with my assistant in the country for three weeks, until that day."

She lived in a suburb of Nemchinovka and from her house on a hill, I could see a dance floor, a grassy volleyball court, and a pond with a boat station. For more than two weeks I swam, was pulling the oars as hard as I could, lightheartedly played volleyball, and danced every night. The dance floor under the open sky was planked, fenced, and, in the absence of rain, dry. If you had no money, you could dance outside on the grass and dirt road, and comment on the happening inside. This new world was in no small degree created for me by Piotr Leshchenko, who officially didn't exist. The country, exhausted by the bloody war, discovered him, and its youth began dancing to his catchy and hot tunes, all in the Gipsy manner so dear to the Russian heart. Soon we started hearing stories about this either White officer or a Gipsy, a Soviet, Rumanian, Nazi or French spy, or a good bandit. We couldn't know that the real Piotr Leshchenko owned a restaurant in Rumania and Soviet military officers loved the place and the singer. They were quietly bringing home and selling his records at the black market in every corner of this vast land. His daring and inviting songs copied from foreign records were scratched onto X-ray film; we called it "on the ribs." Under this avalanche of popularity, the papers and the radio finally recognized his existence and informed us that his songs were vulgar, lacking principles and ideas, devoid not only of ideology but even of a message. That gave us a reasonable explanation of why we loved him so much. He was a foreigner and the Party could not punish him. Years later, we learned that Leshchenko was arrested when Stalin was still alive and died in a Rumanian prison in 1954.

Soon he helped me to fall in love again, and my floor partner was destined to be the choice. Nelly had all the necessary qualities—she was a great dancer with bright eyes, big lips, and a small waist. When Leshchenko sings "Wine of Love," you want to hold her tight. When you hold her tight, Nelly puts her head on your shoulder, and you feel in heaven. When you are in heaven, local boys hate you. When she refuses to dance with anybody else, they want to beat you up.

She lived in a nearby settlement and to catch the last local train, we had to leave the floor a half hour before it closed. As a bona-fide man, I escorted my lady right to her door. She was the first girl I ever kissed. We didn't have Western movies scrupulously instructing youngsters on the correct protocol of kissing. We were incompetently mushing our lips against each other when she accidentally separated hers. I squeezed her in my arms, and all of a sudden began trembling and ejaculated into my pants. She felt every little bit of my paroxysm, did not look at my face, kissed my hand, said, "See you tomorrow," and ran home. In the dark of the night, I stood there, frozen, until realizing that walking two miles back to Nemchinovka in soaked, sticky pants wouldn't be fun. I looked for some grass and leaves, took my underwear off, wrapped my unpredictable organ with a layer of burdock leaves and headed back by the railroad tracks thinking of where I could do laundry and hang my belongings so the lady of the house wouldn't see and smell it.

◈ ◈ ◈

Often we were late for the last train and competed as to who would walk longer on one rail. The loser had to kiss the competing party, and I tried my best to lose as many times as I could. Once we saw three figures running in the dark along the rail track. As they caught up with us, we recognized them. The lean fellow with a stick in hand, said, "If we see you dancing with her again, I'll break your legs." Then he turned to Nelly and asked, "What? There aren't enough Russian boys here for you?"

"I'll report you to the police," she said.

They began laughing, one of them moved behind me with words, "Lame to your synagogue."

Nelly stepped between us, pressed her back against mine and said, "Hit me!" I wanted to hit him first, but thought of my new friend, the boatman Mike recently discharged from the military, and said, "I'll ask this Jew, Mike, to never give you a boat."

It worked. "It was a cultured warning," their chieftain said. "Don't complain tomorrow if we ..." and he delicately touched my knee with the stick. The hoodlum certainly remembered that Mike brought from the bottom of the pond the son of the local police commander when everybody had already taken the kid for dead. Mike's reference from a psychiatrist, the very fact that the buck could lift anybody in the air and hold him aloft, and his famous words, "I can kill anyone I wish," also played an important role. The gang departed, singing in dissonance Leshchenko's "Shot of Vodka."

"You're something!" I said to Nelly.

"So are you!" she said.

"I don't even know where it is, the Moscow synagogue," I said.

We were in love.

The next evening Mike came to the dance floor and said to that lean scum, "I know you can pull a knife, right? And you know I can break your neck. Don't touch these children. Alik is my cousin." He was something, too!

Three days before my departure, Nelly stopped coming to the dances. The first day I thought she was busy. I worried and did not dance the entire second evening. In the morning of the third day, I hung around her house until dark, in vain. Somebody looked at me several times through the drawn curtain. It wasn't she; Nelly would jerk the curtain away and show me her pretty face. To knock at the door was out of the question. I felt shy, did not know how her family would treat Nelly after such a visit, and decided that after going through necessary formalities at the university, I would feel emboldened and talk to whoever opens the door. We did not have telephones.

◈ ◈ ◈

At the Philosophy School, I did not find my name on the dean's list. The blood rushed to my head. I looked for it until my eyes were unable to do it anymore. Everything went black. With effort, I moved away from the bulletin board surrounded by the excited crowd and stood as if petrified on a landing between floors. Every devilry turned in my head. When did all this hate start? Probably when we had not yet turned into bipedal. Darwin was wrong. We descended from the omnivores. Bears? Pigs? I did not realize that I began to mumble when I heard a bit hoarse voice, "Pigs." Fred Solyanov gently tugged at my sleeve. We had chatted before. "Not accepted?"

"What's your score?" I asked dejectedly.

"Twenty-three."

"Mine too."

"It stinks," he said.

"How d'you know?"

"One doesn't need to be very observant," he said. "A couple of people accepted with 22. You better talk with Kosychev." This associate dean dealt with us during the tests.

"I don't want to," I said. "It's not an accident."

"Talk to him," repeated Fred. "As true Marxists, we know, proletarians have nothing to lose but their chains."

"And brains," I said and went to Kosychev.

He told me that these days were the busiest and asked me to come back three days later. Fred waited in the corridor. "He's playing for time," Fred said. "It's still not an official policy; it's still a passion."

"Yeah, a passion of millions, favorite Russian pastime."

"So what? It came at the time when everybody believed that this planet was flat."

"Yeah, a paper called *Pravda* didn't exist then ..." my hand depicted the broken wing of a falling bird.

Two days later Kosychev said, "We are the smallest school at the university. You would have a passing grade if the selection committee didn't admit several war veterans. They are outside of the contest."

"But all who scored 23 points were admitted," I said.

"No, you're wrong. It was up to the selection committee to decide."

Crushed, I muttered under my breath, "Biological selection committee."

He screwed up his eye behind the thick glasses. "What? If the Ministry of Higher Education allows, you can study as an extern, on your own. We do it in certain cases."

This convinced me, the campaign did not have written instructions beyond countless inspiring caricatures, articles, and satires. "We also accept those whose fathers had fallen on the battlefield, for example, Mikhail Grisman," thus demonstrating that there was no discrimination against Jews.

"Can the extern attend the lectures?" I asked.

"Normally, no. However, if a lecturer doesn't mind, one can do it. You won't be allowed to attend seminars or use our facilities for studying."

❖ ❖ ❖

The Ministry did not mind. The large self-confident official looked at me with interest, apparently surprised by my visit. I had a splitting headache, mumbled something about tests and scores, and stared above his head at Stalin sitting on a bench next to Lenin. This is a nervous break-down, I thought. Then I heard, "You'll be permitted to take winter exams, but don't forget, from now on, the military can call you up at any time."

Who knows, maybe he sympathized with this pale boy with the shifty eyes who babbled nonsense. He sure knew why they lowered my grade.

This mortal never worked so hard. At the end of November, I started to worry with a bang—I didn't have proof of being an extern. Reluctantly, I went to Kosychev. "The end-of-term exams are coming up," I said. "How can the lecturers even talk with me, if I don't have any documents?"

"We were sure that you changed your mind," he said. "Why didn't you come here three months ago? We can't do anything now."

"I was studying day and night."

"We call it self-education."

I felt a strong urge to hit his unremarkable face with my chair. I got up, lifted it, dropped it to the floor, and rushed out of his office. It was a break, and I saw Fred Solyanov and his classmate Oleg Rynkov walking toward me.

"I wanted to kill your associate dean," I said.

"Why didn't you come to him after your visit to the ministry?" interrupted Fred.

"I thought the ministry informed him."

Fred touched my shoulder.

"Okay," I said bleakly, "I am going there again. Didn't want to be humiliated again."

He winked at me, and I heard Kosychev's tenor behind me, "You don't need to conduct this public hearing and don't need to go anywhere. Come to me in a week, and you'll receive the student's record book."

At the end of the first semester, I was a high achiever. It was recorded in my brand new student book. The success encouraged me to think of Nelly with renewed passion. How could I explain to her my long absence? It would be difficult for her to understand the hurt and humiliation I went through. She would probably say that those who truly love, walk to the other end of the world just to see their lass. But even if I had traveled to her end of the world, I wouldn't necessarily be able to see her. How many times could I go by train in an attempt to meet her? I didn't even know the name of her street and her last name. By my old habit, I kept looking for Nelly in the streets and vast plaza of the Northern Railway Station.

⊹ ⊹ ⊹

I finished the school year with top marks but wasn't sure that I should continue my struggle under a constant threat of being drafted. Fred and Oleg Rynkov decided to set a rumor afloat that my father during the war saved the life of the incumbent minister of defense Marshal Vasilevskiy. They planted the fake news in the head of their academic group's slick Party Secretary, himself a war veteran. Fred even mentioned a certain Colonel Ivanov who witnessed the exploit with his own eyes. Being interested in formal logic, mathematics, and chess, he calculated that a couple thousand colonels with this most common surname served in the Russian military, and the associate dean might think twice before contacting the military commissar of my district.

Papa giggled and asked about something more realistic. "D'you remember recent elections of the Supreme Soviet?"

"Who cares about this circus?" I gave him a dirty look.

"You should," Papa laughed. "You voted for your University Rector. Our family and all alcoholics of our district voted unanimously for our People's Deputy in the Soviet parliament. Sonny, appeal to him for help."

On the day allotted for the reception of voters, I anticipated seeing a crowd—Nesmeyanov, the world-famous chemist and full member of Academy of Sciences, was a celebrity. However, I was his only visitor and was pleased to find that his pretty assistant was obviously a Jew. She took my handwritten appeal and the record book without saying a word and went into his office. In three minutes, she showed me a one-line resolution on the first page of my record book: "To enroll as a full-time second-year student. Nesmeyanov."

Overwhelmed, I said, "They didn't accept me because I'm a Jew."

She ignored my inappropriate remark.

With this gift from above in sweaty hand, in five minutes, I was knocking at Kosychev's door. All-triumphant love quickly replaced on his face the expression of total devastation. "Alexander Nikolayevich is a great man." He energetically shook my hand. "How did you find your way to his office?"

"That was easy," I said. "You can see his door from your window; it's in the wing in front of us. Just walk up to the second floor."

"Did you have a long conversation with him?"

"Oh yes! We discussed Georg Wilhelm Friedrich Hegel's work *Phänomenologie des Geistes*," I chirped in German. During the recent test in the German language, I borrowed this title from Karl Marx' work. When I left Kosychev's office, I realized that I overdid it. This work still wasn't published in the USSR. After Stalin's death, we learned that the professor Gustav Shpet translated it not long before the NKVD shot him in 1937.

This all of a sudden full-fledged sophomore came to seek the absolute truth of Marxism; he had already learned that Marxism could be distorted and abused, but did not expect disappointment to occur so quickly. Religiously enthusiastic Stalinists tirelessly talked in our narrow corridors about the new community of people with a common goal—the construction of communist society. Each of us was a Soviet Person, a Homo Sovieticus, a particle of the industrial uniform output called the Soviet People. Medieval alchemists working in their teeny laboratories on the creation of homunculus were pathetic amateurs in comparison with trailblazers experimenting in the laboratory between and beyond the Great Chinese and Berlin Walls. What would happen to my family and me if I shared my outrage with someone in my yard or university? This sophomore decided, to hell with philosophy and concentrated on sports. Very soon, I played hockey for the university and resumed my long-abandoned training in boxing.

◈ ◈ ◈

It was the late fall of 1951. After running in a cold drizzle to catch up with the last streetcar, I entered the empty rear car, shook the icy water from my head and shoulders, and saw a young conductress and a not-very-drunk cad sitting in front of her and sneeringly explaining why he did not intend to buy a ticket. I thought, "you shouldn't interfere." The campaign against rootless cosmopolitans and Zionists was in full swing. If the police came, they might prefer to arrest me. The brute recognized who entered the car and said with a curl of the lip, "She's a whore. You're a rich Jew. You can fuck her for cheap. Hey, you! How much?" He got up on his feet and took a step toward the scared woman, holding out both hands with the explicit intention to pull her off the conductor's high seat. I pushed his hands away and said as quietly as I could, "Sit back in your place, you beast."

He sat, and I took a strategic position between them. I heard the woman's "thank you" behind my back, turned with a victorious smile toward her, and immediately felt unbearable pain in my squeezed testicles. Now the animal had a childish smile and his punishing hand, accustomed to heavy work, was firmly in my crotch. He said, "I'll bring you out at my stop and kill you right there."

From the pain, my legs began to buckle. One thought—don't lose consciousness—swept through my head. Before inevitable death, some people are inventive. Trying my best not to move, I groaned, "You're not some sort of a Fascist, you're a Soviet citizen," I moaned. "Kill me but don't torture me," I grunted and promised to go with him without resistance to the edge of the Earth. His still smiling face reflected the workings of patriotic thought, and this intellectual effort caused him unconsciously to relax the stranglehold of my testicles. The next stop had to be mine. When the brute started to get up, I thanked God twice: he did not live ten more torturous stops down the road, and we were of similar height—he did not need efforts to pull the tenderest part of me up or down.

"I'll stop the driver in front of the police station," the conductress said. Apparently, she did not read the newspapers.

"Oh," I sobbed, "please don't!"

I didn't need their involvement. Police station #11 was two hundred yards ahead of the stop, just at the crossroad. She heard my pleading voice and remained in her seat. Perhaps under my positive influence, the drunk tuned into the patriotic mood and while yanking me, moaning and sighing, to the door, he cried, "For the Motherland! For Comrade Stalin! Forward to the victory of communism!" At the door, he fell into a deep meditation; it would be unrealistic to drag me by the balls three-streetcar steps down to the ground and still keep me in one piece. He wanted all of me. When the tram stopped, the sophist released my testicles—I thanked God again—and grabbed the scruff of my neck with both hands. As we stepped onto the ground, he started swinging his weighty fists. I did some classic boxer's diving while keeping an eye on the police station and on a middle-aged couple under an umbrella who stopped at the road crossing. I was anxious about them. The frustrated drunk was swearing—he was missing his target. Suddenly I heard, "Well, show him what else you can do."

I said "thank you" and knocked him down.

"Go home," the middle-aged man said. "The rain is ending, and the police may take to the streets now."

The sobering patriot already was on his feet and threatened me from a safe distance.

"Please go," said the woman.

"Thank you very much," I said. "I will remember you," and moved toward home. Since that encounter, I understand how people survive torture chambers.

The very next day I met again that girl with a gentle face, who had recently come out of nowhere in the Humanities Library. She was the reason why I began frequenting this fount of wisdom. Ready to enter it, she stood on the second floor of the old university building, beside the 200-year-old balustrade. I saw Irina from the ground floor, gracefully waved with both hands to prevent her from entering the library, beautifully galloped up the wide marble staircase, and, while thinking of putting under my sweater some enhancer to make my chest look powerful, continued waving my rakes. No sane girl could take this prancing stallion seriously. This time, I decided not to let her disappear again and, as boxers say, to impose a melee on her.

We already were acquainted; well, to a degree. The first time I had seen Irina was in front of the Philology School column during the last October Revolution demonstration. She and another novice had the honor of carrying the red banner with a quote from Stalin's work *Marxism and Problems of Linguistics*—"Language is a tool by which people communicate with each other. Stalin." I even kind of escorted Irina home several times though she was unaware of this. I shadowed her. This third-year mature student was again stricken by unrequited love at first blush. The love experience does not help if every time you go off your head. I did my best to hide my feelings from this creature with blue-black hair and bright gray eyes with bluish white. I had never seen either a Filipino or an Indian but decided that she must have some of those bloodlines. When she looked at me, I talked a lot of nonsense. Still overwhelmed, I shared with her my last night's experience, but didn't disclose my fear of the police, was very tactful while describing the specifics of the male anatomy, and only mentioned that the brute called me a moneyed Jew. Irina laughed and did not connect it with the politics of the day. "You acted like a fearless knight!" she exclaimed and asked, "Was she beautiful?"

"I don't know," I said dryly. "I'm not to her taste."

"You see, that's what I meant. You're a gentleman."

"You just don't know how lucky you are." I was angry with myself. "Your internal passport has the right word on the ethnicity line #5."

She did not take it seriously. "You're funny."

"You probably don't read newspapers."

"I read classic literature."

To escape the explosive subject, I allowed myself a bit of sacrilegious irony about Stalin's quote, "Your demonstration banner revealed a deep insight into the very nature of linguistics."

A couple of times we went to movies, and on rare occasions, I walked her home and always tried not to show that I was obsessed with her. I did not want to scare her and called Irina no more than three times a month. One day, this brainless fool decided to check her feelings by introducing this 19-year-old lady to a champion of Moscow in boxing with a Mona Lisa La Gioconda smile. This smile was meant to exude a certain shyness and appeared on his face mostly when Arslan Musin wanted to seduce a woman or when unsuspecting ruffians tried to attack him, a bespectacled short fellow. Unaware of my madness, he began dating Irina. I stopped calling her. He was outraged to find out that I was still a virgin. "We'll fix it," Arslan said briskly. Once, at the university sports camp in Krasnovidovo, he said that our cook Kathy was crazy about me. "When you were playing ball, she was watching only you and ignored the game. Dance with her by the bonfire."

That evening, dozens of us danced on the grass by the river. Kathy touched my bare shoulder with her lips in a cross between a bite and a kiss. I felt a minor pain, nothing else, and after the dance, why the hell did I say, "Thank you for the bite. It's time for me to go to bed."

In the middle of the night, Arslan returned to our tent, woke me up and whispered, "What did you tell Kathy to make her cry after you left?"

"I thanked her for the bite."

"You're an ungrateful and cruel nut," he said.

"Should I acquire your Gio-cobra smile?" I turned my back to him and fell asleep again.

◈ ◈ ◈

The Philology School was a floor above my school. We bumped into each other at the narrow stairs. Unable to hide my sadness, I sighed, "Haven't seen you for a century."

Irina looked around at people passing by us, said, "What the heck," and with both hands on my jacket she pulled me close and kissed me on the lips. My cheeks blazed up. In 1952, university students did not dare even to touch each other passionately in public. I had to hug her.

"You're such a ninny," Irina also sighed. "You could've done it a year ago."

This idiot was still holding her in his arms.

"By the way, I heard about your love affair with a pretty cook."

I squeezed her even stronger and kept looking in her one-of-a-kind eyes.

"By the way," she continued, "if we don't move to the wall, this angry crowd won't be able to use these ancient stairs."

Without releasing her from my embrace, I awkwardly took two steps toward the wall.

"Give me your phone number," my girl said. "Immediately."

It was the year when in Lenin Hills, for the first time in the history, were constructed two 12-story university dormitories with smallish individual rooms. The place was shown to foreign dignitaries. The provost emphatically rejected the brazen request of several students to allow their wives to sleep in their cubicles. "Your wives can be with you in the daytime, and at night they must return to their collectives." He spoke these exact words to the young husbands. A newlywed classmate of mine was devastated.

The Communist Youth organizations of both Schools—Philosophy and Philology—could punish us with a stern reprimand for our immoral behavior at the stairs. This stain could affect our professional future.

PART TWO: STEPMOTHER RUSSIA

Alma Mater in the
Days of the Dying God

Somewhere near the very end of 1952, my father came home unusually late. Gloomy as a black cloud, he said at the door, voice trembling, "They are evicting one hundred Jewish families from Davidkovo, not far from Stalin's dacha." Papa had spent the evening with the family of his former colleague and could hardly contain his tears. Police handed subpoenas to every Jewish family head of this Moscow suburb asking them to come to the Kuntsevo City Council for a talk. For security reasons, the authorities decided to resettle all families who lived too close to the route by which Comrade Stalin traveled to his country house. They had 75 days to find new places to live, until mid–January 1953 and could not settle in Moscow, Leningrad, Kharkov, Sverdlovsk, Rostov, the Black Sea resort of Sochi, the capitals of most republics, and in the world's largest border regions of the USSR. No documents changed hands.

Overnight, my parents discussed in their bed what belongings we should take if Stalin made the next step—to evict the Jews from the capital. Mama said, "I think, Alik can work as a teacher somewhere in Siberia."

Papa attempted to comfort her, "It could be just a trial balloon."

But it was not. After the creation of Israel in 1948, the media routinely reminded us of cosmopolitans and Zionists, but we could not believe what had been gradually happening. Many Jews with more or less senior positions in the enterprises and government agencies had been already pushed from Moscow. My sister Maria was pregnant when, in 1951, her husband, not a big shot, had a choice between unemployment and a transfer to a plant similar to the one he was working at, in the Ural Mountains. We interpreted it as an odd unpleasant case. I knew that my schoolmate Simon Markish all of a sudden disappeared in the middle of the 1949 school year, but we could not imagine that he was sent to Siberian exile for ten years with his mother and younger brother David. On January 27 of that year, his father was among some arrested members of the Jewish Anti-Fascist Committee. Three years and seven months later, on August 12, 1952, just a couple of months before Davidkovo Jews were ordered to go, a loyal Soviet patriot Peretz Markish and twelve other writers were shot. All of them wrote in Yiddish. Their families did not know about this execution.

◈ ◈ ◈

When Irina and I met near our favorite bench in the university courtyard, an icy wind blew the drifting December snow. I told her that we could not marry. "I don't want you to end up in Siberia," I said.

She freed her nose out of a thick scarf to say, "Jews are paranoid," and then retreated to the comfort of warmth.

"All of us?"

"Maybe. We lived for three years in Oslo, which is like a well-maintained Siberia with central heating and bathrooms and without gnats and drunken beggars. This Norwegian scarf will be pretty good for Siberia."

"Your parents won't be thrilled with me even in Moscow. They read papers."

"My dad is an old-fashioned communist dreamer. He remembers that Lenin lived in Siberian exile."

"Sure," I said, "with a piano, a personal library, a shotgun, and a hunting dog."

"And his wife," said Irina.

That evening, Papa brought home three pairs of felt *valenki*. Mama said, "We must buy sheepskin coats."

"For Irina, too," I said.

◈ ◈ ◈

On January 13, 1953, at the university, one war veteran, a Party member, gloomily made Fred Solyanov read a copy of *Pravda*, pinned to a wall. An article about the Jewish doctors' plot to poison Stalin and other leaders of the USSR was headlined "Vicious Spies and Killers under the Mask of Academic Physicians." Three days later the same soldier whispered to Fred, "Tell your buddy that he's a candidate for shipment. In his place, I would escape into some wilderness."

Citizens demanding capital punishment for all participants of the Zionist conspiracy kept sending letters to newspapers. Thirty-seven "loathsome reptiles" confessed to shocking crimes in Moscow, Leningrad, Kiev, Kharkov, and Sverdlovsk. Their collaboration with the Jewish bourgeois-nationalist organization from New York called JOINT was unmasked. This Jewish Joint Distribution Committee was "created by American intelligence" under the guise of charity. Jews were attacked in the streets. Patients all over the country were refusing to be treated by "killers and poisoners in white gowns." Several hundred more physicians, mostly Jews, were arrested. It was clear for millions that some conspirators remained free and planned to poison Party officials and generals, pregnant women, and babies. Police continued checking passports of Jewish-looking men and women in the streets.

◈ ◈ ◈

Irina and I sat on our bench when her classmate Bella Chesnokova approached us. She sobbed and could hardly utter, "My father stamped his feet and yelled that I should forget that my mother was a Jew. He yelled, 'You're a Russian! A Russian!'"

Her looks vividly reminded one of anti–Zionist caricatures. I clumsily acted against my conscience and said, "Maybe he worries about your safety. For a couple of years, my parents have been asking me to stay at home in the evenings."

Until recently, Bella's father, Professor Dmitri Ivanovich Chesnokov, was the chair of our Department of Historical Materialism and the editor of the theoretical *Communist Journal*, thus, a big shot. All of a sudden, he became a celestial being, of whose existence we were reminded only by his portraits on the thousands of walls; he became a member of the new Presidium of the Central Committee. If such a person, who daily communicated with Stalin, stomped angrily and blew up hysterically at his 20-year-old daughter, then something threatening his semi–Jewish child was happening. Maybe this newly appointed junior co-emperor was scared no less than my parents.

"Please don't tell anyone about this outburst," Bella began calming down. "Of course, he loves us. He's just ... you know, such a huge responsibility ... such pressure. Sorry, guys."

We never shared this chat with anyone. By now, I was convinced that Stalin could kill anybody with no hesitation. Nevertheless, I sensed that she should know more and feel my pain, too, and said, "My parents wanted me to get a safe Jewish occupation..." "Stop it," Irina interrupted, but I finished, "...to become a physician. Funny, isn't it?"

Bella sobbed again.

Persistent rumors of the imminent expulsion of the Jews to Siberia crawled into the Theater of Satire and our neighbor Alevtina Petrovna came to consult with my father. She looked scared. Papa and I still tried to find something funny in the latest developments.

"Alevtina, as a true Russian, you can divorce this old fart or write a letter to *Pravda* with a promise to re-educate him," Papa said. Her face wrinkled, but my father continued cruelly, "Or, even better, write to Stalin to express your concern about the future of Moscow theaters. Their actors, directors, and musicians are more or less Jewish, and they would be quickly shut down, including the Gypsy Theater where Jews for years pretended to be genuine Gypsies."

"Abram, you mean there is nothing we can do?" she said.

"Papa!" I said reproachfully. "It might be a years-long experiment."

It was clear to me that Stalin and his clique hijacked great Marxist ideas to cement their grip on the country, which still tried to build a socialist society. After Alevtina Petrovna went back to her room, I guessed, "Maybe the privilege of living in Moscow might be extended to the father of the half–Jewish Lev Junior killed at war."

We could not know that soon, at 9:50 a.m. on March 5, 1953, history would change its course and the mood of my family. Stalin died on the floor of his dacha in Davidkovo. The system of total control and subordination created by the most potent dictator worked beautifully; the new doctors saw him only twelve or thirteen hours after his death. They established that Stalin had died from a massive stroke. The head of the secret service Beria selected all of them. All of them had pure Russian blood. Most of them had never seen their patient alive. Half a day later, when the dead man hadn't yet cooled down, the new Presidium of the Party ceased to exist. It was a sad day in the life of Bella's father. His portraits were destined to vanish. The old Politburo was unanimously revived. Their animal fear of the Leader of All Nations disappeared, but all ten of them still feared each other. As a result, the "collective leadership" came to power. Democracy in Russia multiplied ten times.

The next day, March 6, 1953, knowing the mood of Adik Ivanovsky, I crossed our landing and rang twice. Adik, now a student of physics, and called Andrei, was ready to leave for the Hall of Columns to say goodbye to Stalin. I asked his parents to forbid him from doing so. They ignored my request. Ivan Vasilievich still had excellent relations with the Supreme Leader. Today, another Stalin was on the same easel I saw for the first time some 16 years ago. Next to him stood Stalin's photograph divided into smallish squares with a ruler and a sharp pencil.

"You won't see anything except the soldiers," I said to my friend.

"I know your anti–Soviet views," he barked.

"I'm just concerned about your safety," I said, "but it's you who has anti–Soviet views. Society cannot rely exclusively on one genius's acumen and expertise."

Adik was not alone. Many rushed to Moscow to give the mustached god the last tribute of love and devotion. The vast majority of the Soviet citizens, including relatives of two and a half million prisoners, were still worshiping him. I was ahead of my generation. I celebrated his death. I worshiped communism.

❖ ❖ ❖

Late in the evening, white as chalk, Adik returned home with a broken left forearm and wrist. With a contorted grimace, he refused to pull his coat off the affected limb. His voice trembled as he reported, "Thousands screamed.... A boy tried to climb up a drainpipe ... someone on the second floor opened a window for him..." It seemed that Adik could not control his sobs, "The boy dropped down on their heads.... People were falling like dominos.... They budged and jerked right under my boots...." He looked at his feet in horror.

According to rumor, the number killed on the Trubnaya Plaza and adjacent streets range from a few hundred to three thousand. When a similar disaster happened during the coronation celebration of the last tsar in 1896, the official figures of 1,389 dead had quickly been made public.

❖ ❖ ❖

At the Philosophy Department, where every fifth philosopher possessed a Party card, I could share my true feelings only with Nahl Zlobin, the son of a famous writer, and my classmates Fred Solyanov, Oleg Rynkov, and Mike Grisman. Nonetheless, he with a morbid face stopped next to roses on the floor under the portrait, and probably thought of his pregnant cousin's husband killed on that plaza. Oleg, Nahl, and I were just passing by the pious crowd in front of Stalin's portrait framed with a black ribbon. Mike probably thought of overturned truck, which crushed the young lieutenant and several other soldiers. I thought of tumbling trucks with soldiers in beds. "Like this," Adik said, and snapped with his index finger a matchbox on the dining table; it turned over several times and fell to the floor.

All of a sudden, the Faculty of Philosophy was in turmoil. Communists worshiped the Leader's thirty-years impact on Marxism-Leninism and carried banners with the slogan "Stalin Is Today's Lenin." For years, they wrote passionate letters, often anonymous, to Party committees of various levels—from the Faculty of Philosophy to the Central Committee, accusing each other of deviating from the true love of Marxism. They knew Stalin's death would influence their understanding of historical and dialectical materialism, history, economics, literature, arts, biology, agriculture, celebrated Soviet projects of turning the rivers back, linguistics, and, possibly, mathematics and astronomy. The unaffiliated riff-raffs like me did not know of what was going on inside their ranks.

Twenty-five days after Stalin's death the case of the Jewish doctors' plot was dismissed. The physicians who survived torture chambers were released. Almost four months after the Great Helmsman moved in Lenin's Mausoleum, on June 26, 1953, reliable divisions moved to Moscow, and ten generals arrested the powerful head of the KGB despite his outburst of anger. Next month, *Pravda* released the only evidence of Beria's case—a carefully worded part of the Central Committee's decision. Four more months later, in late October 1953, the paper informed us that the agent of numerous Western secret services Beria and several of his assistants had been shot dead. I asked the now-recovered Adik if the judges at that closed trial had considered such unimportant cases as the rape of schoolgirls delivered straight from Moscow's streets to Beria's house behind high walls near the Vosstania Square. We knew a girl who managed to avoid such a fate by going into hiding.

◈ ◈ ◈

To this day, it is not clear if Stalin did indeed plan the total deportation of Jews. Hitler would approve it. Numerous Russian and Israeli authors say he ordered Bella's father D.I. Chesnokov to prepare a Marxist justification of the necessity of this deportation and his book on this subject was ready by the beginning of February 1953. Bella's conversation with my future wife and me shortly before Stalin's death indirectly confirmed this plan. Her father was hysterical and worried of his own family future. The whole print run was destroyed. After the disintegration of the Soviet Union, Russian historian Gennady Kostyrchenko studied this matter and never found a single document confirming the preparation of this expulsion. His opponents argued that freight cars were assembled on the railroad tracks near Moscow, Kiev, Odessa, and Riga and hundreds of thousands would be dead before arriving in uninhabitable barracks constructed thousands of kilometers away. Stalin's verbal order was always sufficient to begin various campaigns—from catching spies in every little town, where people knew each other from infancy, to deporting numerous ethnic groups, though these were relatively small and not dispersed like Jews all over the country. The switchboard telephone nicknamed the "spinner," the bellied red phone on Stalin's desk, had become his primary weapon of mass killing.

Twenty years after Stalin's death, in 1973, the leading philosopher D.I. Chesnokov remained proud of his service to the Leader. Back in 1947, Stalin transferred him from a position of provincial propaganda expert into the holy of holies—the Propaganda and Agitation Department of the Central Committee of the CPSU. In 1973, Chesnokov boastfully recalled the moment when the Leader discussed with his theoretician the most urgent matter of the time—solving the Jewish question. In his words, Leader demanded "to revive the theoretical work in the Party" and "analyze the new processes and the phenomena in the country and the world." "Without theory," Stalin said, "we will die. Our fate without theory is death, death, death!" Stalin was sincere. In his 29 years at the helm, he always needed mortal enemies. In the midst of the Cold War, the need for perfect enemies had been nicely satisfied by the all-powerful American imperialism and crafty Zionism-cosmopolitanism. This double-headed dragon with Uncle Sam's top hat on a fire-breathing head and a yarmulke on a poison-spewing one had to help to unite all countries of the Socialist camp in a monolith. What enemy could be better and more reliable! Yet, twenty years later, our professor shied away from naming the enemies. His stomping and screaming, "You are a Russian! Forget your Jewish mother!" probably were still vibrating in his ears when D.I. Chesnokov was punished by being sent out of Moscow to continue his career on a provincial level again.

Many more years passed after the death of the Great Pilot, but his memory continued to burn in the hearts of those who served him faithfully. Fifty-one years after Stalin's death, in a 2004 interview, when the Soviet Union was very dead, a prominent professor of my philosophy school, Theodor Oizerman, remembered that tumultuous time: the discussions among philosophers had reached a boiling point. To reconcile the seemingly irreconcilable differences among Marxists-Leninists, the faculty members appealed to the university's Party Committee to determine the Truth. The committee said, "Comrades, cease exercising in scholasticism!" Nonetheless, unsatisfied learned comrades did not stop and, to avoid any political shortsightedness, brought the matter to the attention of the Moscow Party Committee. Oizerman was there, and his brilliant memory allowed him to quote its wise men: "Stop this futile debate," they said. "The question of what is the Truth is decided only by the Central Committee of the Party." The burning problem was thus solved at once.

In this 2004 interview, when the nature of necessity and freedom radically changed, the 84-year-old Oizerman was still proud of his bygone times' connections. The academician listed as his friends some top-level luminaries heavily engaged in Stalin's "cult of personality." I was not surprised. He was one of those who in the past had turned philosophy into ideology and always held his hand on the Party's pulse. He interpreted for us the meaning of forbidden works of Western philosophers kept in special book depositories. All we learned were the excerpts Oizerman was feeding us. The so-called Pornographic Department established by the French National Library in the 16th century probably came closest to this institution.

The Most Influential
Writer in My Life

In 1954, my last year at university, political prisoners began returning home, or to what was left of it. The late spring of that first year without Stalin was the time to allot jobs to graduating seniors. Some activists entered postgraduate studies and later became instructors and consultants of the Central Committee. This was the shortest way to a professorship, Academy of Sciences' membership, and high positions in ministries and media. The rest of us got permission to look for jobs by ourselves. Party and state periodicals and dailies were off limits to nonpartisan freelancers, and I was glad to write for the youth paper *Moskovsky Komsomolets* and the *Sovietsky Sport*. Those jobs did not bring enough money, but my parents were happy to feed and clothe their little boy.

When a censor killed my first satire for the *Moskovsky Komsomolets*, the head of the department said, "Don't worry, you get a 50 percent honorarium for the galley."

"Why?" I said. "You liked it. The editor-in-chief liked it, too."

"We never ask censors why they kill this or that piece," the old hand said. "They have their considerations."

"You said it was funny…"

He interrupted me. "It doesn't have anything to do with the quality of your piece. Get used to this."

"What's the big deal!" I couldn't calm down. "There aren't enough teapots, and kitchens are dirty in a workers' dormitory; what does it have to do with the state interests?"

The grizzled veteran of the newspaper business was getting impatient, "Arkady, I'm swamped with work. Get your money and come tomorrow for a new assignment. Goodbye, old man!"

✦ ✦ ✦

Irina's parents refused to read my pieces, began regularly hanging up on me, locking their daughter at home, and even escorting her sometimes to university.

"Your dad reads *Pravda*," I said. "They worry about your future with me. Let's marry after I find a job at a taiga newspaper and you join me there after your graduation."

"In a year and a half?" she said. "Do you really love me?"

"Could you live in one room with my parents? They love you, too."

"No," she admitted. "I'm spoiled. I have my own little room."

"Is it important for you to go to a registry office?"

"I couldn't care less about these bureaucrats."

We decided to sell some of our clothes so we could rent a room for a couple of months and live in heaven. She wanted to sell what was the envy of the Philology School—her Norwegian sweater with reindeer motif and silvery metal buttons. I said, "Never."

Stephan Pavlovich Zlobin, my favorite writer, who happened to be the father of my university friend Nahl, suggested, "Kidnap your sweetheart, bring her here, and live with us until the colonel pulls himself together and forgives you for being a dead-end Jew."

I could not believe my ears. Sacrifice your comfort for some unpredictable boy?

In the fall of 1954, his selfless offer brought me under Irina's window some eight feet above my head. On that day, Irina boycotted her family visit to her uncle, and now she smiled at me from the open window. "They locked the door," she said. I advised her to tie several sheets and tablecloths together and attach one end to a heating radiator. Irina disappeared for a long time, and when she came back, she did not smile anymore. The parents hid her belongings.

"What if this old troublemaker Stephan Zlobin was just joking?" she asked.

"Do you still have shoes?" I asked.

"Yes, I do."

"Good. Put together all you can and throw it to me."

After ten minutes of waiting, I caught a bundle wrapped in a sheet and holding it in my hands, plopped down on the asphalt. She didn't express any sympathy, asking "Do we know how long Zlobin will tolerate our presence?"

"No, we don't. And neither does he."

"Do you have money?"

I was getting impatient, "Come down first."

Irina disappeared again and came back with another load, "This is my escape equipment," she said, "and ... oh, Alik! This is my only brother. Hi Yuri! This is Alik."

I looked over my shoulder and said, while passing the ill-fated bag to the blushing brother, "We don't need to fight over this dowry."

The hefty Yuri took the bundle. "I don't want to participate in this race," he said with embarrassment.

"We'll run away some other day," Irina said.

"That fellow was there, waiting for you," Yuri said.

"Another contender?" I asked.

"This Romeo urgently needs to get married," said Irina. "Otherwise, he won't get the job in the Washington embassy. The secret of my beauty is in our return home after three years in Norway."

"To secure such a job," I said, "he needs a bride with a 20-years Party membership, not an unreliable philology student."

"That's how you view me?"

"No, I view you as a bespectacled angel sticking out of a brick frame with a heavenly load in her arms, probably removable wings."

"Don't worry, brother," said the angel. "You'll get used to this strange person. That's why they like each other."

"Who?" I asked.

"Stephan Pavlovich and you."

"You flatter me. If only you knew his stormy biography!"

◈ ◈ ◈

Several long afternoons I had been waiting for her by the bridge which led to the Zlobins' high-rise on Kotelnicheskaya embankment, one of the three cake-shaped skyscrapers constructed on Stalin's orders to compete with New York. Finally, the prisoner escaped, this time through the door, with a small bag. The highly unqualified guards were at home. To disorient them, she turned on the lights in the bathroom, locked it, and magnanimously left the key at her pillow next to a short letter with the telephone number of Stephan Pavlovich. This was his suggestion. Already on the bridge, I told Irina how this dying Russian prisoner fell down, and the guard, instead of following German instructions and shooting him to death, dragged Stephan for a mile to a concentration camp. The traitor recognized the front-line reporter.

In twenty minutes, we wandered into his luxury apartment. On our room's door hung a sign "Groom and Bride." We walked to the window, looked at the Moscow River, and embraced. Our host was in a good mood. I decided to get drunk.

"For the first time I see Alik drinking," Irina said.

After a few goblets of Armenian cognac, I grew bolder and asked Stephan Pavlovich to tell why Stalin gave him Stalin's Prize First Class for *Stephan Razin,* my favorite historical novel about the legendary Cossack, who led the uprising in the 17th century. From his son I learned that the Writers' Union Secretaries, the most celebrated Simonov and Fadeev, did not include his father in the list of candidates for the prize and Stalin scolded them.

"Is that true?" I said. "How dared they? Big deal Party Central Committee members! Yellow-bellied punks!"

He filled my slender goblet one more time and said, "In the middle of the night, drunk Fadeev woke up all babies in my overcrowded communal apartment. He called me a genius and said that he never read such a beautiful novel."

"I'm drunk like Fadeev," I said. "So, this is how you got this apartment, right from Comrade Stalin."

Stephan Pavlovich was apologetic and explained why Constantine Simonov did not congratulate him. The court poet felt uncomfortable. A couple of years previously not only had he killed Zlobin's manuscript *Rebellion of Dead*, but he also had handed it to a military prosecutor.

"Crud," I said.

"The Nazi guard dragged you for a mile, the great Soviet poet tried to put you in camp again," concluded Irina.

I waved my arms, "Stephan, sorry, Stephan Pavlovich, why did you write a book doomed to die before it was born?"

"Fool!" Zlobin began to make excuses. "This fool was there," he tapped his wide chest. "I can't explain this rationally. I saw many traitors and true heroes."

Irina asked him if he knew what makes people heroes or traitors. He shrugged, "In most cases, circumstances." He shook his head, "Just look at that guard who dragged me risking his own life. Was he a hero or a traitor?"

I got up from the chair and shook my index finger meaningfully to stress to Irina that throughout three years Germans didn't want to enter the barracks where the Russians were dying in droves from typhoid. The nurse Zlobin, I turned emphatically my finger to him, dragged dead prisoners to the hole in the ground, fed and wiped fouled-up wounded, wrote and sent to other camps songs, poems, and leaflets. "Why?" I threw up my hands. "This nonpartisan anarchist," I shook my forefinger vigorously, "even created an underground Communist party organization."

"That wasn't envisioned in the Party Charter," he interjected, "and the Party later didn't recognize those impostors. How do you know all of this?"

"From reliable sources." I felt like an all-knowing sage. "You were chained to the subject like a convict to the galley oar."

Stephan was listening with a certain curiosity to this youngster who pretended to be sober. "Fool!"—he repeated contritely.

"This isn't explanation," I demanded. "Where this suicidal feeling comes from, that tells you to make this illogical choice? No other choice is given."

Stephan tried to fill my goblet again and lowered his head. "I don't know. It's a matter of your esthetics."

Irina was intently silent.

"Why did you need to do it?" I clung to him like a drunk leech. "You don't believe in the salvation. You neglected the instinct of self-preservation. Stalin, Fadeev, and Simonov were guided by this most powerful animal instinct all their lives."

Stephan shook his bush of hair. "Heroes and saints come of fools."

I turned to my future wife. "For this man I can kill. Just tell me whom to kill."

"Kill my chatty son," he said.

Irina smiled silently.

"This man's place is next to the Lord," I explained to her.

"In your Jewish Heaven," she said.

"In a can, as everyone else," Zlobin said.

"Get off the rostrum," Irina lightly slapped me on the bottom, "and don't miss the chair."

They couldn't stop laughing. It was not funny.

Our luxury life did not last long. Irina's father called the next evening. It was a complete surrender. The colonel asked me to come to them to get acquainted. We came. They kept kissing her. He was a deeply religious communist, as I was before entering university. He led political studies at the Ministry of Defense and was depressed—not all of his students in epaulets were disappointed in Stalin. To establish relations with the new kin, I just assented. Irina looked at me with surprise and love. They invited us to stay the night in her room, but we went to my parents' only room. Papa and Mama waited for us and we settled with them. Their neighbors did not object to our temporary invasion of their communal apartment. It lasted for almost two years with long breaks for springs and summers when we rested at the dacha of my in-laws.

Travel to True Russia

Unlike all known-to-me inhabitants of the capital, I had wanted for some time to live away from Moscow and to report about real life in the country, not about the pampered Muscovites. I started writing letters to editors of youth newspapers. Three Siberian papers had no vacancies. Another three never responded to a proposal of the highly educated and sophisticated Moscow reporter to work in a region of his dreams.

In October 1956, this dream came true.

My train was heading north, to Kostroma, a city from where the European taiga stretches for thousands of kilometers to the north and the east—to the Arctic Ocean and the Ural Mountains. From now on, I would be the head of the Correspondence and Satire Department. We would work on the first issue of the just-established regional daily *The Molodoi Leninetz* (*The Young Leninist*). The steam was whistling; the wheels were rhythmically banging. I was thinking of the 20th Congress of the Communist Party. It has already been changing my life and would make my job exciting and meaningful. My bliss felt overwhelming. My fellow passengers were friendly and talkative. It was such a pleasure to get drunk on board in good company and tell my new, already dear friends about intimate details of my life knowing that we will never meet again. I pretend that I am listening and from time to time smile and nod to fit in with the company. They brought on board open-faced sandwiches—white and dark bread with the cheese called Russian, scarce Doctor's sausage placed on a bed of butter, and even more scarce oranges, and also chicken, boiled eggs and potatoes, salted pork fat, biscuits, and waffles of all kinds. Many brought vodka, and to make the morning hangover more bearable, pickled cucumbers and sauerkraut.

To the accompaniment of the railroad's soothing heavy metal music, my thoughts turned to the 20th Congress of the Party. On its last day, at an unscheduled closed session, Nikita Khrushchev, to the surprise of the vast majority of delegates, delivered a report: "On the Personality Cult and

Its Consequences." After four months of silence, ordinary citizens learned about it from *Pravda*. Stephan Pavlovich Zlobin called it an abridged and softened version. Blame for the crimes committed during all the years of my life was put squarely on Stalin's shoulders. Political prisoners kept returning home, and we concluded that Stalinism was dead and nothing in the world could reanimate its stinking corpse.

The benevolent conductor with loads of red and black cosmetics on her round face brought now and then deadly sweet tea in metal glass holders, but refused to take a shot of vodka. "Probably an alcoholic," guessed my neighbor in highly polished, tall boots. Evil tongues said that this tea was so black because the tea leaves were mixed with a pinch of baking soda. I shied away from the vodka and, not to offend anyone, lied that on the previous night bad moonshine had poisoned me. The man exhaling wine fumes compassionately hugged me. I embraced him and a hefty woman wrapped in a gypsy shawl; I gave her my bottom shelf after imagining how her bulk of flesh would squash me if she fell from her narrow upper bed onto poor skinny me. She was constantly laughing, throwing back her head and leaning against the wall, her weighty breasts dangerously rolling up and down like a storm surge. It was now late and, after having a good long talk, everybody was sleeping soundly. The car was not divided into compartments, and the lady's snoring and gurgling drowned out the rich variety of other sounds produced by fellow travelers. Nothing was bothering me. I was busy thinking of the historical Congress. I was able almost not to think about the long separation from my beloved; she would be coming to Kostroma later, to celebrate the New Year with me. On and off, I had been in a state of euphoria for more than seven months, since the Congress.

❖ ❖ ❖

I arrived in Kostroma on time. The editorial staff of *The Young Leninist* was waiting for me. Portraits of Lenin, Khrushchev, and Karl Marx hung in the office of the editor-in-chief Elena Protasova. No Comrade Stalin! Everybody in the room, including her, was young, except a local poet, Alexander Chasovnikov, with a military medal "For Bravery" on a crumpled lapel of his jacket. They treated me like a crackerjack. Protasova had read my satires in the *Soviet Sports* and said that from now on I'd better forget about sports and quickly learn about collective farms, milking cows, weaving mills, and logging. She caught my puzzled gaze at a poster of a stocky woman with a rugged face and two gold stars on her white apron denoting a Hero of Socialist Work. Behind her, several happy cows were peacefully grazing, except the one who was studying my physiognomy. She had the eyes of her milkmaid. That was too much for me.

"Evdokia Isaevna Torsova is our pride!" said my editor. "The best milker in the world."

I caught my new colleague Anna Galun's sharp eye; it was winking at me. I couldn't do the same. Protasova moved her rhapsodic glance from Anna's weather-beaten face onto me and from me onto my new peer again. To suppress the urge to say something inappropriate, I squeezed out, "What a beauty!" They all roared with laughter, even Protasova and Alexander who slapped his knee; before that, he was moving lips and rolling eyes, clearly hatching a new poem. When everybody calmed down, Protasova interpreted my words, "Arkady appreciates inner beauty."

Freckles on Anna's cheeks began to jump, and she nearly fell out of her chair with laughter.

"Anya!" said Protasova reproachfully.

"Sorry!" said Anna.

To help her, I said, "I should talk to young milkmaids with whom this veteran has been sharing her experience."

"Of course!" said Protasova. "And your first assignment will be exactly that—to write an essay about a collective dairy farm in Susanino District; it's not far away, some seventy kilometers. They have a very active *Komsomol* cell."

The formalities were over, and the editor took me to a large desk with an inkstand installed in the middle of it. "The Regional Party Committee allocated to us some of their furniture; this one is yours." With an effort, she pulled out the stubborn upper drawer. We anticipated seeing empty space ready for immediate use, but it was occupied. Small, hateful eyes looked up at us, ready to attack invaders. We both instinctively stepped back. My childhood experience next to refuse boxes helped me to overcome my fear and loathing. I used my foot to shove the drawer backward.

Relieved Protasova yelled, "Rats! We still have rats in this building!"

Anna Galun was the only person in the room who remained calm and began hammering the desk. After five seconds of hard work, she pulled the ill-fated drawer out. It was empty. "Our dormitory in Penza accommodated more fat rats than skinny students," she said. "Please, in the name of our bright communist future, don't put food in your drawers for a while."

In the mornings, all of us kept banging on our desks. To the uninitiated, it could look like a mysterious ritual.

Three days later a three-ton-truck from the Party Regional Committee drove me to Susanino. Before I stepped on the wheel to climb in the truck bed, the man next to the driver raised his hand in the manner of a person accustomed to greeting demonstrators from a podium. The driver warned, "You better keep both hands on your suitcase. We hit a pothole on this very road, and a *Northern Pravda* correspondent's handbag jumped into the mud and drowned there."

The story supported my romantic mood. "Did you find it?" I asked in the hope of hearing "no." He ruined it with his "sure." I sat on a crosspiece plank nailed between the wooden broadsides right behind the cab, put my hard suitcase flat on the muddy bottom, set both feet on it, and pressed my back against the cab. At last, I was going to see the real Russia. In half an hour, by the swollen Kostroma River, I saw the monumental ruins of a monastery. I couldn't believe my eyes, a sign reading "righteous Hierony-mus" on a piece of plywood leaned against a wall of a demolished tower. I pounded on the cab's roof, the truck stopped, I jumped into the liquid mud and squelched to the plywood. With three mistakes in two words, it was written there "Kerosene for sale." When I, disillusioned, came back, the astonished passenger opened the door's window and asked, "What were you looking for?"

"For a saint," I said. (My confusion. You can tell, in the Russian language, the words "righteous" and "sale" begin with the same letters.)

"After the revolution, we blew the whole thing up and drove away all saints," he giggled.

"Are you from the Regional Party Committee?"

"Instructor Petrov," he nodded.

"Responsible for anti-religious propaganda?"

"How did you guess?" he straightened his black tie.

"Because you don't believe in saints."

We both smiled understandingly.

"I still feel sorry for these magnificent ruins," I said.

"As Comrade Khrushchev said, 'when you chop down the tree, the chips go flying,'" the instructor Petrov continued. "It's Ipatievsky Monastery, the former bastion of tsarism. Now it serves people."

"How?" I asked.

"A museum of atheism, machine and repair shops, a garage, a lot of storehouses—cabbage, potatoes, other vegetables, firewood, coal, building materials, you name it, and it's there."

Yet, the driver strengthened my romantic mood again. The famous Susanino was on top of a hill, and we might not be able to climb up there.

"Don't worry, comrade Polishchuk," the instructor misread my happy smile and reassured, "a tractor might be waiting for us, to pull the truck up the hill."

"Only a horse didn't skid in the mud," remarked the driver. "Give it a stronger switch, and it will drag any *telega* uphill."

"I knew an old stableman who never hit a horse," I said.

"Probably a Muscovite," he said, smiling at the instructor.

We stopped for a leak at a vast swamp. A historical place, explained Petrov, the Susanin's swamp, twelve kilometers long and up to four kilometers wide. As a lazy fifth-grader, I had learned that in 1613, Ivan Susanin led Polish invaders into impenetrable swamps and sacrificed his life for the Motherland.

"Recently two cows drowned here," the instructor said. "The drunk herdsman."

"Was he tried?"

"Comrade Muscovite, what can we do nowadays? Under Stalin, he would've got a good seven years."

Now the driver giggled. He knew the cowherd. "The old man sleeps on the go. He can't herd even one goat."

"There is no youth in the village," Petrov explained. "After military service, boys are accepted on construction projects in big cities and Siberia, and then, by hook or by crook, they obtain an internal passport and use it to avoid returning to their village."

I did not know that the villagers did not have such a crucial document and said grimly, "Something should be done about that."

"Yes," the Party veteran wanted to educate this young fellow who didn't know a thing about real problems of the country, "you're probably unaware that days after Stalin's death, Beria, not yet unmasked as a Western agent, attempted to give passports to all peasants. That would be the surest way to destroy the collective farm system. Fortunately, he was tried and shot."

I mentioned the young workers in a Moscow dormitory who couldn't get a residence permit from the police, and as soon as they ended their work, they would have to leave the capital.

"Former soldiers?" he asked.

"Yes, in worn-out uniform shirts. It's a mess."

"Did you write about them?"

"Not really. Only now, thanks to you, I'm beginning to understand the extent of their problems; I wrote a satire about bad conditions in their dormitory."

The instructor did not show interest in my feuilleton butchered by a censor. "We should do something about this," he stressed. "This flight from farms should again become a criminal offense."

"The younger generation wants to live better," I said, but didn't inject in our conversation an explosive memory; my university buddy from Czechoslovakia once amazed me when he said that in Western countries people did not have internal passports.

"There are wider state interests," the instructor continued. "From a historical perspective, every citizen will win if we strengthen the agricultural base of the country. In the long run, this is for their benefit. A villager loves his countryside and dislikes the cities."

He invited me to drop by his office to do more talking. "Just tell me," he asked, "have you seen *Ivan Susanin* in Bolshoi Theater?"

"Yes, I did." This subject gave me a chance to say that this opera was called *A Life for the Czar* before the revolution. In response, he refreshed the Marxist axiom—that art has always been of a class nature and suggested I check out the future home for the Susanin Museum building, at the intersection of Marx and Lenin streets. "In the 17th-century building," proudly stressed Petrov. From textbooks, we knew this Susanin prevented the Poles from entering Kostroma, but we did not know that he sacrificed his life for Mikhail Romanov, proclaimed the first czar of the Romanov dynasty. The ceremony took place in the monastery where I had looked for a saint. Centuries later, the village of this peasant was not able to allow me to enter it in a four-wheeled miracle of the twentieth century. The instructor was right. The tractor was waiting for us at the bottom of the hill.

◈ ◈ ◈

Olga, the First Secretary of Susanino *Komsomol* District Committee, liked how this newcomer gloomily shook my head when she said that milkmaids get up after 3 a.m. and slog to the unheated cow-house through mud, already ice-cold. She hesitated for a second, and continued, "You have smooth and soft hands, a 20-year-old milkmaid's hands are like sandpaper."

I asked if the young Secretary had ever said this to a *Northern Pravda* correspondent. She burst out laughing. "Aren't you scared that at the moment you maybe are the only young male in the district?" she asked.

"I'm painfully aware of this privilege."

"Sorry," Olga paused. "I'm in a bad mood today."

"You're in a perfect mood. I will carry your picture at the May Day demonstration." An idea dawned on me. "Maybe my report should be titled *District Committee and the Farm*."

"You'll describe our difficulties by quoting me, the Secretary?"

"Exactly. A local bureaucrat wouldn't be able to say, 'This effeminate Muscovite probably doesn't know how many teats a cow has.'"

"Do you?" she asked.

I promised to count. We certainly liked each other.

"Criticize manufacturers of milking machines with impunity," the First Secretary suggested, "they don't empty the udder fully and break down. To milk three dozen cows, often by hand, is quite a task."

"Are you local?" I asked.

"Yes. Why?"

"How did you manage to get your education here?"

"My family has passports; my father had been an agronomist for years. I wanted to study obstetrics in Moscow, but the parents were getting old, and I ended up at the Kostroma Pedagogical Institute."

"Do you have second thoughts about your occupation?"

"Yes, I do. Are you happy with yours?"

"Let's talk about that in a couple of years. On the way here I talked with an old school Party instructor; he wouldn't mind solving our problems with Stalin's laws."

"Are you married?"

"Practically, yes."

"What a way of saying it!"

◈ ◈ ◈

My article occupied the entire basement, the horizontal, usually politically important lower part of a newspaper page. Olga called from her District Party Committee to my editor-in-chief, expressed deep satisfaction and asked Protasova to bring me to the phone.

"Well?" Olga asked in a conspiratorial tone.

I said I had to finish a little satire for the next issue and asked her to call in an hour. At that time, my editor had to be in the Regional Party Committee.

"What's it about?" asked Olga.

"About a drunken priest who has fallen into a police drunk tank. Let me tell you, the gray-haired police captain was great! Struggling with this violent preacher of peace and forgiveness, undressing and putting him in an icy shower, and after that—tying him to bed—it was a true humanitarian action."

In an hour, she learned that Protasova praised the heroic part of my report, stabbed the part on backwardness, and murdered my diffident allusions to the farmers' hopeless misery.

◈ ◈ ◈

Sixty years later, in Washington, D.C., I typed "Lisa Ershova" in my laptop and Google delivered an article from the *Rossiyskaya Gazette Nedelya*. Chills ran down my spine; on March 26, 2009, this paper mentioned Lisa in passing as the mother of famous 21st-century Kostroma milkmaid Galina Kokueva. She was from the same village, Golovinskoe, in Susanin District, as the heroine of my first report. I felt the cold of that distant November day of 1956 and saw the nineteen-year-old girl sitting on a three-legged stool, her red fingers squeezing methodically and pulling down the teats, her pink cheek resting against the black-and-white cow. Her high rubber boots are covered with mud almost knee deep.

The article said about Galina the same that I wrote in 1956 about her mother. Galina gets up after 3 a.m., works with 34 cows, and comes home late in the evening. "Golovinskoe, frankly, is better than many other Russian dairy farms," wrote the seasoned reporter Elena Trukhanova, "but it doesn't have a milk line. After milking, Galina carries a can of milk into a room with the refrigerator. Daily she carries more than 1,500 pounds of milk. I'll never know how this small woman, with no biceps and triceps, does it."

At that distant time an athlete, I took an empty milking machine and a can from embarrassed Lisa and realized that I couldn't cope with 34 cows without strengthening my muscles. "Milkmaids' legs and hands are hurting. We cannot force young to work on the farm," wrote the reporter. I saw serious progress behind this remark, even in what a disappointed neighbor dared to say, "We hoped Galina would be given some money; their shabby house is in need of repair and gas."

The winds of change blew over Golovinskoe. Gasification was a tremendous improvement. In 1973, for a record milk yield, Lisa Ershova received her medal from the hands of the Kostroma First Secretary. Her daughter got hers from the President of All Russia right in the Kremlin. "The bouquet presented by President had long wilted, but Galina Kokueva will forever keep it on the table," wrote the correspondent.

Granny's Log House

Anna took me to Zoya Tikhonovna's log house on the day of my arrival in Kostroma. It was possible to find better housing, but her faded eyes framed by countless wrinkles stopped me from saying "no, thanks." A thin chintz curtain divided her only room in two. Our beds stood on both sides of it at the distance of an outstretched arm. Sometimes under the cold rays of the October sun, this shabby wall melted and we pretended that we did not watch a theater of shadows. She was not used to hearing her full name. Neighbors called her simply TikhOnOvna (she was stressing all the Os as befits indigenous inhabitants of the region), their kids called her Granny ZOya. She had neither relatives nor friends in town and wasn't eager to chat with neighbors; they weren't bad, but a bit importunate. "Since you moved here, they stop me in the street with new questions."

"What do they want to know?" I asked.

"Usual. Married or not? Do you drink or not? Why have you traded the rich Moscow for the poor Kostroma? Why you don't smoke; maybe you have tuberculosis? Why your wife didn't come, this kind of stuff. Why do you greet them? We're city dwellers," her shy smile exposed her half-toothless mouth, "not homebodies who greet every new goat. They also wonder why I don't cook for you."

"It's normal; they are interested in what isn't in papers and on the radio. Why don't the two of us have a tea party, and we'll gossip about them."

That first evening, my landlady walked me to the well to teach me how to hook the bucket securely to the chain and lower it to the depth of six yards. After bragging that at the age of twelve I had been able to get water from a well, I lost the bucket. She quickly borrowed a hook attached to a long rope and fished out the galvanized bucket, which, thankfully, was still floating on the dark surface. The old woman tried to keep from smiling, though in vain, and more wrinkles came out around her melancholy eyes.

At first, I wanted to invite Zoya Tikhonovna to the downtown Kostroma Restaurant, but worried that its starched tablecloths, sprightly waitresses, and unaffordable prices might embarrass her. She had never been to a restaurant. Locals who considered themselves intellectuals and the medley of business travelers dining at government expense frequented it. I bought there deep-fried balls with apples and small pies with tripe and in a store—candies, cookies, Georgian tea, and a bottle of local sickly-sweet cherry liqueur. Zoya Tikhonovna retrieved old-fashioned glasses with silvery holders and cut wine glasses from an age-old wooden chest, and we had a feast. She thanked me for the treats, for carrying water, and chopping wood.

"I'm pleased to do this," I said. "In Moscow, I missed the firewood and axes."

"Axes?" She changed a little in the face. "My first husband was hacked to death with an ax. By a drunken lumberjack. Thank God, with one blow. They cut down trees together."

I heard in her voice neither frustration nor pain. It sounded as if she were saying, "It's my fate, and one can't complain about fate. It was what it was." I poured some more liqueur in our glasses. Zoya Tikhonovna drank it like vodka, in one gulp, throwing her head back, without savoring. She said "Tasty," and wiped her mouth with the back of her hand, looked critically at my still half-full glass and said, "You don't like it."

"I'm stretching the pleasure," I faltered.

"My husbands knew how to drink," she said, "but they never hurt me. I had a good life with them."

"When did they die?"

"Way back. Ivan didn't die. He fell asleep in a snowdrift. Drank a little too much that evening. Now I'm glad, it was a good end." She nodded at her feet. "In these *valenki*." Zoya Tikhonovna touched the worn felt boot. "He had small feet. I wear them only at home. They will live with me until my death."

I looked at her gray *valenki* with rumpled bootlegs and had nothing to say. Instead, I pointed at a framed photograph sitting on the chest. "You have a good looking daughter."

"Before the war, she left for big money on the other side of the country, they say not far away from Japan and America. Winter in that Kamchatka Peninsula is year round. Quickly got married to a deputy head of a camp."

"The boys and their father are also good-looking," I said.

"They sent this picture soon after the war."

In the photo, the husband had major's insignia. "What rank does he have now?" I asked.

"I don't know."

I was thinking he might soon lose his job; the hard labor camps had begun shrinking.

"I'm happy for them, a good family." She took the picture from the chest and wiped it off with the edge of her homemade shawl. "The daughter writes once or twice a year and never about him, only about the boys."

"Have you ever had a cow?"

She nodded. "In the forest, we had everything—butter, thick curdled milk, sour cream, and wild honey."

"I thought the bees need oak or maple to make a hive," I confessed.

"No, all they need is a hollow. Once I found a hive even in a hollow log on the edge of the forest," she shook her head, her eyes sparkled. "The girl grew healthy, liked wandering in the forest alone. Loggers bought our milk. Too bad! They stole the cow. Our daughter cried and swore like an adult for several days."

"Who could do such a thing? Probably everybody knew your family."

"Oh sure, they knew. Women in those days didn't work in lumbering. Perhaps logging prisoners killed her. Ivan talked with the guards, but who knows, maybe they got their share of meat."

"Were you afraid of lynxes?"

"Not too much. They are fierce, and if you or a lynx are sick or if you're a child, they might attack, but normally they avoid humans and stay on branches. We carried sticks, looked upwards, and tapped the trees. It could also help with the men, but they knew Ivan would kill for us. He was a fair man."

"One milkmaid said that lynxes sometimes kill cows."

"No, they don't," said the old woman. "What do they know, milkmaids? A lynx can kill a goat and a pig."

I did not want her to lose income and advised to begin looking for a new tenant sometime in May. After graduation, Irina would move to Kostroma.

"I understand," she said. "Today the young don't want to live behind a curtain. When you have more time, I'll ask about Moscow."

"We'll do that. Now I can say only one thing. The forest smells better."

"Life wasn't too bad here until Stalin banned horses, cows, and goats in the city."

"I saw some chickens in the street."

"He allowed it."

Next morning, I was already at the door when she thanked me for the newspapers I kept bringing to the outhouse.

"The same problem in Moscow," I said, and we giggled. "By the way, do you read them?"

She shook her head. I touched her trembling hands with their age spots and quickly shut the door behind myself. I knew she was not used to touching.

◆ ◆ ◆

Soon after my return from Susanino District, we celebrated the launching of the paper. Everybody brought berry wine, vodka, and home-made dishes. I brought a dry Crimean Riesling and only at our party understood why the bottle was so dusty and a saleswoman gave me a strange look; Kostroma disliked its "acidic" taste. Anna Galun brought vodka and got drunk. I helped her to get out into the corridor, opened a window wide, and we had an elaborate discussion about the meaning of life and mutual respect, the favorite subjects of drunken Russians.

"Stop pawing the floor!" I said sternly. "Hold to this windowsill with both hands."

"What a shame!" she said. "You should be shot by a firing squad. To write about Russians and never get drunk? It's tantamount to treason."

"I'm more interested in writing about Soviet people," I confessed.

"You mean there aren't Russians anymore." She waved her hand desperately. "Are we all Soviets?"

"No," I said. "My landlady Zoya Tikhonovna, whom you met at a well, is very Russian. Are you growing sober?"

"Never! Otherwise, I wouldn't talk to this Muscovite who cannot imagine how much moonshine we had to deliver to convince our farm's president to take care of my passport needed for college."

"You're sobering up," I said. "The cold air helps."

"The capital of all progressive humanity just unable to understand the hush-hush high politics of this," she pushed me hard in the shoulder, though lovingly, and explained how the farm president and the chair of the village council delivered moonshine as a tribute for the district big shots. Sometimes, when the Party Committee, the judge, and the police ran out of the gargle, they traveled to her village, sort of not to break away from the simple folks. "They didn't go to my father, a moonshiner, God forbid!" she stressed. "It's a punishable trade. They went to these reputable communists."

"You're getting better," I said again.

Her snub nose jerked up disapprovingly and she tried to close the window. I did not allow it. Only once her dad had a close encounter with the Second Secretary. Anna was doing her homework when her father screamed, "Idiots! They gonna kill themselves!" and rushed outside. A truck was sitting with both front wheels in a ditch. He managed to pull the driver out of the cab and get the car key. "The drunken idiot hit him," she smiled inappropriately. The Secretary attempted to climb into the body, maybe to save broken bottles. "He shifted his feet, and plucked at the sideboard like a frustrated baby at his crossbar." Her strong father dragged them to his house, took their belts from their pants, and said that if they wouldn't sleep on the floor, he'd tie them together with a rope.

I was unable to understand why they could not just buy vodka in their district center. My stupid question made her sober up completely. She gave me a motherly pat on the head and patiently explained, "First, our moonshine is better than vodka. Second, sometimes it's not in the store. Third, you have to pay for vodka." She pressed her index finger against my chest, "D'you, little boy, know what a workday unit is?"

She ignored my class farming experience of several summers. Her family kept earning workday units in the fields, and in the fall, they were given potatoes, carrots, beets, and even wheat—the best material for moonshine. Who didn't work the required number of days, had their private plots trimmed right up to their very houses. Some neighbors wrote anonymous denunciations of her family. "Didn't you learn it so far? We, Russians, hate everyone who lives better than us." The district leadership read these letters while drinking Galun's moonshine.

Anna sighed. "In my dreams, I traveled the world as a reporter. Why did you decide to become a journalist?"

"Frustrated writer. Weren't you all afraid to end up behind bars?"

"When I asked this question, Dad said, 'D'you know any other way to send you to college?'"

Now she was depressingly sober. I had to change her mood, made a dignified face, and warned Anna of an upcoming intoxication test. Her answer would scientifically determine the level of it.

"Go on," she said solemnly.

"If all Polish invaders and their horses, all in armor, and Ivan Susanin, all of them," I said, "drowned in a swamp, no survivors, how could the historians determine that it was that particular 4 by 12 kilometers swamp, not the one ten kilometers away?"

The wrinkles on her forehead reflected the process of hard thinking and then, with a guffaw, like a horse, Anna rushed back into the editorial room to establish the degree of intoxication of all participants of the party. Some modern historians dare to say that the highly regarded Russian patriot Ivan Susanin never existed.

❖ ❖ ❖

Two days before the New Year, Irina came for a week, and she quickly made friends with Zoya Tikhonovna. This New Year's Eve, it was my turn to be on duty at the printing house. Protasova warned me not to drink with the censor, but like any Russian, we thought it was disrespectful to our colleagues and brought a bottle of Soviet champagne. When I refused to join in the celebrations, he gave me a big shrug, filled two tea glasses with champagne to the brim, and said in and edifying way, "You correct the typos and watch out for pictures placed upside down, and after that, you can drink whatever you wish and sleep tight."

Nikita Khrushchev and the Kremlin's Spasskaya Tower bells greeted us with the arrival of the year 1957; Irina and the gray-headed censor emptied their glasses. He laughed when my innocent wife said that he could check all political mistakes during the day, in the silence of his office.

"You're in my office, Irina," he pointed at the noisy printing presses.

A woman in a red headscarf tied at the nape demanded from the wall over his desk, "Don't blurt out a state secret!"

Irina explained that, to keep from drinking, the poor thing over wall pressed her index finger to her already compressed lips. My wife felt that she had to drink for both, for this "thing" and for me. Our new friend filled two glasses again. He was placid. "I brought her before the war from Moscow *Glavlit*, long ago. 'You youngsters don't understand that just a couple of years ago the lack of vigilance could ruin my entire life.'"

"At that time *Glavlit* was a KGB department," I said.

"That's correct. Now it's called the General Directorate for the Protection of Military and State Secrets in the Press."

"And now we have three bottles, thanks to the state secrets," said Irina.

"Now I could lose my job, but not my head," he poured wine into Irina's and his own glass.

"Yeah, it's really a tough job," said Irina and they clinked their glasses again.

"Look closely at this," he passed to her a magnifying glass and a damp control strip of a newspaper page, still with fresh paint. "Now check it by this light on both sides and try to detect, let's say, a little swastika or a suspicious mark on a portrait of a leader."

"It's a real toughie," repeated my wife contritely.

"A preface by a purged person or his photograph, or a quotation from a wrong person, or just his indistinct face in a huge group," the censor said almost plaintively, "it's all easy to detect."

Irina still held the magnifying glass, now with an unsteady hand. She looked through it at him, "I sure hope you're still in the KGB."

"Alas, some fool had pulled off our shoulder straps so as not to pay for our military ranks." He poured more wine into two glasses. "Otherwise, I'd be rich by now."

Irina became terribly indignant. "The enemies of the people aren't asleep! If Comrade Stalin were still alive, we could drink today even more of this fine wine!"

"Yes, my general," he jumped up like a boy and stood at attention. He was clearly an alcoholic.

"At ease!" ordered the general. Then she turned to me, "Rookie Polishchuk, I order you to ask the officer if it's true that mention of natural disasters, bad weather, and anti–Semitism is banned in the USSR."

"Your Excellency," the officer pointed at me with the empty glass, "it's good you brought this fellow here."

"This fellow lied," Irina complained, "that there still is a market in Kostroma where we could buy some hay for our goat."

"Soviet journalists never lie," the censor protected me from the undeserved criticism. "This morning, I'll take you to that hay market."

"Officer, where's your battlefield horse?" the suddenly agitated general asked him.

"A couple of years ago, the working class of this city presented all their horses, goats, and cows as gifts to local collective farms," reported the officer what I already heard from Zoya Tikhonovna.

They were busy clinking glasses.

When Irina woke up in the afternoon, I told her that she pretended to be a KGB general, tried to find out some intimate secrets of that institution, and bragged that we had a goat.

My Journey into
the Forest's Depths

A week later, Irina returned to Moscow. Now, from the same platform, I was looking at a battered pilot engine with a snowplow attached, setting out to clear the rail tracks for my departure, and thinking about the 20th Party Congress promise of a transportation revolution. Diesel and electric locomotives would replace these prehistoric steam locomotives and strengthen my railroading advantages in comparison with the forthcoming flight from Galich. Soon our two half-empty miniature cars were traveling between unfriendly dark-green walls of spruce separated from the tracks by narrow strips of deep snow. Our aging engine caught up with its puffing, snowplowing peer, and we sharply slowed down. When they engaged in the deafening roll call, I began suspecting that the snow had forced both workaholics to turn back.

In six hours we overcame 139 kilometers (about 80 miles) to Galich, my transit point. By now, I knew, local distances should be measured only by the quality of the roads. One could expect this new railroad leg crowned by a brand new station; instead, a shabby door led me inside a dilapidated wooden building. In the tiny waiting room, I passed by the large "Lenin on the rostrum," looking lovingly at me and I stopped on the snow-covered steps, observing the frozen station square. Next to me, an affable bespectacled man in a rough sheepskin coat asked, "Where do you want to go?" He waved to a smiling teen who stood next to an indifferent horse harnessed to a sleigh.

"First to Galichanka Hotel; tomorrow morning to Soligalich."

"Buses won't go there for at least a week. We'll take you to Galichanka. Forgive my curiosity, but who travels to Soligalich at this time of year? Are you on some kind of a mission?"

"Yes, I'm a *Young Leninist's* correspondent."

The boy barely touched the reins; the horse revived and nodding vigorously, passed by two buses turned into giant snowdrifts, and briskly strode through the deep snow. "My son Sergei," the man reached out and touched our driver's shoulder. "I'm the District prosecutor."

"Good. So, if I'm unable to reach that historic town, I'm sure you could help me with some topics in Galich."

"We can do that. It's a relatively quiet place, yet the number of crimes increased after ex-prisoners were able to move relatively freely."

"How relative is their freedom?"

"This isn't a newspaper topic. They did time in taiga just a year ago, still don't have the right to leave the area, and bringing down trees, unfortunately, for little money. Some try to escape, in violation of the law."

"What law?"

"Okay, technically it's not the law; it's a set of recent instructions. In this district, we arrest and send escapees back to logging enterprises."

"Am I correct—there are no guards, barbed wire, or watchtowers anymore?"

He nodded. "In some places, they are tried and get new terms."

"Are you risking your career?" I smiled.

"Are you being ironic?"

"No. Just trying to learn. Shouldn't we let bygones be bygones? Stalin is dead. He'll be even deader ten years from now."

"Maybe in Moscow," the prosecutor said.

I saw concern in his eyes as he looked at the driver's back. The confidence of the man next to me began melting. "It's a serious subject," he said. "Drop by my office tomorrow." Perhaps he didn't want to continue the conversation in the boy's presence.

The horse brought us to the hotel. It looked like a twin sister of the station, the same wooden walls, crooked steps, and the same declining years.

"I didn't question your integrity for a second," I said. "I question the integrity of those instructions."

We shook hands. I also shook Sergei's hand and stepped inside the Galichanka Inn.

An untidy woman with a large kerchief tied on her chest said, "This night you'll be alone in the room. Tomorrow some people will come from across the lake."

"How d'you know?" I asked.

"Some Party meeting."

"About what?"

"I don't know."

In the room, I tried all four narrow iron beds, placed my suitcase under the least squeaky one, and returned to the taciturn woman to ask for a towel.

"You had to bring your own," she said unemotionally.

"And my own firewood?" I muttered.

She gave me a dirty look.

"Do you have a cleaning lady?"

"It's me."

"And the administrator?"

"Yes."

"What color were these sheets when they were new?"

"This is all we have," she said blandly. "They sleep without sheets. The water and the toilet are down the hall. You can buy a cup of tea from me in the morning and in the evening."

In the morning she said, "I work as much as they pay."

"Do the guests complain?"

"They're happy here," a shadow of a smile flitted across her face. "They're villagers or from towns like Chukhloma and Soligalich. We don't save on firewood, and they can dry their foot wraps, socks, and *valenki*."

I decided not to ask if she brought vodka for them. She didn't like my smile and asked, "Why do you have in your passport both Moscow and Kostroma police residence permits?"

"I volunteered for a job in Kostroma."

She got scared. "Are you a prosecutor or a policeman? Please, don't destroy me!" the woman pleaded. "I have a nine-year-old daughter."

"Are you mad? I'm a reporter and have no intentions to harm you in any way."

She sighed. "If the District Party Committee knew that you're in town, they'd invite you to stay in their cozy guest house."

"I prefer it here. Do they have such a guest house in Soligalich?"

"How would I know? I've never been there. It's one hundred kilometers away." (That's 62 miles.)

I felt a pang of conscience, wanting to show her that she was in no way to blame and said, "On my way back I might stay here again."

I knew that on my way back from Soligalich I would travel to this town with a bunch of milkmaids, by road, in a truck hooked to the tractor. The Regional Committee of Communist Youth Organization asked me to chaperone this group traveling to Kostroma to take part in a conference of milk farms' *Komsomol* members.

Not to scare her again, in the morning, I didn't ask how to get to the prosecutor's office, but she caught me at the door. "Are you going to the prosecutor?"

"How d'you know?"

"You two were talking for a long time. That's why you got the best room," she smiled cautiously so I could take her words just for a joke.

"I'll use his phone to call the airport."

She looked approvingly at my knee-high felt *valenki* and pointed at the snowstorm blowing behind a window. "The planes might be grounded for several days."

The prosecutor reserved a seat for me for the following day. "When the weather allows, the AN-2 flies to Soligalich on Tuesdays and Fridays," he said.

"So, if I get stuck here, would you recommend some outrageous crimes?"

"I didn't see anything of this sort in the papers." Three months ago, he said, eighteen girls drowned in the Galich Lake when their scow capsized close to the shore; the youngest was sixteen, the oldest twenty. They were traveling during a storm for a dance evening. Neither the *Galich Pravda* nor the *Northern Pravda* reported it. I was not surprised.

"It looks like none of the girls could swim," the prosecutor continued. "They drowned at the same spot. Partially the explanation is historical. Several generations of Old Believers had lived here; they had fled here, to the upper reaches of the Volga River, from persecution by the Orthodox Church and the tsars. Even now, their women never frivolously dressed, getting in a river half-naked was a sin before God. All of them were virgins."

I was shocked. "Did you need to investigate this?"

"Investigators just follow procedures, no matter what. Here one holds her virginity intact until marriage. If a woman doesn't, her entire family is disgraced. We've had some ugly incidents."

My memory dredged up an event at the university sports camp, a hundred kilometers from Moscow. Arslan Musin, Nahl Zlobin, and I were jogging and accidentally scared a bunch of naked village girls swimming in the river. Clothes in their arms, they fled toward shrubbery, laughing and screaming. We pretended to run after them, whooping and whistling. It was a lot of fun for both parties involved.

"I read a 19th-century book about those who fled," I said. "Even to America. That's why an American river is called the Russian River."

"Melnikov-Pechersky," he said. "*In the forests and mountains.*"

I did not hide my surprise.

"You thought we, prosecutors, read only police reports?"

"I'm sure the girls were atheists," I said.

"We came here twenty years ago, and by that time all churches had been long destroyed."

"Pity," I said. "Isn't it better to store flax and woods in a beautiful ancient building than in their ruins under leaky roofs?"

"Our fathers were in a hurry to get rid of this holy devilry," he said. I told him that my father was a member of the Union of Godless Atheists. He added, "After meeting you, Sergei decided to be a journalist."

"A bad influence."

"He can give you a tour of the town. You'll have a couple of hours to discourage him."

"I'll do my best. Does he like reading?" I asked.

"Yes."

"A bad omen," I said.

After the school day was over, that same chestnut took me along the Galich Lake. As far as one could see, the banks were low and flat, and we went right on the ice. I perked up at the sight of fishing holes in the ice and became envious. Sergei clearly envied me. He fished the whole winter, from the end of October, for almost half a year.

"This side—more than five kilometers," the boy said. "Up to five meters deep. Our side is shallower. Where the girls drowned, the depth was less than two meters. A bit closer to the shore, and they would be alive now." He paused. "Fate."

"Sergei," I said, "tell me something about the town."

He listed a metalworking plant near the airfield, tanneries, a flax mill, the cheese factory, and lumber camps near the city. The cheese was sent to Moscow. Here, you could not buy it. A note of pride sounded in his voice when he said that in the fifteenth and sixteenth centuries this principality controlled most of the Russian trade in salt and furs.

"And now?"

"Nothing. The population is in decline, about 25,000."

"Still one of the largest in the region, thanks to the new railroad link," I remarked.

"Four centuries ago a lot of people lived here. The roads couldn't be worse than now. Our princes captured the Moscow Kremlin several times."

"I wouldn't mind if they did it again," I said.

"Why?"

I thought that the cheese would have remained in Galich, but my answer was cautious. "I prefer princes to tsars. They were less powerful. You could escape from them."

On five hilltops stood the remnants of obscurantism and prejudice and we went up the hills. Soon we stopped in front of an ugly building. Tall, massive doors reminded one that once there was a church here. "Granary," he said. "I read your satire in the *Young Leninist* about a drunken priest. Was the old woman really praying to the police drunk tank?"

"No, but this could happen to a purblind old woman when he, in the morning, came out of it, sober and unhappy."

"It was funny," the teen said politely, clearly reflecting on what he had heard. To distract him from politics, I told the boy that Moscow saleswomen sell ice cream dressed in white cloaks over their winter coats and *valenki*. My political blindness punished me. There was no ice cream in Galich, even in summer. I advised him to prepare, while fishing, what in imperial times was called tsar's ice—frozen milk and cream cut into small pieces. While parting, he asked, "When will we have television here?"

"I think, ten years from now."

The boy was disheartened. "I'll be an old man then, 26 years old."

"Yeah," I said, "just like me."

◈ ◈ ◈

What I saw the next morning from the same sleigh reminded me of Mama's snow-white linen tablecloth with my cute wooden biplane on it. Sergei brought me right to the wide-open door of the single-engine plane on metal skis. I patted the chestnut on the neck, made three steps in the fresh snow right to the aircraft, and ran up into it by a hinged metal staircase, remembering Anna's warning of the vomit smell, which would knock me off my feet.

"Comrade Polishchuk! Have you flown in the AN-2 before?" asked the pilot.

I touched a thin chain separating him from the passengers and nodded. It was the first flight of my life.

"You have to pay the watch, not me," he said kindly.

I looked back through the open door at a little booth. Next to it, a man in a sheepskin from head-to-toe was looking at me with suspicion.

"I'm sorry," I said, "I thought..."

"It's okay, this isn't Moscow," comforted the pilot. "You'll pay the keeper in Soligalich. Here every creature walks right under the propeller—cows, bears, kids, and drunks."

Six unsmiling passengers had already occupied half of the folding seats on both sides of the plane, their belongings beneath and in front of them. I stepped over a bucket of sauerkraut sticking out from under a wooden cover, and, while lowering the first available metal seat, picked up two brown vomit bags pressed against the green wall. Ignorance is a gift from Above. I felt good and safe after we took off. The harsh forest fascinated me. Nothing could stop me from gazing through the small portholes. The noise, gusts of icy wind inside the cabin, and continuous rattling and shaking seemed to be an integral part of the aviation business. Very soon, we began dropping down toward inhospitable fir trees, turbulence shaking the plane. Two passengers started strenuously vomiting. Who could ever imagine that the safe and trustworthy air we breathe in so easily can be full of treacherous holes! I broke into a cold sweat and felt like joining them. In a last-ditch attempt to ignore this urge, I took a mitten off and pressed my palm against the green metal wall; in seconds, it felt like frostbite. I learned to close my eyes whenever the man in front of me, with heavy rattling, bulged his eyes before the next attack of vomiting. It did not help. Nauseated and dizzy, I joined them. The brave adventurer turned into a suffering animal.

After almost two hours' flight, hee pale passengers left the airplane hobbling. I knew I had to do something immediately upon arrival, but could not remember what it was. Five minutes later the pilot approached me at the edge of the white field. I was sitting on my small suitcase. Oh yes, I still hadn't paid for the pleasure! "Some people never get used to this," he said. "Some feel better after a couple of flights."

"Should I eat more or less or nothing before the next one?" I asked.

"Don't gawk at the forest and stop moving around so much," he said. "There are different schools and theories. One guy stopped vomiting after he ate a whole salty herring on an empty stomach and didn't drink any liquid before the flight."

It sounded suicidal. I felt better with every new gulp of the sweet cold air and now could sip it slowly.

"Pass the money to me," the pilot giggled. "You missed the watch again."

My Unhealthy Interest
in Former Prisoners

Once in Soligalich, eager to go to a remote piece of woodland, I postponed a required visit to the District *Komsomol* Secretary and went to Communist Street 19, the office of Soligalich Logging Enterprise. The broad-shouldered director in a knitted gray sweater was all smiles. "Perfect, we have an important meeting at a plot twenty miles from here. It would be great if your newspaper covered this event."

I wanted to put my foot on the hard ice road on which overloaded timber trucks slid.

"They've been in good shape," he said. "We water them after the first layer of snow settles on the ground. Now—it's just maintenance—tamping down fresh snow, adding water. Timber must flow, no matter what!" The man sounded like a cheerful Communist Youth leader, if not for his age, a stubbornly expanding waistline and a slightly unnatural wide smile. He nodded at a snowdrift rising above the wooden windowsill. "If for the first time in my life, the ice crust all of a sudden begins melting in mid–January, then a tractor would pull us to the division."

What is the use pondering over yesterday's prisoners, I thought, and heard myself asking about the ratio of locals to former prisoners. The majority of problems were coming from the recent prisoners, he stressed guardedly. If it had not been for my ridiculous urge, this question shouldn't have been asked or, if asked, only after seeing them and after my notebooks had everything needed for the story. Neither of us had ever read anything in print on the fate of prisoners that had been pardoned or exonerated after Stalin's death. Still, I asked, "Are all of them criminals?"

The man paused, his chest and abdomen under the thick sweater growing larger from a deep sigh, and he said, weighing every word, "How would I know? I've never worked with prisoners. If I had, I'd have shoulder straps and a higher salary than my present one."

I already heard it somewhere. He had undoubtedly seen the barbed wire cut by soldiers and the prisoners' barracks, now called dormitories. He might've been wondering why this correspondent was asking about prisoners? Could it be a kind of calculated provocation or was it just the genuine recklessness of the nosy young? To show my insignificance, he asked solicitously, "Do you know what soft timber is?"

"Birch?" I guessed.

"Pine," the director said quietly, "fir, spruce, all coniferous taiga."

It's all those with cones, I thought. He sounded sarcastic while explaining that birch and spruce were ardent enemies.

"The forest confirms the correctness of Marxism," I said. "Class struggle for existence."

"No, it confirms the correctness of Darwinism," the director sounded a bit too gentle. "Everybody wants to stay alive, no matter what."

After learning of my plan to stay at that plot for three days, he expressed fatherly concern—some unrepentant criminals work there. I disguised my anger as gratitude and inquired about the latest achievements in felling technology.

"It's a revolution," his voice relaxed, the tension almost evaporated. "You'll see the most advanced methods of labor brought to life by the 'Friendship' brand chainsaw. Difficult to believe that until recently we used axes and two-handled saws."

"Just like a century ago?" without knowing it, I touched an open wound again.

"You can say so." Now he was nervous anew. "After the war, no-no, the workers weren't prisoners; they were deportees. The winter in Karelia was harsh. The barracks were built slowly … I was young. Just like you. It was my first job after the Forestry Academy."

As if apologizing for the momentary weakness, he smiled crookedly and explained why he allowed himself this outburst. "The Galich prosecutor, he's a friend of mine, rang me up today; he called you an idealist from Moscow."

"Soviet prosecutors have a long history of poor judgment."

My joke sounded ambiguous, but it did not stop him from returning to his memories. "At first, I took all deported for enemies. They were continually arriving."

I mumbled some sort of soothing nonsense like, "The whole country did. Patriots are blind." After that, I asked a wrong question again, "Who were they?"

He ruffled his hair. "Russians, Poles, Latvians, Estonians, Ukrainians, Volga Germans, and Chechens." He stared at me almost in a panic. "The families with small children…" He looked toward the window, his voice faltering. "Have you ever seen a concert pianist chopping down a pine with an ax? Her fingers were so delicate."

"We all remember what we want to forget." It seemed to me that I was unable to stop my nonsense.

"She was learning to gather cloudberries in the swamp and not to drown; the lumberjacks roared with laughter, she thought because she was a Jew." He repeated, now to himself, "They weren't prisoners. Many died." We both felt awkward and fell silent. "When she fell in the bonfire, the loggers dragged her out, giggling," he paused again. "Her hair, her eyebrows were burned."

"Did she survive?" My abrupt study of the moose antlers on the wall was ill-timed and we knew it.

He sent her to haul out trunks to the warehouse. Easy job! Take the horse by the bridle and force it to drag a long whip in deep snow; then, walk back with the horse, rest, if the blizzard isn't crashing. One joker taught her sheer swearing as commands for the horse. "Even I was laughing," he said, a smile returning to his lips but not to the eyes. He began coming back to his usual self, "The petrol 'Friendship' saw was developed two years ago. More advanced machinery also came to the forest: TDT-40 skidding tractors and ZIL-150 and ZIL-151 timber trucks."

We agreed that the forest covering almost half of the country might become the basis of dying towns and villages' survival and a backbone of economic growth and welfare of the Soviet Union. Now he was strong and determined. We would've writhed with laughter if some fool had told us that the Russian forest industry crisis would last deep into the 21st century. I began to understand why these two mature men were more or less open with me; I wasn't very good at hiding my true feelings.

My face was probably still pale. He said, "Here it's safer to fly, even walking distances."

"My heart loves it, but my stomach hates it."

"We all have a split personality," now he joked.

"After Stalin, the whole country has a split personality," I said. "The struggle between a great idea and its embodiment."

When we shook hands, he screwed up an eye and said, "Don't worry, only firefighters fly there."

I screwed up my eye, "With them, I would go."

◈ ◈ ◈

It was getting dark, and I ran to the Communist Youth Committee, stomping with my sheep wool *valenki* on the narrow path in the snow. The bitter cold made it bounce a little, squeak and clang under my feet.

The tall and wiry secretary was waiting for me. The plump baby lips of this Ivan and his pug nose reminded me of Ivan the Fool, the popular character of Russian fairy tales. With his guileless face, he was so out of place in his position that sympathy at once filled me for his religious belief in the rightness of our common cause. Soon I knew that Ivan's very existence depended on every word in the newspapers; they revealed to him the highest truth of life. His sole concern was the future of working people throughout the world. Yet one wouldn't call him exactly a silver-tongued fellow propagandist; rather, he was tongue-tied, and that was another reason for me to like him. As if to balance his charming ignorance in global issues, he instantly turned into a walking nature encyclopedia. In this boundless world, he celebrated each little blade of grass. Such knowledge one can acquire if he brought up in a remote Russian village or by a mother of a Kalahari Desert hunter.

The next day the trip to the distant plot was postponed. Frustrated, I went for a walk. When a newcomer strolls in Soligalich, all seven thousand of its inhabitants, including newborns, look at how you stomp the snow. They wonder where and for what price you bought your luxurious sheepskin and why this well-fed city dweller kept his earflaps laces tied under the chin when it is such a warm day, only minus ten degrees Celsius (fourteen degrees Fahrenheit).

I stood under the gray sky by the frozen Kostroma River, looked at the opposite bank, and guessed which way the water flowed. Then I recognized the blurred contours of the medieval fortress' former ramparts; reading helps, the 16th-century fortress was on the left bank. The Secretary running toward me like an antelope interrupted this moment of my glory.

"Ivan, you're a good runner," I said.

"It helps to stay in touch with the grass-roots organizations." He did not joke.

"You ought to share your experience with *Komsomol* and Party leaders throughout the country." I tried not to smile.

"When summoned to Kostroma and the roads are impassable, I usually walk to Galich."

"Ninety-five kilometers?" It was no longer funny, and I shook my head. Like a Christian hermit of the past, he did not attach much importance to the small inconveniences of daily life. "How often do you walk there?" I asked. They had here three seasons of roads in the worst state ever and one short season when the roads were occasionally dry.

"At least four times a year." Ivan did not see a reason for boasting.

"Thank God!" I abandoned my efforts not to raise my voice. "I thought of ten times."

"Why do you thank this god? It's a relic of past superstitions. I keep asking my parents not to do this. I thought that in the capital of all progressive mankind they don't do it."

"It's just an ancient expression of positive emotions," I said and declared my firm intention to ask the Regional *Komsomol* Committee to give him a new pair of *valenki* and shoes or, at least, high rubber boots, once a year. Ivan begged me not to do that. I promised and asked how he found out that I've been touring the town.

"The *Komsomol* members came running to me."

"Perhaps they took me for a spy," I suggested. "The color of my *valenki* differs slightly from the local ones."

"Spies don't wear *valenki*," Ivan said confidently.

I argued, "Any child would recognize a spy walking in his casual black-lacquered shoes in the deep snow."

His reasons for not smiling were related to the security of the country, surrounded by its sworn enemies. In the end, he laughed and invited me to the local history museum. Before the revolution, this 19th-century house belonged to the family of a salt-and-timber merchant. After the young principal of the local school unlocked the museum's heavy door, I asked what happened to the merchant. The teacher shrugged, but he knew that from the 14th to the 18th century Soligalich was a major center for Russian salt production. His abridged history of the town included close ranks of smoky log cabins of the salt works, the destitute folk, civil wars, poor villages around fat monasteries, nine-yard-high battlements of the fort, and the lone kerosene lantern remaining in the downtown. In conclusion, he said that the bulwark of obscurantism, the Church of the Assumption, did not exist any longer, and its fate was instructive. "In 1930 its stones were used for socialist construction."

The eyes of the *Komsomol* leader sparkled and he exclaimed, "Great!"

"I was born in that year," I said.

The principal was showing portraits of the October Revolution participants when I pointed at three light spots on the wooden walls, "They're square. Probably there hanged the portraits of local revolutionaries persecuted by Stalin."

He smoothed his thinning hair and looked at Ivan in confusion. I wondered why there were no pictures of the tsarist times' lumberjacks.

"Probably they were prisoners," said Ivan.

I suggested brazenly, "*Komsomol* could hold cultural and educational work among prisoners released after Stalin's death."

"There are former criminals among loggers," the principal said.

"Many of them didn't commit crimes," I said.

"We never received any instructions from the District Party Committee," he said and looked at the contemplative Ivan again.

At the very end of the last century, during the rise of Russian post-communist nationalism, the Soligalich History Museum was closed due to "chronic lack of visitors."

When You Chop Wood, Chips Fly

A day later, a trucker in a sailor's striped vest under his quilted jacket knocked on my door. Only criminals or former sailors could boast the precious white-and-blue vest. The director of the enterprise and the District Party Committee instructor were waiting in the cab, and I climbed into the body. The dashing driver insisted that he could make it faster just with the chains attached to the wheels, but they wanted to play it safe, and a tractor pulled us. The icy road was in good shape, it reminded me of my ice skating experience; in three hours we reached the little forest village. I declined my companions' offer to go to the canteen. In January, the working days are short, and after losing a day in Soligalich, I wanted to go to the cutting area right away.

Everything foreshadowed the imminent onset of darkness. The dull sky aggressively dropped closer to the sharp treetops. A flatbed ZIL-151 with a trailer had just delivered a load of long, ponderous whips to the depot, and now we were heading back to the harvesting area. Squeezed between the silent master of the forest and the whistling driver in the oiled jacket, I listened to the rattling side racks of the empty truck. The dried pine needles colored the snow a light brown. We quickly covered the two-mile slippery ice strip.

The lunch break had just ended and I could see a tall feller with a heavy "Friendship" chainsaw approaching an eighty or ninety-foot pine, straight as a mast. He was pointedly looking at something over his head while shifting from foot to foot like a wildcat before jumping on its prey. His assistant was trampling the snow around the brown pine. The working area had already been cleared, shrubs and brushwood around the tree cut away and removed. I stood some sixty yards away, as ordered by the foreman, trying to determine what the feller was looking for and saw nothing but the snow-laden powerful branches. Then I heard, "You want this fucking limb to kill me!"

The feller's blaring voice drowned the howl of two chainsaws in the strips of the neighboring crews.

"Come on, Rail!" yelled his assistant, who was moving a fuel tank to the side and seemed to be at a safe distance. "You've handled more dangerous branches!"

"I don't like this one!" shouted Rail. "This widow-maker has a weird curve. Maybe I should change the direction a bit, so it will still land in our strip!"

I finally noticed the overhanging loose limb; it was thicker in the middle than at the base. The foreman behind me yelled, "Hey Rail, what's going on here? Here is a correspondent waiting for you!" He was definitely using foul language under his breath.

"You want the correspondent to write a nice obituary?" Rail roared.

I yelled, pointing at my notebook, "Give me your real name, just in case!"

The lumberjack smiled broadly, turned his back to me, and with both hands leaned the saw forward against the trunk, but did not pull the drive; instead, he stepped back again, never taking his eyes off the tree, still looking for the best spot for the first undercut. I had already learned that a tree should fall on this deep gash called the "face." After determining the right spot, Rail resolutely stepped slightly to the left, leaned the saw against the trunk again, and finally turned the motor on. The saw squealed. To get a better view of his movements, I jumped on a smelly stump nearby. Rail was making a wedge-shaped cutout. I congratulated myself for realizing that this notch would control the direction of the fall. He springily, almost leisurely, walked halfway around the wounded tree. So far, it had ignored the challenge. The feller looked again at the branches high above and disappeared behind the pine. Now nothing other than the white gap of its "face" was visible. The saw squealed anew; he was placing the final cutout, a "back-cut," opposite to the "face." The pine resisted, angrily groaned, crackled, and shook threateningly. The saw stopped. Rail was in my view afresh, now with lots of snow on his head and shoulders. For a second, he studied the jaded trunk and the trembling top of his antagonist and then quickly, without looking back—such a show-off—walked toward me by a path trodden in the deep snow by his assistant. Rail blithely smiled. The tree, crackling behind him, was on its noisy way down. He glanced at it only some four yards away from the pine, a split second before it hit the ground. The earth trembled. I felt unstable on the stump sixty yards away. The fallen giant was now moving in the snowy dust with pine needles rising from the ground, then subsided and froze.

Rail looked at me, "A good tree is never dead," he said. "I'm Ivan Kotov."

✦ ✦ ✦

On the way back to the camp, the six of us stood close to each other in a narrow space between the cab and the wall of fragrant tree butts towering behind us. Several times, the tops hanging behind the trailer danced violently like giant merciless whips. They would do it even if we were traveling across a polished hardwood floor. We chatted excitedly as if returning from an outing. The unlucky once stomped two miles of the icy road. I kept patting a wet butt tenderly while busily gushing with Rail and others.

"I overheard you talking with the foreman," a girl next to me said.

"How could you hear us with your earflaps covering your ears?" I said. "Yes, he asked me to sit in the cab."

"I read your hands," she laughed. "Why did you refuse?"

I wanted to know how it feels riding on a slippery road without sideboards, but didn't say it. Nobody seemed to think that if the truck stumbled on a pothole or if the chains or wire ropes binding the logs broke, these butts could turn all of us into one good chop.

"We all have little dirty secrets," interjected Rail. "Even if you're squeaky clean."

I wondered to whom he referred by that remark.

"So, how was it?" he asked.

"Windy," I said and sought and answer to why, when the pine was in free fall, he walked away without looking back.

"I did look at it," he said. "You just didn't see it. Besides, I don't want a heavy limb to fly right into my pretty face. When a tree goes down, funny things happen when it hits another tree; even lying in the snow, it can kill. So, why look back? It slows you down when you run for life."

✦ ✦ ✦

That evening, the director, the instructor in a black skirt covering her black *valenki*, and the camp supervisor were sitting at a desk on the modest creaking stage, under portraits of Lenin and Khrushchev. A front-rank worker with a blue tie, still in pants stuffed with batting, a crusty foreman, and I sat next to the desk. The mess hall was full of loggers; it smelled of spicy sawdust, sweat, and thick pancakes. The director opened the meeting and quickly gave the floor to the instructor. She stressed the many achievements of the 20th Party Congress held less than a year ago and condemned ideological dogmatism and the practice of separating ideological work from communist construction. I had heard similar sentiments at Moscow University. All of a sudden, there was a pleasant strumming of guitar strings. I could not believe my ears, looked in the direction of the sound and saw Rail wistfully confirming the instructor's statements with unobtrusive chimes. Neither the speaker nor the audience paid attention. In Moscow, the intruder, the provocateur, would've already been arrested. The undisturbed instructor continued her peroration. The nice fingering of Rail's guitar accompanied the lecture on the role of socialism as a world system, its struggle with imperialism, the collapse of the colonial system, and the emergence of new developing countries in Asia. A redhead with two short braids sticking out to the sides gently hugged the guitarist and rolled her eyes up to the wooden ceiling; she enjoyed the strumming.

Meanwhile, the instructor denounced Stalin and stressed that Nikita Sergeevich Khrushchev praised the strength of the Party, which withstood the adverse effects of imaginary crimes and false accusations. The Party, in other words, had been Stalin's victim, not an accessory to his crimes. After this vital statement, Rail added a question to his fingering, "How 'bout the 21st Congress?"

She did not respond to the inquiry, but the musician gently insisted, "When will the 21st Congress be held?"

"The Central Committee will decide it at the appropriate time," said the instructor, visibly pleased with the high political activity of Soviet workers.

"And how 'bout the 22nd Congress? I'd love to know."

Some in the audience began to chuckle, and those on the stage smiled graciously. She ignored Rail's next question, "Tell me please, would Lenin be pleased to see Stalin lying next to him in Mausoleum?"

I anticipated a question about the 23rd Congress when the camp supervisor took the floor. He cleared his throat and, in contrast to the previous verbose speaker, in five seconds, elegantly tied together the two most important problems of our life. "The international situation is extremely fraught," he stressed and concluded, "This obliges us even more."

The political logic of this short-lived ritual dance overweighed its blatant disregard for basic grammar. The audience and the genius himself did not notice a penetrating insight, highly valued by me. Now he elegantly switched to the advantages of cutting branches in the upper depot instead of doing it between fallen trees. Just this innovation, he said, would increase the loggers' productivity four- or five-fold and decrease injuries. The numbers and such a late arrival of the idea surprised me. It should occur, I thought, when humans began using horses for hauling logs. Electric saws with cumbersome cables and expensive mobile power stations became a thing of the past, stressed the supervisor, since the enterprise mastered felling with the "Friendship" chainsaw and introduced an innovation that improved the work of its engine.

"The 'Friendship' is still too heavy—12 kilograms," one man interjected.

"Add to this two liters of gasoline," said the most productive worker with the tie. "This weight exceeds safety standards by more than two times."

"True friendship cannot be too heavy," remarked Rail affectionately, but without changing his facial expression; in a low voice he sang a line from a popular song, "Behind a good friendship hides the true love."

The director said that he already asked the manufacturer to solve this weight problem.

"Comrade Director," said Rail, "we've long been promised a public bath. My guitar is getting dirty."

"Next spring we'll get it," the director said.

"I solemnly pledge," said Rail with an impassive face, "to make beautiful frames for the new portraits of our leaders on the walls of our new public bath."

"Thank you," said the instructor.

"You're welcome," said Rail. "It's as easy as falling off a log."

The director, trying not to laugh, buried his face in his hands.

All of a sudden, the redhead began yelling, "Why is everyone afraid to tell the truth?" She jumped to her feet. "I fear nothing! It can't get worse!" Her braids kept jumping. "Why can we buy in our shop no milk, no butter, no kerosene, not even a winter hat or a spoon?" She turned pale.

Rail stopped strumming.

"The District Committee will take the necessary action," the instructor said.

But the girl continued yelling. "We still get water from the stream! We need a well!"

"Sit down, Natasha," Rail said quietly.

She sat but did not stop yelling. "Give us all this, start showing me movies, and then I might stop getting drunk and playing cold deck!"

Rail placed his guitar on the floor and held Natasha tight.

The director's face flushed. "A great deal depends on how much money Moscow allocates to us."

Now the supervisor could continue. When he talked about the increase in injuries, the director interfered again. "Safety is still almost absent; even the lumber station's chief engineer and the master of the forest violate safety requirements."

"The plan is forcing us to neglect safety," the chief said in a trembling voice. He did not anticipate that his boss would dare to say such things in the presence of the instructor and the correspondent. To help the director and myself, I did not write about the plan. Everybody knew that it came from Moscow state planners. If you want to lose your job, object to this planning.

After the meeting was over, I approached the Board of Honor on the log wall to select the best workers for an interview. Rail walked up to me in his exaggerated, muscle-bound swagger and said, "My mug should be on this one and the District Board of Honor."

"In a beautiful new frame?" I repeated his words.

"'Cause it's me, Ivan Kotov, who invented that hole in the saw," said my new friend.

It was his idea to drill a hole at the bottom of the saw case to drain the melting snow; since then the motors had been working flawlessly.

"The director said," continued Rail, "'here's your bonus for this invention, and please, shut up; otherwise they might finally open criminal proceedings against you.' Why did the supervisor not even mention the name of the inventor? Cause I'm a criminal. Cause I'm already framed here. Cause I knocked down a local jerk for stalking my girl."

An hour later I walked by a long panopticon, a barrack now called a dormitory, and heard muffled voices from the barely lit window of the little garret everybody called "Rail's birdhouse." An inhospitable, almost vertical ladder nailed to the outer wall of the well-worn building spoke tons about its inventor. I climbed the round steps with remnants of bark, reached out to the tiny door, and knocked. In seconds, I was facing the red-head's knees and heard her icy voice, "What d'you want, citizen comrade?"

It looked as if she were ready to kick me in the face.

Then I heard the familiar deep baritone. "Hey-hey, Natasha; I invited him."

She leaned down, stretched out her rough hand, and pulled me inside the teeny room; it looked more spacious thanks to the triangular ceiling attached to the sloping roof and smelled like a perfume shop. A party was going on. It accommodated six people sitting on two rusty metal beds. One of the guys gave up his place to the guest and flopped to the floor. I nodded at the door with the original single-pane window incorporated into it and asked how drunk men managed to go down by this ladder without breaking their necks.

"We're loggers," Natasha explained.

"We drink what the Lord provides," Rail said. "Anything goes—any cologne, 'triple' cologne is the best, ladies powder, tooth powder, talcum baby powder, and Cognac Blue Night." He pointed at a bottle of methylated spirit on the floor. "We can only dream of ethanol and lotions."

"I'm not wasting powder on my nose," giggled the mellowed Natasha.

"One boy managed to swallow shaving cream and was spitting out the foam like a fire extinguisher."

The guest on the floor vigorously stirred stubborn tooth powder with an aluminum fork in faceted glass and invited me to join the party. "Boss, this is for you."

"No offense," I moved his hand aside.

He gulped it cheerfully and said, "Soap is better."

"One little girl," said Rail, "wanted to rob the pharmacy in Soligalich, but I forbade it. Even if they had vodka, we wouldn't be able to afford it. What's your pay?"

"Pretty low," I said. "Eighty-eight rubles."

"Mine is three times less."

"You're kidding."

"Ask the Director."

"In Moscow, a street cleaner gets forty rubles."

"I wouldn't do such a job even for one hundred."

"Why? To handle a broom is easier than to fell trees."

"Ivan has his pride," his girlfriend explained. "He's the best feller around here."

Rail patted her on the butt and changed the subject, "Have you eaten our thick pancakes?"

"Yes, why? They're cheap and good."

"Yeah, good for a month. Hell, we stuffed with the pancakes every day, the whole year 'round. But if tomorrow they deliver sausage, cheese, and chocolate, check it out, we'll be able to eat it only after the final construction of communism."

"So, when they abolish restrictions, you'll move somewhere else?"

"To Siberia; the boys say the pay and the digs are much better over there."

One of the guests pointed at the floor. "Have you seen this intestine divided with plywood into rooms? With ten bunks?"

"Yes," the other one said, "just bring a girl into your room, she settles under your blanket, and at once all ten stallions want to help you."

"The girls are better," said the powder lover. "They only neigh and give advice."

"Where did you get these iron beds?" I asked.

"A gift of Comrade Stalin," chuckled Rail.

"I see you love him as dearly as I do." I found my company the most suitable for the story of the Ukrainian doctor Alexander Bogomolets. He promised to extend Stalin's life to 150 years and to transplant young testicles in him. Stalin offered to select the best ones among lumberjacks. The fraud received highest government awards, but just in case, died at 65, soon after the war. After the thundering laughter subsided, the skeptical girl asked, "How did you dig out this state secret?"

"One Stalin Prize winner shared it with me," I did no mention Stephan Zlobin.

Rail tapped his bed's metal frame. "The first lieutenant didn't want to drag this heap to another camp. We'll make a large one out of them; the supervisor promised to give me the welding equipment. In the spring, we'll open the roof anew."

"What a show for the whole forest!" I said.

"Natasha," he stroked her thigh, "and the boys will help me to drag it back in."

"I've already been sewing a soft feather bed," she said.

"Where did you get the feathers?" I was surprised.

Everybody laughed—the hosts with delight, the guests with envy.

"We'll fill this pallet with hay," now she stroked Rail's thigh, "and love each other until we faint."

I thought of Romeo, Juliet, and Shakespeare's narrow horizons.

Adventures
in the Wilderness

In Soligalich, several milkmaids were waiting for my return from the forest. If they were lucky, their first ever vacation would last up to five days. They were to participate in the regional two-day rally of the best young milkers. On behalf of the Regional Communist Youth leadership, I had to teach the girls how to ride a train, and upon arrival in Kostroma, to take them directly to the Committee.

And the day had come. The intense snow had been falling ferociously for the second day in a row. Sitting on the spruce branches in the bed of a truck hooked to a tractor, we were about to head for a great adventure, to a big city with people dressed as townsfolk, with shining asphalt roads, and two, three or even five-story brick houses with lots of entrances. None of them had ever seen a city bus or a train and before their eyes loomed luxurious fast-speed trains and cozy public buses. Ivan the Secretary, in a motherly fashion threw a huge matting on us and, waving an ax, began cutting off nearby massive fir branches and putting them on top of it; the strong wind could blow away even this reinforced cover, he warned us.

Everything looked beautiful. Blizzard, beating us in the eyes, confirmed my hopes—driving snow and strong wind promised 95 kilometers of combat with unwavering nature. The day before, Ivan reaffirmed my anticipation. "Not to miss the paramount event, you should leave Soligalich on the eve of the train's departure from Galich."

The girls, all in headscarves and *valenki,* both homemade and grey, huddled together, pressing tightly to each other. We began moving. Ivan was walking in the deep snow next to our truck. When he stopped, our tractor driver did not increase the speed. The clearing in front of us looked like a plain, with no road in sight. My glasses, already plastered with snow, helped me to imagine this narrow clearing and the endless trees merging soon into one giant white blanket under the leaden skies and our drivers

no longer able to navigate in this boundless space. Their behavior supported my hope; instead of saying how long it would take to reach Galich,
they just shrugged. Soon a new encouraging idea flashed in my mind: the
snowstorm blinds the driver, he can no longer see the live walls, the tractor run into the thick pine, the engine stalls, and the wayfarers are waiting
for rescue in the white wilderness. Until spring.

The first hour my team felt shy sitting so close to this urban sophisticate; during the second hour, they began asking questions. Their faces
were under our coarse covering, and this encouraged them.

"Is it true that every Moscow family has its phone?" was the first
question.

"In my apartment," I said, "four families use a phone on the corridor
wall; my aunt shares one phone with a dozen neighbors. When the thing
rings, everybody runs to it, they're happy about the innovation." I did not
tell them about an anti–Semitic neighbor of my parents who kept telling
the callers that we weren't home.

One girl, impressed to learn that almost all Muscovites had central
heating, said, "Jeez!" and asked, "Do you often eat oranges and caviar?"
She obviously saw some connections between the central heating and
the food of rich Muscovites. Our companions burst out laughing. I didn't
admit that I ate both, only said that caviar was much easier to buy in Moscow than oranges, but the queues were just for oranges.

"Is it permissible to walk through Red Square at night?" another
milkmaid asked.

"Sure," I said. "You can do it with impunity."

The next question was—is it true that Moscow movie theaters have
bands and everybody can dance there?

"My relative is a leader of such a band," I replied, "but if you try to
dance in there, you might end up dancing in a police station."

"In Moscow, they don't interrupt movies every twenty minutes while
changing the reels, isn't that true?" the disenchanted girl said. After learning that Moscow projectionists, to avoid riots, use no less than two pro-
jectors, she added, "When a projectionist is on the way to our club, even if
we've seen the movie before, folks come from the distant villages."

"Snowstorms or thunderstorms won't stop our grandmas," inserted
another movie fan. "It's good that we captured many movies as a war prize."

We lifted the heavy cover a bit to gulp air mixed with the relentlessly
falling snow. The only milkmaid whose hair was not hidden, but flirta-
tiously covered her forehead, drew in the fresh air and said dreamily, "I
loved Marika Rokk from *The Woman of My Dreams*."

Here in the middle of Russian snowy nowhere, to hear this from a girl
in self-woven shawl sounded weird. "She's a German," I said.

"They say big chunks were cut out of it. Could it be some Fascist propaganda?"

"I don't think so," I said. "I've heard there were some erotic scenes."

"What's erotic?"

"It's some…" I was looking for a sanitized explanation, and they knew it. "Well, this is when a man and a woman are naked in the same bed." Then I reconsidered my explanation, "Or almost naked."

In different parts of the country, the censors were cutting different scenes out of this movie, including the opening song "At night man hates being alone," the heroine dancing the cancan, bathing in a vat, and other items of the same innocent kind. In fact, the first censor of Soviet and foreign films was Stalin himself; all his *dachas* had cinema halls.

To my surprise, another girl asked, "Who's buried in the Kremlin Wall?"

"Not only in the wall," I said, "but also next to it."

"Next to it?" She clearly conveyed everyone's surprise. "So, all military parades and festivities take place at the cemetery?"

"Not between the graves but close to them." I had never looked at it from this angle. "Right in front of Lenin's Mausoleum, I mean, now it's Lenin's and Stalin's Mausoleum."

They ignored my correction and I decided to wait for questions about Stalin. After discovering festivities at the cemetery, this girl became bold and asked, "Why are foreigners admitted inside the Mausoleum?"

"They could put a bomb when Nikita Sergeevich Khrushchev welcomes the demonstrators from its rostrum," supported another politically astute girl.

One more milker expressed similar concern, "Is it true that there are many foreigners in Moscow? Can their presence harm our country?"

I only said, "I never met a person who would dare to mingle with foreigners."

I anticipated the next question, though not immediately. A shy girl next to me asked with embarrassment, "Is it true that the majority of Muscovites has never seen a cow?" All through the trip she had been trying unsuccessfully not to sit or lie too close to me.

"Yep, I still don't feel comfortable next to a cow," I said and blurted out, in a Freudian slip, "I feel much more comfortable next to you." While this urban sophisticate thought why the hell did he say it, the girls laughed approvingly. Suddenly they felt like women, and I completed my reflections assuming that they would notice some ambiguity of my joke. "She's, I mean, the cow, is very heavy and has horns."

After eight hours on the invisible road, the snowfall stopped. I got up on my numb feet, gingerly picked up one corner of the cover with a layer of snow and stood hunched waiting until the girls grasped three other ends of the matting. We shook most of the snow and fir limbs—survivors of the wind's assault—over the sideboard; a small pile of snow powdered the warm branches on the bottom of the truck. Now, the one who had discovered a cemetery on Red Square, asked with awe in her voice, "Is it true that Lenin looks like a living person?"

"Not quite," I said delicately.

"Does he look old?" she continued.

"Not too young," I said. "By now he must've been about ninety."

Four years after Stalin's death, they still would not dare to ask something about him. It reminded me of my fear of the dark. They feared him as Gogol's Khoma Brut and I were afraid of a dead witch flying in a coffin in an abandoned church. They talked only about Lenin.

"When did you see him last?" a new girl chimed in.

"Sixteen years ago. With my school class."

"If I lived in Moscow," she said, "I would see him often."

I wanted to defuse and challenge their nervousness and said, "After they put Stalin next to Lenin, I didn't want to go there anymore."

The girl interested in oranges and caviar was the first to mention Stalin, though without calling him by name. "Is it true that he began to create collective farms only after Lenin's death?"

"Yes," I said. They looked at each other with understanding; I was not going to give a lecture on Lenin's critical attitude towards the peasantry and, to entertain them, told them about John Reed, Lenin's friend from America, buried in Kremlin Wall. The milkmaids were impressed. "So, America could become one of our fraternal republics," one of them said.

"Yes, like Uzbekistan and Latvia, only bigger," I pulled the mat over my snide smile. "He died from typhus soon after the revolution."

A girl who had not said a word so far plucked up her courage and asked if it was true that spitting out the sunflower seeds husks or throwing dog-ends on the movie theatre's floor ends up with fines in Moscow.

"Possibly," I said.

✦ ✦ ✦

The journey through the wilderness continued and, eventually, we drifted to sleep. Two neighbors clutched me too tightly and, trying not to wake them, I gently released my hand pressed to the fir branches by the wheezing one, rose on my elbows and raised the matting. We stood in a small village. Myriad stars were winking either to me or to each other. The air was getting warmer; I felt its soporific fragrance as rare snowflakes were lazily dancing over my face. Our drivers stood in an open doorway in wisps of vapor. A flickering kerosene lamp illuminated their silhouettes from inside the house. The door quickly closed behind them, and they turned into two dark shadows; a minute later, they acquired drivers' features. They switched places and the new tractor driver was pulling us ahead without turning on the headlights. In the deliciously cool air, the monotonous roar of the tractors acted as a lullaby. I fell asleep again.

We reached Galich after nineteen hours of travel. "Nineteen" was a magic number. The milkmaids' *Komsomol* leader, traveling on foot, covered the same distance in as many hours as we did. My troop stepped on the same creaky steps where recently the prosecutor had offered me a ride, and before my mouth opened, they rushed to the railroad tracks. The workaday locomotive and the train disillusioned them. They could not know that the carriages with luxurious shiny nickel parts, inlays, and paintings they saw in Soviet movies belonged to the first Russian train and the railroad built in the nineteenth century by European engineers for Nicholas I to travel from Saint Petersburg to the nearby Tsar's Village. At the station, our party found a pair of battered cars with no compartments and with rows of wooden berths instead of the sumptuous leather sofas of the royal family and mirrors in golden frames. Nonetheless, the familiar scenery—boundless snow and endless forest—all of a sudden became beautiful. The girls took pleasure in the journey with its rhythmic music of iron, steel and cast iron and the exotic smells of lubricants and locomotive smoke penetrating the car. While the grave conductor was dozing in the second carriage, our band, under my direction, went on a couple of daredevil expeditions to the shaking platforms at both ends of our car. We opened the door and, in turn, bravely poked our heads outside and breathed the cocktail of the wind and locomotive soot.

Upon arriving in Kostroma, not to disappoint the milkmaids, I did not tell them that the station had been built in 1913 to celebrate the tercentenary of the Romanov Royal House. Never in their lives had the girls seen such a sea of unfamiliar faces. No one greeted anyone; in this city of 200,000 inhabitants, everyone behaved as if they were on a desert island, even when bumping into each other.

When the bus came, people pushed my troop with its homemade bags aside from the narrow doors. We managed to get in when the aisle was already overcrowded, and the girls were unable to move a limb. The pretty face of the youngest one rested in someone's smelly jacket. Soon we were on Lenin Street, and some milkmaids could observe this main thoroughfare of the town and a Lenin's statue overlooking the Volga River. They surely did not see the contradiction between the absolute simplicity of the concrete figure and the cylindrical 120-feet high tower of the picturesque pedestal in the form of a shrine. Even the townspeople did not know that it was a part of the monument for the tercentenary of the ruling dynasty. In 1924, the year of Lenin's death, all 28 cast bronze statues, mainly the tsars, were melted down. One of the statues depicted the peasant Ivan Susanin.

The biggest girl was lucky. She stood next to the bus door and perused the city. The only inconvenience she experienced was when passengers, some cursing, waded to the door next to her powerful torso. When the bus stopped at a red light, I announced, "This is our stop." The milkmaid pushed the door, but it did not give in to her mighty hand. And the unpredictable happened. She turned sideways and began using her torso as medieval warriors used a battering ram to open the forged gates of an enemy fortress. The pneumatic door still did not obey, and the warrior turned into a bird in terror, trying to escape from a cage. The driver began swearing. I began yelling, "Wait! It's not a stop! The door will open at the stop!"

A minute later, it magically opened. She was stunned. The girl never saw streetlights and pneumatic doors.

❖ ❖ ❖

Within three days after my return, I finished an essay called "The Guys and Gals from the Dense Forest." Rail—I called him Ivan Kotov—and two Volga Germans were there among the best loggers of the Soligalich Logging Enterprise. I played it safe and did not say a word to my editor-in-chief how all three became loggers and had to remain in the forest until someone somewhere at the top of the country would cancel the decision to keep them there. I described their skills and efforts in the unending struggle between humans and nature. The word "ecology" did not exist yet in the Russian lexicon, and my heroes looked like good Red Warriors though, in fact, they were gladiators fighting against two-legged predators. My reader did not need to be smart to understand that Karl Schmidt and Heinrich Kohl were Volga Germans; he knew that if something positive was published about Karl and Heinrich, it meant that from now on they were good fellows. Elena Protasova didn't ask me about these sensitive matters; she too smelled the political turnabout.

Neither did I say that the best logger of that lumber station, Ivan Kotov, robbed a food store as a teenager. Rail did not feel remorse while telling me how he and his partner made the night watchman of the store help them to load their factory cart with stolen food. After that, as their "victim" told the police, they tied his hands and feet, blindfolded him for no reason, forced him to quickly finish a bottle of vodka, put him on the counter, planted his head on a sack of barley, put a burning cigarette in his mouth, and locked the store. It wasn't his fault that in the morning he was reeking of vodka fumes and an unopened vodka bottle was found hidden in an empty jug in the shop window—when a robber puts a sharp knife to your heart, you'll agree to drink any poison to save your life. "Don't you see my jacket notched right in front of the heart?"

"I'm sure," said Rail, "what we didn't take, was pinched by the store manager and his salespeople, and by the police, no doubt. They found most of the shit in my partner's basement, next to his own sacks of potatoes. The watch, such a good man, winked at me during the identification parade and didn't recognize us."

Two weeks after my romantic description of their labor achievements reached the Soligalich lumberjacks, I received a short letter from the 21-year-old Karl Schmidt. He cried when he read the report. For the first time in his life, somebody praised him and had not called him a fascist. Karl had been five years old when the war broke out. Three days after the first letter, he wrote again, this time a one-liner: "Rail killed in a drunken brawl with the locals."

Poor talented Rail! It was not a newsworthy event. You don't need a censor to know it. The internal editor had already planted his roots in my soul. Otherwise, I would not be a journalist. Frustrated, I was rummaging in my notebooks, trying to dig up something which, without mentioning him by name, would remind his devoted little girl, friends, and enemies of Ivan Kotov. All I found never fit in my future reports; it could fit only into his obituary. The last time we talked, he put his saw in the fresh snow, leaned with one hand on a mighty pine, and said, "It's easy as shit to clear forest trails in winter. The swamps, wetlands, and bogs are frozen; they're like firm ground." His face was wet with sweat and snow. "Throughout the rest of the year we cannot use tractors or bulldozers in such places."

Snow kept falling. We stood silent for a while, studying the pine. He slapped the trunk. "It's good now; if I'm tired and refuse, they can no longer beat me down or lock me up in the cooler, or cut my rations."

"No watchtowers and barbed wire in sight anymore," I remarked, stating the obvious.

Snowflakes fell into his eyes and those who didn't know him could have thought that he was crying. A solitary ray of sunshine made its way through the clouds and for a moment turned the tree from brown to red. The foreman looked at us from a distance disapprovingly. Rail looked back at him and said, "They don't like it when I give 'em a stink eye. I don't want to get in a wreck. I've had enough of it."

He smiled at me, unable to disengage his teeth. Rather, it was a savage grin, as if he were gritting his choppers.

PART THREE: THE ROAD TO REBELLION

Not Newsworthy Events

The snow had already melted in Kostroma and the air smelled of spring and the upcoming sowing campaign when I invented a compelling reason to visit the place of Rail's killing. At an editorial briefing, I reminded everyone that the Regional Committee criticized our lack of coverage of the youth activities in the remote areas. The spring sowing campaign, I said, would give us a chance to compare the socialist competition in opposite northern corners of the region—Soligalich in the west versus the eastern Bogovarovo and Vokhma. With one stone, we'd kill two birds. I did not utter a word about Rail and the fearless rafters, of whom I daydreamed in Moscow.

Our editorial poet Alexander Chasovnikov and Anna Galun enthusiastically suggested that Arkady should take on this task. Everybody knew the poet never wanted to go beyond the city where he was born. "Poets," he spoke loftily, "don't need to travel to exercise their knowledge of human nature."

"How true," said Anna. "If Shakespeare and Tolstoy traveled, they would've had much less time for writing."

The poet nodded thoughtfully.

"And humanity might not have *Hamlet* and *War and Peace* under its belt," I said.

Chasovnikov nodded again.

Protasova giggled and said, "Arkady, it's about time Anna and you joined the Party. You both work hard. The very day your first year with us is over, I'll give you a recommendation to the Party. A journalist must be a Party member."

"Thank you, Elena," I said.

"I also want a recommendation," said Anna.

"We'll do something about that, too," Protasova said.

To cement my new assignment, I demonstrated my erudition, "Isn't it amazing, Soligalich and Bogovarovo are over 250 miles apart, but snow covers them roughly the same 150 days, until mid–April. So, the sowing campaign all over the North begins at the earliest at the end of April, but most probably, in May. Meteorologists warn this year flooding will be rough and rapid."

The old soldier Chasovnikov asked with a skeptical smile, "What does it have to do with the planting?"

I decided to prolong the pleasure. "First, ice on the rivers has to break up."

To Anna's delight, our fish swallowed the worm on the hook—he repeated his question for the ignorant Muscovite.

After a pause, I declared, "They deliver the seed only after logs accumulated over the winter move from waterlogged shores down the forest streams."

"I know that," he lied. "I just wanted to check the knowledge of the novice."

"I know that you know," I lied, too. "You probably saw with your own eyes how the logs torpedo the barges with the seed here, on Kostroma River."

"Sure," Chasovnikov said.

"If you don't mind," I continued our entertainment, "I'll use your poem as an epigraph to my future report from the northern milk farms; it so convincingly reflects the heroic struggle for high milk yields."

"What poem?" he asked kindly.

"Your pitch to the cows for decisive action. Remember? 'Double the yield! Triple the yield! Or else you'll end up being killed.'"

"Sure," the poet said. "Feel free."

Anna suddenly bit her fist and jumped to the door. We distinctly heard her sobs in the corridor.

"Women!" the storm-beaten poet said philosophically.

"Something has been happening to them," I said with a profound understanding of female psychology.

My new colleague and now friend Boris Klitsa looked with deep compassion at all of us, and spoke noble words, "Real poetry always evokes great emotions in women."

Chasovnikov looked happy.

After the briefing, Anna came to my desk and whispered, "You're a bad boy! You know that Kostroma River has never been used for delivering seed. We have to join the Party as soon as possible."

"I know that."

"Without the Party membership card, we'll never find a new job."

"Don't worry; we still have one more year to remain young and beautiful."

"And innocent," Anna added.

The Charter allowed us to remain members of the *Komsomol* until the age of 28.

◈ ◈ ◈

I knew this self-imposed task would be grueling and tried not to think about my long flight to northeastern Bogovarovo and Vokhma. Instead, I thought about their rafters. I wanted to run with them from shore to shore, with a long stick, on logs floating down the local streams. I wanted to crawl inside their skin, to try my fate with them. To complete my trip around the Kostroma world under the guise of the sowing campaign, I would have to return back to Kostroma and from there to fly to the opposite northwestern corner of the region. It was the only way to collect material about the murder of Rail in Soligalich. This was why that AN-2 pilot's herring reemerged in my head. To fight fire with fire, I decided to buy this salted-through-and-through medicine as a motion sickness remedy.

Even twenty years later, before my final flight from the USSR, my country was unaware of the very existence of motion sickness pills, of LifeSaver Peppermints, peppermint candies, and Gingersnap cookies. A Russian who isn't out of his mind would never believe that in effete America they had motion sickness pills for dogs.

I called the Kostroma airport, and a beautiful husky man quickly ruined my self-sacrificing plans. "What are you man, completely mad? We fly to Bogovarovo only in summer. Don't you know that the flights beyond one hundred kilometers are canceled in winter and spring?"

He heard my faltering breath of relief and probably thought I was terribly upset. "Use Sharya as a transit point. Go there by train," he suggested, "and try to take a short flight to Bogovarovo by a mail plane. But I think the postman won't take you, why would he want to?"

Even if he were hinting at money, I was ready to kiss him and just said, "I'm a correspondent."

"Well, if you frighten him," said my well-wisher, "he might take you." He paused. "But you better say that Peter is your buddy."

"Who's Peter?"

"Me."

"Pete, I owe you a bottle! What's your last name?"

"I'm not a fool to give my name to a correspondent. First, come here with this bottle, we'll finish it together. Everybody knows me here. There's no village in the region over which I haven't dumped a bag with newspapers and mail."

"So Bogovarovo and Vokhma read my reports only in summer? The lucky devils!" When he finished chuckling, I said, "My name is Arkady Polishchuk. Thank you very much, buddy!"

The year was 1957. In 2014, I read in the *Northern Pravda:* "The establishment of regular flights between Kostroma and Bogovarovo again postponed indefinitely."

❖ ❖ ❖

The first thing I saw from the steps of Sharya railroad station was rushing floes, menacingly protruding from the water, crawling upon each other, colliding and breaking. Sharya Rivulet loudly agreed with the instructor of the Regional Party Committee who told me in confidence, "We can't sow panic among the citizens. Bogovarovo and Vokhma don't have enough seed grain for the sowing campaign," he stumbled, before adding the word "sometimes" and continued, "Upon completion of timber floating, two barges deliver it—a barge for every district. You cannot use this information in your article. You certainly understand that." In his tired eyes, I read, "Why did these idiots sent you there?" I did not ask this man with a peasant's face where their own seeds were. Eaten up? He knew, peasants, even hungry, always leave some wheat and potatoes for the next planting season.

Now I saw it with my own eyes. The high temperatures quickly melted ice and snow, the fast floodwaters in forest streams, just as quickly as in this rivulet, were moving down the hills to bigger rivers and could be gone soon. The barges, trying to make it upstream, would not be able to climb up with impunity to Bogovarovo and Vokhma. Logs scattered by high water in the bushes could torpedo them.

Straight from the station, I walked by a dirt road to the airfield surrounded by the forest. There was another passenger. A soldier with a medal for bravery and sergeant's stripes slept arms and legs akimbo on the waterproof cape thrown upon the young grass, his face shielded from the sun by a field cap.

"I love this hooded cloak," I said quietly as if to myself.

The sergeant removed the cap and showed me chubby child-like cheeks.

"It's both my bedding and my blanket," he said. "No military in the world has such a handy thing." He definitely wanted to talk. "You can make a tent out of it and carry the wounded and the dead."

I asked how he got this medal in peacetime.

"What peacetime? It's for the war."

"Where?"

"In Hungary."

"I read in *Pravda* that some counter-revolutionary hooligans..."

He interrupted me. "Yeah, someone cheated the correspondent; the hooligans had tanks and were armed to the teeth. America and England gave Hungarian Fascists billions of dollars."

"Many of our boys were killed?"

"I don't know; at least a thousand, I guess. Two boys from my crew burned in the tank. I jumped out."

"Wounded? Burnt?"

"No, just two broken arms and bruises all over."

"A shell?"

"No, petrol bombs, several bottles. We crushed almost all of them," he said with a serene smile. "In a tank, you don't hear how the bones crunch."

"Are you on leave?"

"Yeah. It's good here in the sun. Only pines rustle."

"How long have you been here?"

"The second day, waiting for a passing aircraft. The time on the road doesn't count."

The ground still was wet and cold. I asked the soldier if he had a knife. He pulled a dagger out of his backpack and said, "Hungarian." I advised him to cut some branches and put them under his cape. The rising roar of a single engine broke the silence, and soon a low-flying plane emerged from behind the forest.

"They fought in Hungary," he said.

The descending AN-2 quickly touched down on the field, taxied some seventy yards, and stopped not far from us. The propeller blades made several lazy turns and froze. The pilot raised the cockpit's left lantern-like hood and waved to us. We went to the aircraft.

"Arkady Polishchuk?" the pilot said. "Greetings from Peter, the pilot, our veteran."

A creaking cart was slowly moving toward us, the driver, with reins in his hands, walking at an easy pace next to the horse.

"He's bringing the mail from the railroad," the pilot explained. "They accumulate the mail and then call us. We'll take off after I fetch the bags for Bogovarovo and Vokhma Party Committees."

"This sergeant is trying to get home," I said.

"Where's your home?" he asked.

"Kadiy."

"A soldier with a medal will be taken on board. Sit down here for a couple of days. The guys will pick you up, I promise."

Fascinated, I sat next to the pilot, and we waved to the sergeant. We moved, first towards the woods, and soon, slowly, seemingly reluctantly, soared over it. When I pulled from my backpack the herring wrapped in a newspaper, the pilot sniffed the air and said reflectively, "I'm afraid we'll need to make an emergency landing to buy a vodka bottle."

I now thought I should not fly with this lunatic. After a theatrical pause he added, "The herring works only with vodka."

With a pitiful smile, I put my medicine back into my knapsack next to two canvas mailbags behind us and said, "I'm a timid passenger."

The pilot chuckled. "Enjoy the ride!" He slapped me on the back. "I'm Andrei. We'll make you a pilot." He patted the dashboard. "She's the only aircraft that can return out of a spiral mode back to horizontal flight." The sadist checked whether his victim was still alive. "I'll show it to you."

"Oh, no!" I begged him for mercy.

He ignored my noise. "She's a very forgiving girl, and forgives terrible blunders. If one day this baby flaps her wings and sings like a nightingale, I won't be surprised."

He carried on rambling, but for some reason, I didn't feel sick and only begged, "Could we move a little higher? We might catch on those spikes."

"If you wish, we can hover over them with the engine running at full power." His tone became businesslike.

It was too much for me. "Andrei, are you crazy? Don't you have a loving family?"

Andrei ignored my pleading. "What I suggest, never land on a frozen lake."

"Why?" My curiosity turned out to be stronger than fear.

"Skis don't hold up to the landing on hard ice. On floats in summer— it's a different ballgame."

I looked at him with suspicion. "Are you trying to hypnotize me? I'm already obsessed with what you're saying; only a bit burping."

The flier definitely did not hear me. "A nice girl has been waiting in Bogovarovo for me. I'm sure she can find a nice chick for you, too. Men run away from here."

"After an AN-2 flight, I need to stay in bed alone for a while."

"D'you still want me to fly backward?" He definitely kept me in suspense.

"No, no," I pleaded, "better show that trick to your girl. Birds can't do that. Even more advanced crocodiles and alligators cannot step backwards."

Andrei looked at me in surprise. "A good idea! I'll show it to her. The whole trick is in the slow speed of the aircraft. Have you ever made love in a cockpit?"

It was the most comfortable flight of my life. Nonetheless, when we landed in Bogovarovo, I vowed not to fly to Vokhma.

"It's a five-minute flight," he said.

"I will walk. Just twenty-something kilometers. I dream of walking in the impassable taiga."

"People go astray when they have to circumvent fallen trees," Andrei warned.

On the same day, I faced the anticipated obstacle. Logs accumulated through the winter on the banks moved. When the riverbeds packed with wood were cleared, it was too late—only one barge with seed, instead of two, was dragged upstream. Until next spring, I could say goodbye to rafters from my future book. I called my editor-in-chief from the Bogovarovo Party Committee to say that we could not cover the planting campaign. The farms did not have seed.

"Don't they work hard?" she said.

"Oh, yes, they do."

"So, why don't you write about hard-working people overcoming the difficult spring?" She was smarter than I was.

"They say a war broke out between two districts over seed grain. The belligerents attacked the barge from both banks; they were pushing and hitting, heavy sacks fell into the water."

"Arkady, I don't recognize you. You're there to cover the socialist competition, not the unfortunate incident."

"Fields will stay barren," my voice dropped.

"Arkady," she was getting angry, "you're there with a specific assignment and must perform this task."

She hung up on me when I said that party committees of both districts led this bloody battle.

In that early afternoon, I walked along virgin woods back to the small inn called the Inn and while passing by the ruins of an 18th century church thought about the degree of religiosity of the locals. Its builders dropped an icon in a cauldron of boiling tar and renamed this village *Bogovarovo* (Where God was cooked). I forgot the God-fearing men of yore when I entered my room. Bold steps, the gnashing of furniture dragged across the adjacent room, and the deep voice of a drunken dame quickly moved me from the holy to romantic. We already had had a quick word outside the inn. The wallpapered barrier was not high enough to separate me from this head with a thick braid wrapped around it and black eyes peering over the barrier.

"Hi neighbor," the head crooned. "Want a drink?"

"No, thank you," I said. "I have to go."

"It's all right," she said. "I'll wait for you."

She was an agent of some collective farm from Southern Ukraine—in Russian terms, a pusher (*tolkach*). Her job was to buy timber for the construction of a new dairy farm and stables, of course, if she was telling me the truth.

"Are'ye here to get some raw wood?" the head asked.

"No."

"Live wood? Logs?"

"No."

"It's great," she said.

"What's so great?" I said.

"It's great that you aren't here for the timber. Are'ye a prosecutor or a policeman?"

"No, I'm a pediatrician."

"Is that the type who helps pregnant women?"

"Kind of."

"Could you help me?"

"Are you pregnant?"

She whinnied like a breeding stallion.

"Do you have a child here?" I asked.

"No, my children are in Moldova."

"I can't treat children from a distance."

"You can treat their mama right here."

"I have to go," I said. "A child is waiting for me."

In Western terms, she could be called an expediter or even a mover and shaker. The law did not back her activity though it was as necessary for the Soviet economy as a lubricant for trucks and trains. These agents traveled across the country to get scarce material and parts for plants, factories, and farms, whatever the cost. Their primary tools were bribes and what could be delicately called barter arrangements. If in the interests of authorities or an extortionist, these pushers could easily fall under the penal code. Without them, though, the five-year plans of the USSR would not have been implemented. No doubt, this proprietress of the luxurious black tresses did not know a thing about the very existence of the State Planning Commission. However, this powerful institution has always conceptually known of her existence. The Socialist system worked!

To my relief there came a knock on the door. It was a coachman from a nearby collective farm Great October Revolution.

"We have a nimble mare," he said and fixed his eyes on her.

I could not restrain myself and said, "Me too."

She liked it and neighed again.

On my way to the farm, the horse's rump somehow reminded me of this *tolkach*. She certainly could bribe her way through felling, warehousing, loading, and delivering the timber to rivers and railroads, and transporting it to whomever she was sending or reselling it. With such combat experience, she could make a career as a kosher capitalist entrepreneur, as an oligarch in modern Russia or as a lobbyist in Washington, D.C., but the woman was unaware of this, unaware even of these very words, including "kosher," of course.

I came back from the Great October Revolution late, and didn't turn on the light for fear that it might wake my neighbor's passion. In the dark, however, I bumped into a chair, and it loudly fell to the floor. I heard mumbling, shuffling steps, the light in the adjusting room lit, and my beauty, drunk like a lumberjack, appeared behind the barrier staring at me from a chair with once-in-a-lifetime love in her sparkling eyes. She was holding to the partition with both hands, and her heavy braid, now on a white nightgown, was swaying along with the woman herself and the wooden obstruction.

"Go to bed!" I said and heard the trumpets of Jericho.

"Only with you, my dear."

"I hate drunken women," I said.

"I'm climbing over," she turned to recitative. "Move a little to the side, my dear."

I sat on my bed and watched her bouncing on a chair in an attempt to fly right into my arms. After a minute of struggling, she disappeared, and I heard her groaning, swearing, and dragging another piece of furniture to the barrier. Now I saw a much larger part of her nightgown with Ukrainian hand embroidery on her voluminous chest—she obviously placed the chair on the desk. The show turned into a deadly balancing act and I rushed to the barrier. She interpreted this humanitarian gesture as a manifestation of my unrestrained desire and held her bare arms out to me while exclaiming, "I knew, my..." and collapsed noisily down. I heard the curses and groans again. A minute or two later came scary silence. I swore and ran into her unlocked room. The femme fatale lay motionless on her back, next to the broken chair. Her breathing was fine, red roses were moving up and down on her chest as if alive. I removed the blanket from her bed and covered the sleeping beauty. Even a fairy-tale prince would not be able to awaken her with a kiss. In the end, she knew, I wasn't a prince; I was just a pediatrician.

◈ ◈ ◈

In the morning, to the accompaniment of her mighty snoring, a forester from the neighboring room tapped at my door. The day before, he had promised to instruct me on how to get to Vokhma and now drew a map in my notebook. I had to come to the forest edge twice and cross two meadows at the points, he described with precision. The forester feared foreign spies; local and Moscow maps didn't exist because spies could use them. We did not know that the crafty CIA had already produced the most reliable map of our capital. Thirty years later, the liberal president Mikhail Gorbachev admitted that all maps of the aging Soviet Union were distorted.

It was about time for me to go when the forest man's eyes flashed, and he asked if I remembered Old Believers. They had lived in the nearby woods before the revolution, a three or four hour walk from the inn, as the crow flies. Some seven miles before Vokhma, there would be a little village, a bit out of my way, called Brooks; some call it Swamp. During the rainy seasons, you couldn't get there—two narrow streams kind of surround Brooks, they begin and end up in swamps. Recently, to replace rotted logs, he brought and tossed three new pine trunks over one of the streams with a tractor-driver.

I became interested. "Were you born here?"

He studied my face and replied, "No, I'm from the White Sea." He kept talking about that village and its inhabitants, who generation after generation, keep fighting the forest to save their livelihood—the fields, the crops, pigs, and cows. I gathered my strength not to be dragged into this quagmire, and said, "My paper is interested only in the crop planting campaign."

A dying hope slipped in his voice. "Do you think it's better not to go there?"

"I will not," I said in exasperation.

His face fell. "Okay," he said, "so there is nothing for you to do there. Wetland, not good timber, a poor farm with only one man, a crippled chairman." He waited for my reaction. I didn't intend to react and heard the despair in his voice when he said, "And every child there looks like him."

I made a mistake and said, "You said he's crippled."

"Yes," his eyes flashed again, "you just have to turn sharply south almost at the edge of the second meadow; you'll see a grove of young fir trees, three dozen 20-year-olds and from that tiny knoll a sharp eye can see the path on the other side of the stream." Hope returned to his voice. "Maybe the water is already subsiding."

"How nice to be a Muscovite," I said. "Everyone thinks that you're able to work miracles."

The forester grew morbid and mumbled, "Their medicine women still take delivery, they treat the whole area, even from the evil eye. By the way, that whore with golden rings has an evil eye, he-he!" My face expressed astonishment and he hurried to explain, "Her door was slightly ajar, and I opened mine."

"You heard?"

"Yes. In radio plays and movies, men have no members, only party membership cards, and women—with no vagina. And here—it was real life."

"Not exactly," I said. "The member was hers."

A Village in the Midst of Swamps

Soon after this enlightening conversation, I was walking to Vokhma, enjoying the uniquely resinous scent of pine trees. The forest road looked more like a damp trail, occasionally barely discernable, sometimes like a pathway that still could be used as a dray road. Patches of settling snow were lying in the dense shade of some trees, and some crept to the trail in the lowland. A sleepy beetle crawled out from under the dried needles, and, what a little fool, stopped in front of me. I stepped aside and nearly crushed an innocent snowdrop in the melting strip of snow. Following the forester's instructions, in almost four hours I reached the meadow and the young fir trees at the edge of the forest. Covered with dense little cones, they gave off a spicy fragrance. From a distance, the hard cones looked more like oblong green-brown fruit or exotic flowers. I decided to send a unique bouquet to my beloved, opened my knife and started to cut a bunch, thinking that its wonderful smell could reconcile Irina with the inevitability of her moving to this godforsaken hole called Kostroma. I finished the job and suddenly felt that someone on the other side of the tree was studying me through the branches. It was still light in the field, but it was getting dark on the forest side, and my fear of the dark once again came into play. Very slowly, I parted the thorny branches. Any abrupt move would make the animal attack me. Suddenly, the boughs in front of me began shaking, crackling and breaking. I shuddered with fear. Before I could think of the sharp knife still in my hand, a great beast, judging by the noise, began to exit the spot, destroying everything in its path. It could be only a bear or a moose. Perhaps the animal was eating the soft young fir shoots when I approached it. My plans quickly changed. I decided to spend the night in the village called Swamp and Brooks.

✦ ✦ ✦

The water had burst both banks and was now reluctantly returning to its course. On this low bank the three thick logs not yet cleared of pine bark settled a little in the soaked ground. Stepping on them, I felt like I was walking uphill. The closer I got to the opposite higher bank, the more the makeshift bridge crawled out of the swift stream and now, though still slippery, was above the water. I looked back. Could that one-legged chairman walk here? I was going to stay overnight at the farm where all the kids looked like him.

A soggy foot trail led to a thick stripe of the seemingly impassable sickly forest. The small village was hiding behind it. Then I saw two boys and a girl running toward me. They politely greeted the stranger. My bouquet puzzled them.

"A gift," I said.

The kids glanced at each other in bewilderment. "Where's your cow?" the younger boy asked. In the springtime, to save cows from starvation, many farms fed them young spruce needles.

"It's not a cow," I assured him. "It's a lassie."

They took it for a joke, giggled and led me to the house of the farm's head. The girl pointed at the three abandoned dwellings; the village men, she said, had long taken up logging and some have been constructing buildings in big cities.

The chairman did not budge when he saw me. Two heavy-set comely women on a bench in the corner of the room greeted me, looked at my bouquet and each other, and continued to repair the fishing net spread on their knees. The man knocked on his wooden leg, explaining why he did not rise and said, "Thank you for coming. Only moose and wolves drop in here."

"And bears," one of the women said darkly without taking her eyes off the net. For some reason, the children smiled.

In the middle of the room, a thin sliver of wood was burning, inserted into a bent nail on the side of a wide stump. An ember fell in a flat metal dish with water and quietly hissed.

"A *luchina*?" I was seeing this item for the first time in my life. The light of a candle would be lifeless in comparison. "Don't you have kerosene lamps?"

"We don't have kerosene," explained the other woman, also still looking at her work.

"You look like sisters."

"We are," she said.

"Your children?"

"No, but we have many," she said.

"How many are many?" I anticipated a stunning number.

"Five. All girls, except a boy who's in Stalingrad."

"He managed to remain there after military service," said the father.

"Does he visit you?"

"Once. Now he's saving money for the road again. We pick up his letters in Vokhma."

The women still did not look at us. I blamed it on the Old Believer's traditions.

"You probably heard that I have two dozen of them," the chair said.

"More. They say all the children here look like you."

"Even in the District Party Committee, some serious folks asked if I sleep with all the women here."

"Envious," I said. "They speak their dreams."

"Exactly. It would be difficult to catch up with them all with this leg. I had enough problems just with this one," he nodded at his wife.

She said gloomily, "Once he ran very well."

"If I were that bear, I'd run from her," the chair said. "She ran straight at the bear and stopped him with a shot for hunting birds. Right in the muzzle. He screamed in pain, and then I shot him."

"I was in such fear," the woman said.

The kids laughed louder than the rest of the company. She glanced at them and joined us.

"Who are the hunters?" I asked.

"We all are. We have two hunting guns and two shotguns," the chair turned to the children, "Who went on the hunt with me the last time?"

"I did," the girl said.

The man read my mind and said that he made shots from old cables lead. "One good fellow was afraid that we would use a wrong metal and kill ourselves." The old soldier did not tell how they get ammunition for their hunting guns. I suspected the forester of being privy to this secret when the chair hurriedly added that his birth women had been paid by ammo in the villages where they take delivery. Now he felt more comfortable and turned to fish. "With my piece of wood it's easier to drag the dragnet. It doesn't slip in the mud."

"Sure." Irony sounded now in the wife's voice.

He ignored the irony. "Where the mud is too deep, I use a trap net."

"Sure," her sister said. "And what if you were stuck there again?"

"That mudcat," he turned to me to explain, "buried itself in the slime. I grabbed that log right by his mustache as big as marshal Budenny's."

"Yeah." The sister stopped mending the net and said, "And the children dragged them all—the marshal, the net, and this stubborn old chair—out of that ooze."

He just shrugged. "These women, they always exaggerate." The man looked almost fearfully at the women and moved to a safer subject. "The District gave up on us—our fields are small and waterlogged, our only wheel tractor breathed his last two years ago, but we haven't lost the metal, thanks to our forge."

"Tell this correspondent how we bake cakes from beet leaves with chaff, in winter—from cabbage leaves with the chaff again." Irritation could be heard in his wife's voice. "Put it in your notebook, too."

Chair clearly decided to put an end to an unpleasant conversation. "We live on bear, moose, hare and wild hog," he said, "on milk and whatever grows in the forest."

An unframed small photograph on the wall attracted my attention.

"Yes, that's me," he said. "I was a sniper, angry like a winter wolf. Celebrated every kill. That's why I have this iconostasis. It still comes back at night."

His sister-in-law asked him to make more lights, so that the guest could see his many medals. He rose with an effort from the bench, stumped loudly across the floor, picked up another long splinter, lit it in the flame of the burning *luchina,* and inserted it into another bent nail driven into the opposite side of the same woodblock. His wife brought a clay bowl with water and placed it under the new *luchina.* Water multiplied the light like a mirror.

"Great!" I liked it. "So, you're the only man around here, aren't you?"

"Yeah, two-legged creatures run away from here, but after returning from the military, boys from distant villages come here looking for brides." Mindful of my unhealthy interest in his ammunition, he added, "They are required to bring cartridges."

Buried in their work again, the women smiled.

"Why?" My question sounded ambiguous.

"Our girls—the most beautiful," he explained, perhaps suspecting that my question was about ammunition. "We have this breed from the old times. Our stallions were Old Believers; they learned to guzzle moonshine only recently, so they haven't spoiled the herd."

"Have you, Andrei Ivanych, found another groom?" his wife asked calmly.

"Of course, right from Moscow. Don't you hear the way he speaks?"

"He won't survive here one day." Her sister nodded without looking at me. "Probably isn't able to plant a potato or collect cranberry in a bog."

They were talking about me as if I weren't in the room and there was nothing offensive in it; I even liked it. How often do people have the opportunity to hear an impartial opinion about them in their presence?

"He can teach our children to read and write." The chair defended his choice and maybe felt obliged to give me some objective information about my future place of residence. "The forester who sent you here gave us a crumpled fuel oil drum for tanning hairy skins," he said. "We soak it in piss."

His wife looked at my bewildered face and tried to calm the Muscovite a little. "He keeps this stinking stuff away from the village."

His sister-in-law offered me even a more positive view of things. "He teaches kids to make the fishing tackle, hooks, and fishing line."

This could not stop the old hunter. "After the piss," he said almost vindictively, "just scrape the hair off with a knife, salt the fresh hides quickly, and soon you can use it to repair the harness and the shoes."

Their life reminded me of the books of James Fenimore Cooper, of the American Indians of two hundred years ago. I planned to travel soon to Moscow and promised to send them *The Deer-slayer, or The First Warpath* and *The Last of the Mohicans*. Unexpectedly a boy cried aloud, "Uncle Andrei! Don't you remember? The last winter!" The children on the floor started bouncing on their butts like rubber balls. "They didn't talk in Russian!"

"Yes, in the loggers club," Andrei Ivanych said, "they still show American movies captured during the war."

"I saw them in Moscow," I said.

"All the warriors and their women," the girl said, "are walking in the skins like ours."

"Maybe not anymore," I said.

"We don't wear the horns of our cattle." The older boy updated me.

Now I was fired up no less than the children. "Have you seen the movies about Tarzan?"

"We have! We have!" they cried, interrupting each other. "How he was looking for his son!"

"And what else did you see?," I asked.

They shook their heads sadly. "Nothing," the girl said and all three began shouting shrilly at once, "Oh please, tell us, tell us!"

Genuinely fascinated by the topic, I began to list, "*Tarzan in a Trap, The Rescue of Tarzan, The Adventures of Tarzan in New York,* and how he found his son, of course. The famous American swimmer Johnny Weissmuller played Tarzan."

"Who else? Who? Wow!" They nudged each other and cried even more loudly. There were no names in the captions and titles—no actors, no directors, no one.

"How often do you go to movies?" I settled myself down.

"We can't afford this," Andrei Ivanych said. "Some kids lay for free before the first row and sit on the floor by the walls, but there isn't enough space over there."

He had touched a sore spot. "We can walk to Vokhma before dark and sit on the floor waiting till evening," the girl said. "No wolf would attack us."

I couldn't help asking, "How do you pay Party membership dues? You earn nothing here."

"I do pay dues—a sacred thing. We sell wild honey, herbs, berries, and roots at the Saturday fair in Vokhma, sometimes, fish, bear, and moose meat. We buy needles, matches, thread, salt, and kerosene for holidays in town." A sly smile appeared on his face. "Thank God, the methylated spirit is cheap and is almost always there. It's better than vodka."

After some thought, I asked, "Why are you reasoning so boldly?"

"What should I be afraid of? They won't send another chair to this swamp; if they do, the women will kill him."

"Who else drinks here?"

"I don't allow that. Well, for holidays my women brew moonshine from beets, potatoes, and grass."

"The whole village sings and dances," said his wife.

I nodded toward the children.

"Yeah, we give'em a little," she said.

"Uncle Andrei loves dancing," said the girl and blushed.

"We see you keep writing," the sister-in-law, suddenly nervous, interrupted. "Write that the decorated war veteran with a peg leg keeps 52 females, a dozen of them barely alive, and 40 children from starving to death—we'll all be looking forward to your report..."

The women and children looked at me at point blank range. I looked at the floor.

"Don't be ashamed, son," the soldier said. "We all should be ashamed. I saw how the Germans live. As I drink my cheap spirit, I always tell my women how well they were under Hitler."

"Why didn't you rot in the Gulag?"

"I was silent as a fish while the Boss was alive."

"Me too," I didn't want to ask questions anymore; his wife tried to help this grim reporter and broke the silence. "The children go to school in Vokhma. Three girls are *Komsomol* members."

"They walk," her husband said, "when our two horses are busy or the road is bad."

✦ ✦ ✦

In the dark, the children brought me to stay overnight with two sisters. Why did he put me up there? Everybody saw my prickly bouquet. The siblings' log house had only one room and a small kitchen. One of them, the farm forewoman about thirty years old, looked like a creature from a

Thousand and One Nights, only blue-eyed. She could not know that she belonged to the chimerical world of glossy magazines, which did not exist in our country. It is likely the woman were not acquainted with the word "cosmetics" either. In these places, a woman older than twenty and still single was suspected of having a hidden defect. The sisters' long necks and legs did not match the local concepts of a broad-hipped and busty beauty. They lowered their bottomless eyes while talking to me, did not ask questions, and offered their iron bed where they slept together. I don't remember any other furniture in the room, only this tall bed with a high headboard of black metal tubes with silvery knobs and a simple silvery, tubular ornament in the middle. I refused their offer and slept on the floor, just a yard away from their squeaky bed.

When the women were stuffing my mattress with hay, their long fingers, rough and reddish, told me the story of their life; they certainly were not sensitive to touch, the nails weren't well kept and had ill-kept cuticles. The right thumb of the older sister, broken probably long ago, was crippled and its nail was bluish.

I could not sleep and was thinking about their looks that would soon fade and hands that would soon ache constantly, and about the good man who, wishing the sisters well, put me up for this night in their tiny house. Judging by their pensive eyes, I had no doubt they understood his intentions.

It was still dark when the creaking of their bed awakened me. The sisters were going to the barn for milking.

In the morning, I found on the rough kitchen table a note under three raw eggs still smelling of a brood hen, a pinch of grayish large salt crystals in a tin spoon, and a faceted greenish glass of fresh milk. The note said, "Orkady, do not be hard on us for this country breakfast." I liked this name Orkady; they obviously heard that Muscovites always pronounce the letter O as A.

I put the note in my backpack, tore a sheet from my notebook and wrote, "Thank you so much! The eggs and milk were perfect. Everything was perfect." And it was perfect. After a moment of hesitation, I added, "And you both are beautiful." At first, I wanted to leave a piece of my hard smoked sausage, but changed my mind—something was humiliating about this. I went out on the porch, closed the door, which had only an inner bolt, and immediately returned. I looked at my note and thought maybe I should cross out "beautiful" and write "perfect" instead, but changed nothing, put my cool clasp-knife and a branch with cones on my note and went out again. They knew that we would never meet again.

I left Brooks, also called Swamps, with a heavy heart and a feeling of guilt. Walking through the spring taiga in broad daylight, stumbling and

avoiding fallen trees and their limbs, cheered me up and I began thinking of the next Great October Revolution farm. It had participated in the
socialist competition with a farm under the same name, which I visited
near Bogovarovo. That was a perfect choice for my story and its miracles.
I thought of barren fields, of hundreds of farms so named in honor of the
Bolshevik Revolution, and decided to tease my editor a little by proposing
a dangerous headline: "Two Great October Revolutions."

Two days later, I called the *Young Leninist* office, as usual, from a District Party Committee, this time from Vokhma, to dictate my report on
the socialist competition. In the middle of the dictation, Elena Protasova
took the phone from our typist, "From what I already see it's a good report.
Of course, I'll ignore the headline; you're pulling my leg again. Please stop
doing it, one day someone might take it seriously, and not only you, but
also some innocent people will pay the price for your inappropriate jokes."

Then she changed my assignment. The Party decided to conduct
preparations for the World Youth Festival to open in Moscow on July 28.
The entire country was right away required to begin in-the-field compe-
titions for the best dancers, singers, musicians, magicians, choirs, acro-
bats, young poets and writers on the subject of international solidarity,
friendship, and world peace. The best of the best would participate in this
momentous event. My trip to Soligalich was canceled. I must go to Galich,
which was known for its amateur theatrical and choral groups. I was three
yards from the office of the Party Secretary.

"Go immediately to him to request a truck," she said.

To return to Bogovarovo made no sense, no one knew when one
could catch a plane. A hundred miles of dirt road to Sharya was drying up.
"Somehow I'll get there," I said, "and will take a train to Galich, whatever it
is, military or cargo. We must glorify our theatrical traditions." No doubt,
hearing my suddenly broken voice, Protasova understood in her own way.
She cheered up. "Tell the Secretary that you're working on latest orders
from the Central Committee."

An hour later, I was sitting next to a disgruntled driver of a
three-ton-truck. "Somebody is out of his mind," he said. "Like in war.
Wasn't even allowed to have my breakfast."

"It's all the fault of the world youth and progressive students," I said
and gave him a chunk of my Moscow sausage.

"In a hundred years I haven't seen such a beauty," he said. "I suppose
it's from the dining room of the Regional Party Committee."

To stress my importance, I nodded, even though I had actually received it in a parcel from my parents. My plan to visit the place of Rail's
murder had failed.

My Questionable
Activities

In Sharya, I spotted a ready-to-depart freight train with logs and a small bi-axial car hooked to it. I approached the engine and started to climb its metal ladder when threats and swearing coming from above and from the ground hit me like a dirty tornado. The driver and a railwayman with signal flags yelled as if I had stepped on their pet peeves. After the failure of my plan to investigate the murder of Ivan Kotov and a sad visit to Swamps, I was in the mood to prank and politely asked, "To Galich?"

Nobody in their right mind would send logs from here to Galich. Usually, such cargoes headed south or for the Baltic or wherever, but not to places like this town, which itself was busy sending local timber to far-away places.

"Who told you this bull!" yelled the driver.

People are aggressive to reporters on occasion. To them, we represent the state. We can be arrogant or sensitive, intelligent or stupid, but nobody doubts that the government has authorized us to do what we do. I waved my press card, and the man on the ground with red and yellow flags acted like a locomotive that all of a sudden lost its steam; he began to seek a peaceful way out. It made me think that the timber was stolen. "Without a special permit even a reporter has no right to be here," he spread his hands politely, but still grumbled, "The railways operate by the war rules. The purpose of this cargo is a military secret."

I stared at him haughtily from the step, "Look, I know about this destination for a reason. It doesn't have anything to do with your operation. All you have to do is to deliver me to Galich where the district prosecutor is waiting for me...." During my dramatic pause the man was turning pale; I slowly shifted my spruce bouquet from one hand to the other and, while smoothly putting my ID back in my pocket, finished the sentence, "in connection with a murder."

Now, his face lit up; this "murder" made him happy. "Of course, in this important matter, we'll help you. Get down and go to the covered wagon at the end of the train." He pushed his uniform cap deeper and ran ahead of me to that bi-axial car.

When I, forcing myself to walk with dignity, approached it, three gallows birds gently smiled at me from the wide-open sliding doorway. One of them offered me his hand, and with the other hand as if by accident, he tried to put pressure on my priceless bouquet, covered and wrapped by one of my shirts. I quickly took it away, and he almost fell out of the car. "Watch out!" I said. "Can't you smell the white roses?"

"Looks like a human head," he said. We laughed airily; a gold crown on his tooth reminded me about this sign of belonging to the criminal world of my childhood.

In the middle of the little car sat a cast-iron *vremyanka*, like the one that we had during the war, only our stovepipe ran out of our window, and this one—straight through the roof. With a cabin and toilet, it did not look like a wagon for livestock. I said, "Nice." Without saying a word, one of them poured a full glass of vodka for me. Clearly, they already obtained some information.

"No, thank you, bro," I said. "I'm gonna talk to a prosecutor soon."

"So what?" he said.

"You know, they aren't always friendly; although I have nothing to do with the case."

"Why do they need these roses?"

"Beats me. These are sample cones for some criminal investigation."

The train began to pick up speed; I needed to add something more convincing and said, "I lied to that good man with flags."

"What d'you mean?" The golden tooth flashed again.

Their eyes bored into me.

"I needed to take a look at preparations for the World Youth Festival."

They looked at each other in disbelief.

"You say that in shitty Galich will be held some kind of world fair?" squinted the golden tooth.

"No!" I started to laugh heartily. "This summer, all over the country, local performers compete for the chance to participate in that festival."

After a pause, they joined in. Through the raucous laughter, I finished, "That's why I asked that railroader about Galich."

One of them squeezed out of his mouth, "And so he divulged a state secret?"

"Yeah," I snarled and laughed even louder. When we all calmed down, the one who greeted me with vodka asked, "Aren't you afraid that the appropriate authorities could investigate you for this?"

"Not really, it was one of those innocent tricks a reporter does to carry out his duties."

"Couldn't you wait for a passenger train?"

"Sure, but I just decided to give it a try to make it sooner."

"And pocket the transportation allowance you were granted for the road?"

"And why not?"

"So now you're rich?"

"Uh-huh."

Upon parting, all three men shook my hand. The tooth said, "It's soft; one can tell this person engages in hard mental labor."

"You would've made a good investigator," I said.

"I am," he waved his hands.

"That's what I suspected," I said, and again we had fun laughing.

"Do you know how we use such evidence?" he asked.

By now, I was better prepared. "They found a body next to a railway track, and the man had a cone in his pocket. Probably to determine the exact place of killing, they're collecting cones along the tracks. Perhaps the nature of the soil is somehow reflected in the composition of the minerals in them."

"Alright, buddy, I'll share with you our professional secret." The "investigator" slapped me on the back and said, "We conduct chemical analyses to determine the location of a murder."

⊕ ⊕ ⊕

The Galich prosecutor had a visitor. When I spotted the director of Soligalich Logging Enterprise, I forgot what I wanted to say upon arrival and said instead, "You can't escape your fate. My trip to your town was canceled on the occasion of the upcoming World Youth Festival."

"I know why you're here, don't be cunning," the director said. "All witnesses say, Rail attacked first and knocked that local guy down."

"Ivan was terribly offended," I said. "I'm sure during the interrogation, his girlfriend Natasha said that that logger had provoked him. He had done it before, insulted her, and made lewd advances. Not to upset her man, she kept it secret from Rail, but not from me. Once, after he pinched her butt, she had tried to fight him."

"Look, that logger is on the run. They both were drunk. I'm sure Rail wouldn't continue beating him."

"I planned to see Natasha," I said. "It's not in the cards."

"I went to his funeral," the director sighed.

"I have nothing to say," said the prosecutor and invited us for dinner. "My son caught a lot of fish."

Ultimately, I told them about six platforms of stolen timber. The guardian of law immediately called the station; someone told him that such a train had never arrived. He hung up the phone, and I briefed him in detail. He called the police and apologized for leaving such good company.

"The invitation stands," our host said. "You tricked them. Kudos, Arkady! They could've killed you without hesitation." I was a witness they would want to get rid of and he asked me not to get acquainted with anyone on the train to Kostroma. Just in case, a good police officer would cover me in Galich. "These gangsters are smart and by now might have second thoughts." At the door, he promised not to give them a chance to unload and to be back in an hour. At dinner, he said, "I'll let you know if we need you to identify the perpetrators. You won't be needed if they start a shootout."

"What a nice dilemma!" I said.

◈ ◈ ◈

After two or three uneventful days, another unpredictable encounter waited for me at the railroad station. In its small waiting room, I noticed a pale boy sitting on the dirty floor under the awful young-looking, despite a goatee, "Lenin on the Rostrum." He hid behind a bench occupied by passengers. I moved closer; the eyes of the ragged fellow were closed, his eyelids twitched, he wasn't asleep. At the time of boarding, I stopped behind the first car door and left it a bit open so I could watch the only way out from the station. When the two-car train started, he burst out and jumped up on the footsteps of my car. Half a minute later, I walked out onto its platform and opened the door. He was sitting on a step. I raised my voice just enough so the boy could hear me through the noise and din. "Please, get in the car. Don't jump! We'll think of something."

When the boy, still on the footstep, got up, behind me was a stocky man. He used his shoulder to move me aside and firmly grabbed the youngster's jacket with one hand, "Come in, come!" he said. "We'll help you. Now I see why your friend decided to play it safe and asked the regional prosecutor's office to take care of this." My fear of a new threat evaporated. The man closed the door and released the stinking jacket. "He's fine. I will go with you to Kostroma."

When we came back inside, the detective ordered us to move further away from the door and took a position near the opposite window of the car, this way he could simultaneously see the passage between the rows of seats and us.

"I've seen many children running, but we don't deal with that," he said. "Fella, never hide next to the wheel! If you only knew how many boys are killed by trains; they don't even stop."

The detective did not listen to our conversation; at least, such was my impression. He sprang to his feet only once, when the fare collector came up to us. The man showed his identity card and said, "The boy's with me." Not "with us"—such a circumspect conspirator. The stowaway had escaped from a vocational school in Kirov, a big city, the capital of the neighboring region. His dull hair and faded eyes were typical of the elderly. He was constantly swearing.

"Stop swearing!" I said.

He looked at me in surprise. "I don't swear." The fugitive slowed down in a futile attempt not to embarrass this strange four-eyes. "I won't go back to my village; my fucking parents felt lucky because they put me into this fucking school."

"D'you have a passport?" I asked.

"No, I'm fifteen."

"What did you learn there?"

"Carpentry. Want to find a job at a warm place."

"Let's go to my place for a couple of days. We'll look for work somewhere in the south. My landlady wouldn't object."

"Why d'you need such a hassle?"

"I feel sorry for you."

"Nobody feels sorry for me." He turned to our silent companion. "Are you a policeman?"

"A carpenter," said the detective, smiling for the first time.

In Kostroma, before leaving the train, he said, "You didn't obey your friend's orders. But maybe it wasn't a bad idea."

"What?"

"To take the kid to your home. I'm sure he's always hungry."

The officer asked us to stay a minute inside, and after we came out, did not approach us anymore. He stood as if a gaper with a hand in his right pocket, a few yards from the bus stop until we boarded it.

"What did he want from you? Does he know your friends?" asked the boy. "It's good you were careful; he was plotting something against us."

◈ ◈ ◈

The next day I brought the fugitive to the office. I was writing my report, and the youngster in a new shirt and pants was looking in the *Pravda* editorial binder for collective farms in the south. I kept repeating, "This doesn't fit either."

Anna was morosely silent. Protasova asked what we were doing. I said, "Looking for a place for him to live and work." I already knew that my paper and *Northern Pravda* were not unique in giving a glossy picture of our life, but I trusted *Pravda*. It did not need to lie about our historic experiment to which all progressive humankind was looking up, to a future without the selfishness of capitalism and its warmongers. Yes, I reasoned, we just got rid of the tyrant; now we needed to weed out all culprits of the last thirty years.

Finally, the boy found an article by the twice Hero of Socialist Labor, the chairman of an integrated farm formed by several *kolkhozes* in the southern Krasnodar Territory next to the Black Sea. Its horses and bulls were presented at the All-Union Agricultural Exhibition in Moscow. A new barn for a hundred thoroughbred horses and many new buildings, including housing, were under construction. Each farmer was paid on the merits of his work. Foreigners visited the *kolkhoz*.

"This is the place for you," I said. "You'll eat more fruit than Muscovites, a good six months of the year. They need carpenters."

"Cool!" said the boy.

I dipped my pen in the inkwell, wrote several lines under editorial letterhead, suggested he take this letter to the chairman personally, and began collecting money for the road and the ticket.

"Good for you, kid!" the poet Alexander Chasovnikov said. "High time to send our youth back to the collective farms." He solemnly passed five rubles to me. Anna shook her head. "You're a simpleton, my friend," and laid three rubles on my desk. "Can't give more."

"I know one thing," I said. "Without a passport, he'll never get any job in a city."

Lena Protasova contributed a ten and said to the boy, "Don't break laws. Write a letter to us." She asked me to come to her office and when I came, said, "Please don't collect money at the Regional *Komsomol* Committee. Just imagine if all kids were running from vocational schools."

I thought of Anna who should be returned to her village and said, "I don't intend to."

The boy promised to write to me and never did. I hoped that he did not face a year of imprisonment for escaping from a vocational school. This law existed when my two childhood friends attended such an institution.

The World Youth Festival;
or, How Hollywood
Tried to Destroy Russia

For the first time in ten months, I returned to Moscow. I burst out laughing as soon as I stepped onto the platform—the Northern Railroad Station was welcoming foreign visitors with banners in several languages. It would be easier to meet a bear than a foreigner north of Moscow. A police sergeant, aglow from his badge to his boots, looked at me with interest. I stopped by him with a sassy remark: "Hi, I don't see your usual clients here."

Surprised, he said, "Who are you?"

"A correspondent. Accredited to cover the festival."

"Show me your ID," he said dryly.

"It's good, sergeant, you're so vigilant." I got out my gray pass.

At this point, Irina emerged from behind my back, kissed my cheek and said, "Comrade officer, it's so good you've detained him! This impostor escaped from his bride."

The smiling policeman was in good spirits. During the next few days, it was the KGB's job to deal with the avalanche of aliens. He explained, "We put all the scum into freight cars and sent them beyond the hundred and first kilometer from Moscow. The order was to mop up all nine city railroad stations."

We shook his honest hand.

On the vast Komsomolskaya Square, where two more railway stations were located, we did not see the usually ever-present vagrants, prostitutes, beggars, alcoholics, and Gypsies. The word "Peace" in many languages, large five-color flowers where each of the petals represented a continent, and white Picasso doves dominated the city landscape. These peace-loving doves were everywhere—they covered trucks, buses, trolleys, streetcars, and even some roofs. Many buildings had gotten a facelift; some were fenced off with solid barriers with cheerful colors, flowers, and slogans appealing for peace in the world. The capital had been transformed from gray and dirty to colorful and clean.

Nowadays, looking back, I allow myself to be ironic, but then I was a different person and reported on that time with the excitement of a traveler to a planet of the peace-loving populace that had beaten swords into plowshares. My country was opening its doors! How beautiful it was to see this young blood, often in traditional African, Arab and Asian garb, or uniformly dressed delegations of our East European allies! They rode through the streets, standing in the cyan blue and pink trucks, greeting us, smiling, laughing, and crying with joy. Crowds went mad. The bold Khrushchev Thaw allowed us to meet with foreigners—what an exciting step forward! This planet was not hopeless.

◆ ◆ ◆

I loved the opening ceremony in the new Lenin Stadium in Luzhniki. Just days before most Muscovites had not even known of the very existence of these countries, and today we met 34,000 comrades-in-the-struggle-for-peace from 131 countries. The standard-bearers, the best Soviet athletes, with the 131 different flags on high staffs opened the festive procession. I would not be able to hold such a huge flag for a minute. After them, delegations with banners entered the stadium, many in multicolored national costumes. Dancers and musicians with exotic instruments accompanied them. Politburo members and other senior officials, three dozen males and a tiny girl, apparently someone's granddaughter, synchronized their applause with Khrushchev, a little bold man, almost invisible in the tightly packed government box. If not for the military binoculars of my father, I wouldn't have seen anyone from my seat high in the back row. To end the ceremony, five young men representing continents—white, brown, yellow, black, and another white (probably politically incorrectly representing Australia) greeted the 70,000-strong crowd. Hundreds of white doves flew above us.

To write about the festivities and friendship was easy. The difficulties began with reporting on the cultural programs. For the first time in our lives, we saw works of Western art, which were questionable from the Socialist Realism point of view. Abstract American paintings shocked us with their challenge to our understanding of art. The first American musician to visit Russia since the war, the pianist Glenn Gould, played the music of Schoenberg and Berg, prohibited in my country. For the first time, the sound of a Western-built electric guitar penetrated our ears and souls. Every decent Russian would be shocked to learn that a member of the American delegation, Shel Silverstein, wrote his children's books while drawing cartoons for *Playboy* magazine, a symbol of Western degradation and pornography. Even more subversive for our way of life were three symbols of the West introduced by unsuspecting Westerners sympathetic to communism—jeans, sneakers, and rock 'n' roll. Their impact was devastating—all three words became a part of Russian vocabulary.

◈ ◈ ◈

I had just finished dictating a lighthearted report about the Paris Pantomime Theater and our young jazzmen (the music now almost legalized) playing with Western jazz musicians. In a good mood, I exited a telephone booth at the Central Telegraph Station and headed for the door when an unremarkable man caught up with me and called me by name and patronymic, for the first time in my life, "Hello, Arkady Abramovich! We need to talk."

He asked me to turn from the main Gorki Street into a nearby lane. When we turned the corner, he showed his KGB ID in a dark red leather cover. No blood rushed to my head, and my heart didn't begin pounding. Millions of prisoners were already released, millions of dead, rehabilitated. The influence of the secret police had been weakening. I was just curious.

"Looking for spies?" I asked acidly.

"We need your help and want to talk with you tomorrow at 10:00 a.m." He was emphatically polite. After years of breaking down locked doors at night and taking innocent people away forever, the KGB needed my help. I had to enter the ill-famed building not through the main entrance, but from the front, overlooking Dzerzhinsky Square, and to go to the fourth floor; he asked me to bring my passport and gave me the office number.

I had no idea what was going on but nevertheless slept well.

Everything at the headquarters looked opposite to what I had learned about the KGB. A guard ticked my name in a leather-bound notebook attached by a thin chain to his desk, recorded the time of my arrival, walked me to an old-fashioned pre-revolutionary elevator, and even opened its cast-iron door for me. I traveled up on my own and found myself in an empty spacious corridor with high double doors on both sides. I could have blown up the whole building, but instead, knocked on the door. A gloomy man in a civilian suit opened it and greeted me with a wry smile.

"We want to ask you some questions about Anatoly Mikhailovich Kulkin," he said.

"What happened to him? Is he okay?" I asked.

"He's in good physical condition," the man said dryly. That was strange.

"You mean, in good health? Where is he?"

His face displayed a mixture of condescension and anger. "Today I am asking the questions."

Nonetheless, I asked again, "Has he been arrested?"

"I wouldn't call it an arrest." The wry smile returned to his face. "We know that you weren't among Kulkin's close friends, but you both participated in the discussions of Lazar's argumentative writings."

"Yes," I said, "that's fair to say."

We met with Lazar only several times. With his high forehead, piercing eyes and sharp tongue, he looked like a true thinker. This sophomore, four or five years older than us, studied screenwriting and already had quite a biography—he worked as a longshoreman, a seaman, and a qualified fitter at the Odessa shipyard.

"Who introduced you to Lazar?"

"I don't remember," I said, though I knew that Lazar was Kulkin's friend, and asked again the same question, now about Lazar: "What happened to him?" and again heard about "good physical condition" and the word "arrest" was rejected. (I never used and forgot Lazar's last name; could it be Lifshitz? It certainly was a Jewish one.)

The investigative officer asked, "How often did you see Anatoly Kulkin?"

"He left Moscow a year before my graduation and soon after he came back from the Ural Mountains area, I moved to Kostroma. All I know is that for about three years he taught Marxism in a closed city near Chelyabinsk."

"What did he tell you about that closed city?" It seemed he was interested in whether Kulkin had blabbed state secrets.

"Well, nothing. We didn't meet for three years. When he got his job, somebody in the university corridor told me that Kulkin was teaching at some research center dealing with atomic bombs. We decided that from the KGB's point of view he had an impeccable biography. He taught us Historical Materialism," I said, while thinking of his Jewish daughter.

"Can you describe his political views?"

"Oh yes, we met at the university two days after Stalin's death. To my surprise, he cried."

"Why were you surprised?"

"I couldn't understand why a true communist mourned the death of the..." I almost said "dictator" but caught myself in time and said, "Stalin. Kulkin called his death a severe blow to the country."

Here I stopped lying about Anatoly's love for the monster and let this inquisitor digest what I already came up with, as it probably resonated with his own feelings and could work for Anatoly's release. Now, in 1957, about a year after Khrushchev's speech on the personality cult of Stalin, in this heart of the KGB, I was riding high.

The interrogator asked my opinion of Lazar's writings. I said we liked his thought-provoking articles and proposals stressing the need for an urgent restructuring of the socialist economy. We had some disagreements with him, and he was open to criticism. As a Marxist-Leninist and Party member, Lazar had been sending his articles to the Central Committee and to *The Communist*, but never got any response. I was beginning to revel in my peace of mind and our cat-and-mouse game and asked if professor Chesnokov, *The Communist's* former editor-in-chief, transferred Lazar's articles to the KGB.

"You don't understand where you are." The investigator frowned, wrote something down, and, to my surprise, almost whispered, "You can go."

The questioning was over. He suddenly seemed to lose interest in me. No questions were asked about Nahl Zlobin who studied philosophy with Anatoly and the fourth member of our group—Lazar's classmate from his Cinematography Institute. At the door, I made an innocent face and roused the officer again. "Is it true," I asked, "that Lavrenti Pavlovich Beria was shot dead in the basement of this building?"

"Nonsense!" he said with a twisted face. "By the way, Chesnokov had nothing to do with the case."

⚜ ⚜ ⚜

I closed the solid door and stood on the polished parquet of the empty corridor thinking of Oleg Milovidov's father who was killed by the KGB, of Nahl's father whose manuscript the KGB destroyed, and of the lumberjack Ivan Kotov called Rail. Overwhelmed with a sense of victory over the defeated enemies that lurked behind every door here, I grasped the first patterned door handle on my way and pulled it. I wanted to show them that their time was ending. You're nuts, flashed in my blurred mind. I quickly closed the half-opened heavy door and continued on my triumphant way out, when it opened again and out popped an angry middle-aged woman. "What are you up to?" she hissed.

"Nothing," I explained. "I was looking for the way out."

In the street, I called myself an idiot, decided to play it safe, and postponed visiting Nahl. That hot summer day, I was busy running from one cultural event to another when I saw two fellows pushing a smartly dressed girl inside the entrance of an ordinary looking apartment house. She screamed, "Let me go, bastards! I like him!"

A snappy policeman inside the building, unimpressed by the press card on my lapel, pushed me outside. "D'you want them to deliver black babies?" he said. "Go, go, before you are stripped of your accreditation!"

Soon I found out how mild the punishment was for such desperate females. At an art show, two dressed-up pusses were loudly expressing their admiration of the Western abstract paintings; I wouldn't be surprised if it were the first gallery they had ever visited. The dyed hair of one girl was combed diligently from left to right, the other had hers from right to left. "What a fashionable haircut you two have," I said, to maintain the universal ecstatic state. One of them pushed a strand of hair to its natural position and showed hair shorn at the root on a strip in the middle of her head, saying, "This is the job of *Komsomol* morons—they clipped out these tracks on our heads for meeting with foreigners."

My parents' neighbor asked with compassion how I felt after I received a shot of an anti-plague vaccine. She believed that some participants of the festival were bringing vials of the plague bacteria to Moscow. Such rumors did not scare anyone. I learned my first English word when a gray-haired coach of our basketball team, screaming "Change! Change! Change!" approached a group of French athletes, who would not recognize this magic word even if a true Anglo-Saxon pronounced it. Soon the foreigners learned—the Russian battle cry "Cheynch!" simply meant "give me your badge or a pen or a cigarette or jeans, t-shirts, sneakers, and baseball caps in exchange for my Soviet pins, stamps, brightly painted wooden spoons, our nesting *matryoshka* dolls, and polished caskets." To turn this gesture of friendship into a trade operation was a punishable crime.

The festival organizers ignored a simple fact: we were already prepared to hold hands with foreigners. Soon after the war, our Great Helmsman inadvertently delivered the first blow to our total isolation. He allowed us to watch some copyrighted foreign films captured in 1939 in Poland and in 1940—in Romania and the Baltic states. Perhaps the maintenance of the state treasury was among Stalin's main concerns. In thousands of small clubs like the ones in Galich and Vokhma, these movies, along with the sale of vodka, were yielding a steady income for the state. I grew up with them. They showed us how Americans looked, dressed and acted. *Charley's Aunt, Sun Valley Serenade,* and *His Butler's Sister* with Deanna Durbin conveyed the sense that the good life and entertainment were available to all Americans. When the lights went off, for one hundred minutes, we were living in a different world, leaving our xenophobia at the door of the movie theater. My favorite was *The Roaring Twenties* (1939) renamed by our ideologues *The Fate of the Soldier in America.* I still remember its melodies and lyrics, which I sang in Russian at my sweet sixteen. Even nowadays the Russians see some similarities between the fate of three World War I veterans turned gangsters and Russian veterans who joined criminal groups after fighting in Afghanistan (1979–1989) and later—in Chechnya. For Russians, this film is still a gangster melodrama and a social commentary.

✦ ✦ ✦

After the festival was over, convinced that not a soul followed me, I rushed to Nahl Zlobin. Lazar exploded with rage when it became clear that nobody was going to respond to his writings. In his latest letters to the Central Committee, he had called the apparatchiks Stalin heirs and enemies of the people. Nahl was interrogated twice and assumed that Lazar and Anatoly had been held in the KGB's prison no more than two or three months. Once a stranger brought Anatoly's note to Nahl, he was now in a regular madhouse near Moscow known under the name White Poles. Lazar was in a psychiatric prison, no one knew where.

Nahl sometimes visited Anatoly and played soccer with him, male nurses, and two young doctors. Thank God, they did not force Kulkin to take medication; he was not expelled from the Party and waited when the KGB would tell his partners in soccer that he was healed. When Nahl asked how long he was kept in prison, Anatoly kicked the grass and said, "I don't want to talk about it."

We could not figure out why the KGB decided to talk with me so late. When a year later unforeseeable events forced me to return to Moscow, Kulkin was a Party member again and supervised the philosophy department of the Academy of Sciences' publishing house. One could only dream of such a job. Less than four years later, he became this giant publisher's deputy editor-in-chief for social sciences. It was a rapid career rise. This not very talkative and dull fellow obviously had the right connections. A couple of times we met by chance and never talked about the past. It didn't exist anymore.

We never saw Lazar again. There were rumors that after an unknown number of years in the psychiatric prison, his mother brought him back to Odessa, where he, dressed in rags, walked the streets looking at his feet and muttering to himself.

Fifty-five years later, in 2012, I was working on this memoir and wanted to find out Lazar's fate. I began looking for Anatoly Mikhailovich Kulkin. According to his short biography in *The Great Biographical Encyclopedia*, after graduating from university, he taught Marxism from 1953 to 1957 in the so-called "closed" city Chelyabinsk-70, which you would never find on Soviet maps. No doubt, his students worked on the production of Soviet H-bombs. His incarceration was not mentioned.

I called Anatoly from Washington, D.C. For more than 40 years, he, now a Doctor of Philosophy, had been the head of the Research Center for Science, Education, and Technology at the huge Federal Institute of Social Sciences (INION). He did not immediately recognize me and didn't express much delight when he did. I asked him about Lazar's last name and when he had been released from the psychiatric prison. After a long pause, Kulkin promised to send me a chapter of his memoir. We talked at length about our medical problems; he was approaching 84 and I discussed his condition with an American doctor, then emailed Anatoly an article on the latest achievements in treating his problem. I did not want to irritate him, and no longer mentioned Lazar.

Ten days later, to my delight, I received a friendly return email. He called me Alik, saying that this was the way Nahl and his father Stephan Pavlovich Zlobin referred to me; this indicated that his memory wasn't bad and he certainly remembered Lazar's last name. That was strange. The two dozen pages from his memoir, attached to his email, had nothing to do with my reason for resuming our acquaintance. They were devoted to the ways Anatoly had helped the famous sculptor Ernst Neizvestny to survive in 1963–1964 after Khrushchev expressed disapproval of his works in the language of a criminal showdown. I was baffled to learn from that attachment that precisely at that time, Kulkin "worked at the Central Committee editing a text for Secretary L.F. Il'ichev," who headed the ideological war against dissidents. This Number One inquisitor delivered it at a Party plenum; he identified art among the main weapons of the class enemy. "Our ideological opponents," he proclaimed, "include in their arsenal formalism, abstract art, and decadence; they want to clog our socialist field with ideological weeds produced by capitalist breeders." Ernst Neizvestny was one of "poisonous mushrooms" that Ilyichev exposed. Such was the inexplicable twist of a psychiatric institution prisoner's fate—six years later to become an assistant to the chief Party ideologue.

In a stubborn hope to find a word about Lazar, I asked Kulkin to send me his full memoir; in a couple of months he emailed a co-authored book, *The System of State Support for Scientific and Technological Activities: The U.S. Experience*, published 16 years previously. My patience was running thin. I asked him again to send the promised memoir, Lazar's last name, and the time of his release from the psychiatric prison. After one more month of waiting, in a short note, I reminded him of my request. Kulkin never responded. I was not bewildered anymore. I had reasons to suspect him of being a not very smart KGB provocateur specializing in the creative intelligentsia. His handlers had known that I was arriving to cover the festival and, to strengthen the credentials of their agent, faked an unnecessary interrogation of Arkady Polishchuk.

The Rise of the Adventurer

Three new friends were waiting for my return from the festival. One of them had called my editor-in-chief to ask about that day, and the moment Protasova saw me, she exclaimed, "It's recognition! Our paper has become a household publication in the family of this outstanding statesman."

I was flattered, and it would have been wiser if I had swallowed my loose tongue when I asked her, "Do you know him personally?"

"No," she said with dignity, "but what I know of him amply shows the scope of his merits."

The man, whose name inspired awe in the hearts of Kostroma officials, was the father of the caller. If the American president were to call me today and ask, "Arkady, would you do me a favor and drop by the White House any time, even late at night?" I would've been less impressed. I don't know with what security escort Dwight Eisenhower traveled in 1957 in Washington, D.C., but the pot-bellied car of Leonid Yakovlevich Florentyev needed neither escort nor armor. The whole town knew the black vehicle of the First Secretary of the Regional Party Committee. All of a sudden, I got a chance to whisper something in the reigning ear of the Commander, the Hand and, to some extent, the Brain of the Central Committee in the Kostroma Region.

"His daughter—she has such a lovely voice!—might call you today or tomorrow." Protasova's voice was sweeter than ever. She asked me not to make any personal plans for a couple of evenings and stay in the office until Florentyev's daughter talked to me. She knew that Irina had come with me from Moscow and spent two evenings there with me. She witnessed that historical call.

Three days after our arrival, a policeman studied Moscow stamps in our passports at the Father-of-the-Region's cast-iron gate. His daughter and son-in-law, both small, thin and featureless, met us in their enormous garden. We entered a spacious living room and saw a gloomy man in a black jacket at the head of the table in a massive armchair; its carved backrest was towering over this baldhead. A woman with a thoroughly ironed apron, not glancing in our direction, was arranging on a linen tablecloth a porcelain tea set and homemade cakes, candies, and cookies of Moscow origin. Leonid Yakovlevich rose from his chair, and with this, the large man with tightly clenched lips turned out to be an amicable shorty with a big belly. He said with a pleasant smile, "I read your essay about the girl-loggers in the *Working Woman*. Written with much love. The whole country reads this publication. Do you plan to write more about us? It's quite important."

"Yes, I do," I said. "Even a children's book about rafters."

"Interested in exotic?" Leonid Yakovlevich smiled.

"Yes. They risk their lives every day."

"They shouldn't drink," he smiled again.

"Poor things," said Irina.

His daughter and her husband faintly smiled and slowly, in small sips, were drinking tea with their mouths barely open. The daughter asked Irina, "Where did you get such a beautiful skirt?"

"In Norway," my wife said.

The master of the house asked, "What were you doing there?"

"Dad was the Soviet trade representative."

"Oh, then you have," he looked at me, "a rich wife."

"Yes," I said. "My wife has a lot of skirts."

Florentyev clearly didn't like my answer. He looked again like a bulldog.

"It was right after the war; I was a little girl," Irina said.

"During the war, Norway was Hitler's ally," he said.

"Quisling," she said and took an apple from a bulky vase.

"Where did you fight?" I politely inquired.

"The Party sent me to lead important work in the rear."

"In the rear of the enemy!" cried my wife with a look of false delight on her face, recognizable only by me.

"No. We had to quickly reorganize the Party work away from the enemy, beyond the Volga, near the Ural Mountains." He turned to me. "Have you joined the Party?"

"I'll submit an application in a couple of months."

"Do you know who'll give you a recommendation?"

"Yes, that was the intention of my editor-in-chief."

"Very good."

"I hope you two have already joined?" asked my wife of our peers in the manner of a strict teacher.

"What?" the daughter asked.

"The Party."

"Yes," they said almost simultaneously.

"Do you pay the Party dues on time?" asked unruly Irina in the same didactic mode.

They responded with "yes" almost in sync again.

That was too much, and I told them that my wife was always late in paying *Komsomol* penny dues. Florentyev had already been losing interest in our conversation when his face lit up. "Tell me, Arkady, honestly, what you think of our writers?"

"You mean local writers?"

"Yes."

"What I read, hasn't impressed me."

"You're a diplomat."

"I just don't feel comfortable giving you names."

"Why?"

"Because your opinion matters much more than mine. Your judgment knows no appeal."

He stroked his baldhead. "Yes, the Party is always right."

"None of them inspire confidence in me," said my wife without batting an eye.

Irina giggled senselessly. His daughter kept touching my hand and asking me about the festival. I told her about music, paintings, and theater, which had nothing to do with our canons of socialist realism; she was more interested in security problems of our country—some festival participants might hold unacceptable views.

◈ ◈ ◈

On the way home, Irina said, "Your father at the age of fifty volunteered for the war, this thirty-five-year-old boar was fighting hungry women in villages thousands of kilometers from the front line. This family is a sad bore; they didn't even feed us. I was ready to consume caviar with a ladle."

In the morning Protasova asked, "So, how was it?"

"He enthusiastically approved of your decision to give me a recommendation."

"How long were you there?"

"Couple of hours."

"For such a busy person, every minute is important."

Soon her phone rang. Elena picked it up, and her face expressed devotion, "Of course! Of course! My dear friend just told me how strong an impression your father and you made on him."

The daughter invited Irina and me to take part in a fishing expedition with the mighty of this world. At the last moment, Florentyev and the gray-haired Second Secretary, the Propaganda Tsar, had to cancel their participation—they headed to Moscow to fry bigger fish. The Chairman of the Regional Executive Committee, in abbreviated bureaucratic New-speak, a single, very simple word *predoblispolkoma*, led our crew, which included his deputy, and the head of the Regional Propaganda Department. We traveled in the First Secretary's bellied car with his daughter and son-in-law. The police in the empty streets stood at attention and saluted. The driver boasted to Irina, who sat next to him, "They stop all autos even when I'm alone in this car."

The mighty Volga River rolled lazily to the south, to the distant Caspian Sea. There were no signs of approaching fall floods. Everybody enjoyed the early September tender sun. At first, the *predoblispolkoma*, the third person in the Kostroma hierarchy, gathered all of us on the bright grass of the low bank and said, clearly for two of us, "Our gang must obey these fishermen from the Red Banner, as we say here on the Volga, *artel*, or, as they say in Moscow, cooperative. Muscovites love foreign words."

We liked the man and the relaxed Irina allowed herself to interfere. "Linguists believe that the word *artel* came from the Turks and was related to mutual aid in a criminal gang."

"Please forgive my wife," I mockingly pleaded. "She just graduated from university and still thinks she passes the Old Church Slavonic language exam."

"I like the explanation," he said. "But don't tell me that *ukha* also is an ancient word."

"Oh yes," said my omniscient wife, "it's present in all Slavic languages."

Meanwhile, the three drivers and two policemen placed in the cool water a sturdy potato sack with several bottles of vodka and fenced them with heavy stones. They put together a dozen dry logs brought from the city and mounted a deep rectangular pot over them. In comparison with this metal pool, a Chinese wok and American baking pan would look like utensils from a toy store. They filled this giant pot with a few buckets of river water and skillfully lit the bonfire.

"With us today are two newcomers," the *predoblispolkoma* continued. "Good guys, who probably have never fished with a professional fishing net or eaten the Volga ancient fish soup called *ukha*." He smiled at us. "If the day gets hot, fish will move down to the river bed. We have to hurry."

Two professionals, one in rubber boots covering his knees, the other barefoot, lay the bulk of a trawl net on the wide stern of their wooden boat; it was painstakingly folded into a flat stack. One end of it stayed with the rest of the *artel*. After that, one fisherman began rowing away from the shore while his partner kept unwinding the net until all its 550 yards were in the water. Soon they were paddling along in the middle of the river, parallel with the shore. To keep up with them, our magnificent seven, all knee-deep in the water—some in pants rolled up above the knees, others in swimsuits—started to haul in the net, happily clutching at our end of it. We cried out, sniggered, ran into each other, and groaned. My frantic cries resounded over the indifferent shiny river.

"Why is this beauty a restricted area?" I asked Florentyev's daughter and bumped into her while catching my breath. She fell in the water, I held out my hand, she clasped it with both hands, rose, and her weightless body leaned against me. She pointedly looked into my eyes. "No one should bother us," she said, leisurely came unstuck from my wet body, and concluded, "when we're fishing."

"Very well said!" yelled Irina. "Ordinary citizens are so inconsiderate!" her voice was heard far beyond the zone forbidden for the citizens. The Propaganda Department head looked at her reproachfully.

"This net is for bigger fish only," I explained to her coldly. "It's a punishable crime to use an industrial net."

The fishermen waved to us to stop moving, and the bow of the boat turned slowly toward the bank. We started dragging our end of the net out of the water. Irina yelled, "Hooray!"

When the boat moored to the shore, we were already pulling the net ashore, yard by yard, and more and more fish, small and big, were jumping inside it, bending back and forth like shiny steel springs. I galloped in the water and grass around the catch and shouted, "Irina, see how many different fish have been caught!"

"Before the construction of the hydroelectric power plant," a grim fisherman said, "we usually pulled up to a thousand pounds of fish with this net, and here there are only some forty pounds. Let's throw it one more time."

Now I frowned. Recently I had raved about this power plant in our paper.

"Bad passes," he continued. "The dam either doesn't allow fish to pass or cuts them up."

"Nobody told me that," I said dejectedly.

After delivering fifty more pounds of fish, the fisherman said darkly, "It's the right time to shut down the Red Banner."

I looked at the placid face of the Comrade-Propaganda-Department and clarified, "He meant his cooperative."

We gutted the bigger fish; we cut off the heads, tails, and fins, removed the ridges, and wrapped it all in surgical gauze.

"Why the gauze?" I asked.

The members of the expedition failed to hide their contempt. Only the son-in-law showed compassion for this strange creature and explained,

"This is what we throw back into the Volga after boiling the strong stock out of it."

After that, we washed the small fry in the river without removing the scales and, finally, sent all of this treasure into our vessel; the bonfire was already blazing. We cut big fish into pieces and added it all to the stock. The son-in-law, to educate us, stated the obvious: "The more different kinds of fish, the tastier the *ukha*."

"I know," I said but judging by the laughter, no one believed me, so I added, "We shouldn't boil it rapidly. We better scatter the embers and firebrands a little."

Predoblispolkoma looked at me with respect and picked up an ember with a sapper shovel. I proudly looked at our *artel*, when he did something weird; he threw that ember in the *ukha*. I tried not to react, but when he poured a whole bottle of vodka into the broth, I couldn't hold back my feelings and asked, "Why?"

"To cool the broth down," said my malicious wife.

The laughing Deputy Chairman rolled on the grass. By now, the whole crew was slightly drunk. Our wait staff was welcomed to participate in the crowning stage of the event—in eating *ukha*.

"It's good that you don't take your wives on such trips," my wife began to orate. "They're perfectly replaced by the police," she pointed at an officer with the manners of a maidservant who tried to remind everybody of his devotion to our cause. An hour earlier, he was parading a tiny bay leaf he brought from home like a red banner. Now, the policeman confessed that he accidentally dropped it in the fire. For his calculated honesty, the guy was rewarded with extra chunks of fish and plenty of the thick broth.

Then I said what I shouldn't say, "One Moscow traffic cop told me that he always carries a bay leaf in his breast pocket." Our lawman almost choked on a piece of fish he had just stuffed into his mouth. I explained, "Nothing beats the smell of vodka better than chewing the laurel."

Long neighing roared over fading fire. With his mouthful of fish, the officer couldn't join us. He shyly smiled through clenched lips.

My Life with a Gravedigger

Zoya Tikhonovna couldn't hide her sadness when we said we were moving to a more comfortable place near my office.

"He's tired of this old woman and of her groaning at night," she said to Irina. In fact, she never complained about her health. Only at nights did I hear her groaning, probably from arthritis pain and the thought of her husband's *valenki* with crumpled tops.

"No," I said. "I enjoyed your company, even when you kicked my butt through this curtain."

They embraced and looked at each other with understanding unavailable to hard-hearted males.

"I almost fell out of bed," I insisted.

The house where we moved belonged before the revolution to the vice-governor of the *guberniya,* a territorial division of imperial Russia. To mark the tercentenary of the Romanov dynasty, these several two-story buildings were constructed in the neo-classic style fashionable at the last century's beginning. Often crowned with a two-windowed attic for the servants, with pilasters projecting from the walls and differently shaped windows on each floor, they competed in height with modern four-story buildings. They fell into disrepair long before the war; a multitude of new walls had partitioned the rooms, packed now with numerous families.

The only reminders of the glorious past were the graceful proportions and tall stucco ceilings. For some forgotten reason our new host's spacious room wasn't divided into family canisters. He lived alone since his son had moved in with his young wife, though they continued working together as diggers. Kostya's mother died 27 years ago, after delivering him. To make some more money, the 70-year-old Uncle Peter and his son built a colossal platform six feet above the floor and no less than six feet under the ceiling. The smooth unpainted deck was made of long square logs, carefully hand-hewn on all four sides. The very first day, I walked, stomped, danced, and ran around my new dwelling, nothing bent or creaked under my feet; the old man enjoyed the show, "Dance with your wife! I won't hear you anyway, as I was struck on the ear by a shovel."

"What an accident!" I exclaimed.

"No," Uncle Peter said, his voice suddenly thick with sadness. "A hungry man wanted to take away my ration."

Deepening wrinkles on his forehead testified that the old digger unwittingly revealed something that he would prefer not to discuss. I restrained myself and pointed at his arm with swollen veins, "You're strong."

◈ ◈ ◈

After we settled in, he and I fought long philosophical battles about the meaning of life. I avoided clever words; his opinions were predictive and free of the verbal garbage typical of such discussions.

"Here you're a journalist, a man of culture," he said once. "But take away your ink from you and what will you do then? Are you going, cap in hand, to ask for a piece of bread at a street corner?"

Uncle Peter did not wait for my response; for him, eagerly joined by my wife on every issue, I was wrong before opening my mouth. "My work," he continued, "has been always there, it was there a thousand years ago and still will be in demand in a thousand years. No instrument can replace a shovel and a pickax."

"Any fool can learn calligraphy," said Irina, not bothering to conceal her contempt for her beloved husband. "The shovel needs a brainy man."

"My wife loves strange words," I apologized.

He agreed with her. "At every moment there was, there is, and there will be someone buried and someone in need of digging a can."

"Good for you, Uncle Peter," I said. "Besides that, we all have to use a hole in an outhouse."

"An outhouse was needed long before the Russian language was born," Irina proclaimed gleefully, "and it will be needed after our language will die."

"Why? How did we talk then? With fingers?" The old man did not sound ironic.

"We spoke a different language," she said.

"The Tatar?"

"Possibly. For example, Tatars gave us all of our filthy words."

"This isn't true," he strongly objected. "We taught the whole world how to swear. Our swear words are the best in the world. Anyway, who taught you such rubbish?"

"The books," I said. "They also say that the outhouse is a relatively new invention."

"This is exactly why I never read them." Uncle Peter and Irina for quite a while could not contain their laughter.

"My wife is a phony," I said.

"Don't get angry, Arkady," said the old man, patting my shoulder with his five-fingered shovel. "The last time I read papers was in the fall of 1933, after I was freed, and I'm sure they still say the same thing today."

Irina patted my forehead and said, "Same goes for your books."

"You have a cunning wife," said Uncle Peter and asked, "What do you need for peace of mind?"

"Her," I nodded at my wife, "to be honest in my writing, many other things."

"How about a piece of bread?" he asked. "You, the cultural, are funny."

"And this bread will give you peace of mind?"

"Oh yeah! I see you've never gone hungry."

"Romantic!" Irina threw up her hands. "A good word for the well-fed man."

"So, kids," the old man said, "I'm still alive because I always had a piece of bread. I wouldn't be here if I weren't a good gravedigger, I'd have died soon after you and my son were born. Still, it wouldn't be too bad to end up in a quiet grave..." he wiggled the fingers of both hands. "I saw people left to die on the stony bottom of the future canal and the dead sliding down the slope of a 12-foot deep trench," he spread his hands to the sides as if he did not want to see his fingers anymore. "Like a bag of sand. White Sea-Baltic Canal ... but soon we were ordered to bury the stiffs at the shores."

The camp bosses feared that the dead would start floating to the surface. They were readying for the visit of some famous writers, explained the digger, but prisoners learned about that when the major stamped and shouted, "You idiots! Don't want an early release? Wanna starve to death?" He pointed at a corpse in a hole-ridden wheelbarrow with clay petrified around his body. "Yeah," Uncle Peter kind of smiled, "his feet sticking out of the clay didn't bother us; They bother me more today, those black toes out."

Irina covered her ears with her hands. The old man fell silent, looked at her attentively, and explained, "Someone needed his boots after he fell dead in that wheelbarrow." He raised his voice. "Before, this Jew, this major, yelled only at the guards and never hit anybody, but suddenly, he screamed and ordered that corpse reburied. When the canal was ready, he got the Order of the Red Banner of Labor."

"A toiler," my wife said with disgust.

"Why aren't you a bitter man?" I asked.

"That major was a bitter man, with the skewed face. People say he and other NKVD chiefs were executed in 1937 for espionage and Trotskyism."

I asked, "What is Trotskyism?"

"I get up early." He looked at our gloomy faces. "We'll talk tomorrow. For years, I didn't talk. You should know."

Irina touched his rough hand, and we climbed up the log ladder to our ship deck, but could not sleep.

"I'm not sure that I want to join the Party," I said.

"It's all right," she said, "if you're ready to become a gravedigger."

"Would you marry me if I were one?"

She no longer uttered a word.

❖ ❖ ❖

The next evening we learned that for three winter months he was digging sheer granite, removing the large boulders with crowbars, hammers, and iron rods.

"Why didn't you use dynamite?" I asked.

"Who would give a prisoner dynamite?" He shook his head and laughed like a child. For another three months, they were working in swampland. If you lost consciousness, winter or summer, you were dead—you'd either freeze to death or drown in the swamp.

"I don't want to hear it anymore." Irina winced as if in pain, but we couldn't stop.

"Who was the first to die?" I asked.

"The smart ones—political workers, professors, scientists ... a writer," he frowned as if trying to remember the face of that writer, "...engineers, musicians, a priest." Self-employed peasants and factory workers toiled better, and thus they had better rations and lasted longer.

"You promised to talk about Trotskyites."

He nodded. "They kept dying like flies." By the end of the construction, that Jew and another officer, both with belts crosswise over their shoulders, with brand new medals on their chests, stopped by the still-digging Uncle Peter. The Jew said that they didn't need Marxists but more men such as him. The other officer got funky and yelled, "What are you, crazy!" "Don't worry," said the major, "he's quite deaf," and yelled, "Yeah! The Trotskyites are no good, lazy bums!"

The old man smiled. His only deaf ear was turned toward the military band playing to spur prisoners to work harder. Only one Trotskyite was good, almost like Uncle Peter. At the interrogation, this plowman learned that he was a Troshkyite—that is how he uttered the word. Uncle Peter already knew it was the name of a traitor.

"He was from Ukraine," I said.

"How do you know? Oh, Irina, he's smart!"

"The 'troshky' in Ukrainian means 'a little bit,'" I said. "And who were you?"

"Class enemy, a small exploiter."

"Why?"

"Because I had a partner whom I paid. Two men in black came to our pit at a graveyard. Leather caps, leather jackets, and knee-high boots."

"A uniform for an undertaker."

"Yes," he scowled, "if not for the brown holsters on the side. They asked, 'What's the baby doing here?' 'Playing in the fresh air with a doll, don't you see?' I said. 'My wife died during childbirth.'" He explained to us, "Little Kostya grew on a neighbor's milk, but that day she couldn't take him in." He told the men with pistols, "When Kostya goes with me, she gives us this bottle with her milk." The men in black whispered to each other and took all of them to the NKVD, with the child in Uncle Peter's arms. "They ordered my partner to take the boy to that woman," he said. "I was so glad and said 'Thank you.' They ordered my partner to come back in two hours."

The old man fell silent. After a long pause, he said, "I couldn't let go. My son cried."

His partner ran away from Kostroma that same day, but first, he brought the child to that woman. She thought Uncle Peter would never come back. The boy lived with her for three years. A wooden doll was his favorite toy. Uncle Peter was among those few freed after over-fulfilling their daily quotas. This was a unique Socialist experiment in "re-forging class enemies." The job was done four months ahead of schedule.

The canal named after Stalin was glorified in poetry and prose, music and movies, in newspapers, books, posters, and paintings. A comedy by the famous writer Nikolai Pogodin was devoted to this triumph of socialist re-education. The packaging of the popular cigarette brand named *Belomorkanal* (White-Sea-Baltic-Canal), flaunted a map of it. Newspapers called Moscow the capital of five seas. The whole country rejoiced. Shortly after its completion, Stalin, with the head of the secret police Yezhov and members of Politburo Molotov and Voroshilov, rode the canal on a steamer. Leader probably knew that since the 17th century, every tsar had rejected all the options for constructing it because of the high costs. Stalin found the way to build it in record time. The Main Administration of Corrective Labor Camps (*GULAG*) at first estimated that the project would require 100,000 convicts. Historians say that in twenty months of construction (1931–1933) the same number of inmates died. Some say 170,000 perished; the lowest estimate of the dead came from the KGB archives—11,000.

Since the Soviet Union's collapse, the local historian Yuri Dmitriev and his team have discovered 360 mass graves of the executed builders along the 141-miles long canal. They turned the graves into places of remembrance and began setting up cemeteries for prisoners. For a quarter-century, the Karelian authorities had not shown interest in the remains. On December 13, 2016, they arrested Dmitriev on charges of sexual abuse of his foster daughter Natasha based on an anonymous denunciation. Aggressively questioned, neither she nor her grandmother testified against him. The girl insisted that she loved Dmitriev, considered him her father, and her pictures were taken for the guardianship authorities since she suffered from dystrophy. Petrozavodsk City Court concluded that the photographs were not pornographic. In April 2018, the trial ended with his acquittal. High-ranking officials, not accustomed to losing, could not anticipate such a turn of events, and Karelian Supreme Court overruled the verdict of Petrozavodsk Court. The charges were renewed. After more than a year in prison and international protests, Dmitriev was put in a psychiatric clinic for five months and then detained again. From September to December 2019, monthly, and in February 2020 to the end of March, the tactics of repeatedly adjourning the trial continued. Hearings were often held behind closed doors. Who could have guessed that such a trial would happen almost ninety years after the completion of White-Sea-Baltic-Canal's construction? Yuri Dmitriev, the old man in poor health, prevents the heirs of those whose job was to pull the trigger, from rewriting history.

The Fall of the Adventurer

From time to time Florentyev's daughter called us. Fortunately, like everybody else in town, we didn't have a home phone, but my wife was working in a small paper of the regional timber industry, and they talked about clothing; with me, she discussed Babaevsky's books, three times a Stalin Prize winner. To read this mix of honey, sugar, and syrup within the parameters of Party directives would be a cruel punishment, but luckily, a movie based on one of his jewels helped me to stick to the subject for a few minutes. To the delight of the highly charged editorial audience, in the end, I learned to turn from the happy collective farm idyll to the captured German film with Marika Rokk bathing in a barrel. Unlike the Soligalich milkmaids, the First Secretary's daughter knew the word "erotic" and was quite aroused when I sang the actress's seductive song under the accompaniment of Anna's and Boris Klitza's hysterical giggling. She gasped and laughed as women do only in bed. When I asked her not to tell my wife about my aphrodisiac singing, she murmured, "Yes, of course." My new best friend Elena Protasova vulgarized a charming situation. She came out of her office to say, "Arkady, you're a great singer."

In November 1957, Anna and I became candidates for Party membership. She dreamed of using this achievement for moving to warm places and eating grapes; I was determined to stay here until my book was accomplished. Meanwhile, I'd been gathering material for a lampoon of local Literary Association leaders. In comparison with their swamp of dribbling socialist pathos, Babaevsky's creations were masterpieces. Anna worried that this narcissistic gang with pals in high places would eat me alive. If they were merely three vulgar hacks, I wouldn't be interested in them, but they were also scammers admitting no one to their manger. The only publishing house of the region was under their full control.

"Nearly seventy percent of its royalties," I said, "end up in their pockets."

Anna could not believe it.

"Its accountant copied for me the necessary documents," I said.

"Copies?" Nervous concern lit up her eyes. Neither the *Northern Pravda* nor we had a manual duplicating machine. We heard that Florentyev's office had one, but had never seen such a device.

"She didn't make the copies." I kissed Anna's temple.

"If someone helped her in their print shop," Anna sobered, "then you all could end up in Gulag."

"Don't worry," I said, "these are just amateur photos, not copies."

She cheered up, but after a few seconds gloomily said that I should kiss goodbye to a Party card.

The chairman of the regional Literary Association, novelist Nikitin, controlled all approaches to the Kostroma press, his deputy, Chasovnikov, headed our department of culture, and the executive secretary of the Association, Starshinov, led a similar department at our elder brother—*Northern Pravda*. Thus, they kept the perimeter defense of all possible sources of literary income in the region. The Party did not notice the flaws in art devoted to the implementation of its decisions and was determined to establish a branch of the Soviet Writers' Union instead of this lousy Association. I undermined this effort. In the early summer of 1958, Moscow *Literary Gazette* published my lampoon. I stepped on the regal toes while the workforce of the Propaganda Secretary labored on his article for *Pravda* praising the achievements of my trio. The coincidence was painful for both battling parties, and the full-scale war began. A leading Soviet newspaper definitely goofed something, but its editor, just like Florentyev, was a member of the Central Committee and this complicated the hostilities. Father-of-the-Region accused the paper of publishing politically immature and misleading material and demanded the creation of a commission to investigate the case. The perturbed newspaper, under the rarely appearing section "In the Footsteps of our Reports," insisted that the facts given in the feuilleton were fully confirmed. The battle between the two titans was held without my participation. To pacify the Kostroma lion, I was thrown to the wolves. Without explanation, Elena Protasova moved me from the post of a department supervisor to a writer's job with a decrease in salary. It became clear that at the end of the one-year trial period for my candidacy, the Party would blacklist me and no publication under the sun would hire this outcast, even as a doorman.

In these difficult days, a dark-haired woman with a confident gait approached me at the Kostroma Restaurant; she worked at the regional prosecutor's office and had just returned from Galich. "The district KGB representative visited your friend, my Galich colleague," she said, "and asked him some strange questions about you. We are convinced that this directly related to your skit. We had fun reading it and are ready to help you."

"I was illegally demoted," I said.

"Sue the editor. It's important."

This woman in a prosecutorial suit knew about my railway adventure in detail and said that the criminals had abandoned the cargo train with the stolen lumber on a long stretch in the midst of the forest. The railway track was blocked for hours. A bunch of criminals, including the locomotive driver and train station manager, had been on the run and declared on the nationwide wanted list. Maybe an accomplice on the nearest station used a telephone and a self-propelled handcar to inform those gallows birds on the cargo train that Galich prosecutor called the station. We agreed to meet at the restaurant again in three days.

Encouraged, I filed a claim with the city court. The court refused to consider it. On the way from the courthouse back to work, I met two novice poets from the Teacher Training Institute. They anxiously looked up and down the street, thanked me for the skit, said, "Sorry, you can return to Moscow, but we live here," and disappeared. Some of my colleagues avoided talking with me in the presence of our staff poet and Protasova. Soon she was appointed the deputy editor of *Northern Pravda*. The new editor Ivan Ivanov was not an evil man and did not quarrel with me, but I didn't doubt that after the imminent failure of my Party trial period, he would be told to fire me as non–Party scum. A couple of times nervous Ivanov said, "You cannot sue a newspaper. It's like suing the Party." To continue with my lawsuit, I needed to stay in Kostroma, but, by order of high authorities, he kept me busy with out-of-town assignments.

I appealed the municipal court's decision in the regional court. For three hours, its employees kept passing by me as if I were not there. I pretended to study criminal code when an agitated clerk warned me that no one would talk to me. My case wasn't subject to judicial review, she explained in a quivering voice. My guardian angel in the prosecutorial jacket recommended complaining to her office. One day my wife and I came to the restaurant at the agreed time. She was sitting with a colleague. We didn't know him and, just in case, tried to slip past their table, when she said to my retreating back, "Please sit down with us. This is my friend. He's been working on your case."

"People now shun me like a leper," I said.

She stared grimly at a menu.

"The Regional Court also refused to hear my case," I said.

"We know," the man in uniform said.

"What do these two little stars in your collar tabs mean?" Irina asked him.

"They mean that we won't become big bosses soon," he said.

My guardian angel thoughtfully poked her fork at her plate and remarked gloomily, "This undermines confidence in the legal system. The Party has jurisdiction over cases of dismissal and reinstatement of senior officials."

"What an achievement!" I exclaimed. "They consider me a senior official. The supervisor of a department, which employs only the supervisor himself."

"The issue of your reinstatement lies outside the purview of the court system," her colleague said. "Since 1928, there is a list of positions that aren't subject to judicial review. The Chair of the Regional Court informed me that the department's supervisor position in a newspaper is on this list."

Irina clearly pronounced, "Bitches."

"Does this mean that I have to get out of here before the end of my probationary period in the Party?"

"Probably," he said. "We never dealt with such a case."

"Finally, this non–Party bastard became a member of the Party's *nomenklatura*," I said.

"I think this law will soon be revised," guessed my guardian angel. She was optimistic. The practice, with some softening of the Party control during the last years of Mikhail Gorbachev's rule, remained in force for 32 more years, until the collapse of the Soviet Union.

Neither the two prosecutors nor I thought of seeking help from a defense lawyer. That occupation was a joke: prosecutors and judges, as a rule, ignored their presence in a case. I attended a district court case where the judge simply refused to listen to the counsel of the murderer. The majority of defense advocates were Jews. I never saw a Jewish judge in Russia, and only once did I see a Jew in a prosecutor's uniform. He sat in front of me in the Kostroma Restaurant. His colleague's pretty face reflected guilt. "Don't worry about the KGB," she said, "at least, we stopped this nonsense. They aren't interested in you anymore."

We were gravely consuming our pork chops when the door opened, and all heroes of my lampoon saw me chatting friendly with two prosecutors. Fear froze on their faces. I triumphed and roared, "At a time like this I'd love to be an executioner with an ax."

The novelist was the first to come to his senses and, passing by us, said threateningly "So, so..." They went into a small room, adjacent to the main dining room, and closed the door. The next day, the Second Secretary's Assistant called me on the carpet. On the way to his office, I heard a familiar bass voice saying through the wide open door, "In short, he's not our man."

Probably my fellow trawler, the Propaganda Department's head, was alluding to my Jewish heritage in a politically correct manner. When I entered the scene, he said, "We've become aware that you're pestering government agencies to confuse a perfectly clear case."

I couldn't utter a word. Hateful men in black jackets looked at me like that rat on the day of my arrival in Kostroma. My lips quivered. I turned around and left the office. A cacophony of indignant voices accompanied my escape from the scaffold.

The next morning, my new boss Ivanov said, "Arkady, don't make your situation more difficult than it already is."

"I just didn't want to get bogged down in the mud."

"You have insulted four prominent Party workers," he sighed. He was not looking for a fight. "You're to leave on a new assignment tomorrow morning for ten days. Your seat to Soligalich is already reserved."

I blurted out, "Another ten-day exile."

Only when I returned to the editorial room did I understand that, in fact, black jackets, without knowing it, were helping me to say a last goodbye to some friends in and around Soligalich. They could not know that after the killing of Rail I unsuccessfully tried to go there but surely knew that I had recently reported from there. I no longer perceived this new assignment as an unintentional gift from Comrade Florentyev.

The Most Dangerous Assignment

Sending me to Soligalich again meant only one thing—something nasty was awaiting me in the old northern town. It would be better for the young newspaper to send me to a place where its correspondents had not traveled so far. Determined to survive this long flight, I bought the over-salted herring again. Approaching the ramp of the AN-2, I held it, wrapped in the *Northern Pravda,* in one hand and a small suitcase in the other. A broad-shouldered man in a long shabby cloak serenely flopped down on the unfolded metal seat in front of me, laid his shotgun on the floor, sniffed the air, and bellowed, "You can't get such fish in Soligalich for love or money."

"Your town has been known for good salted fish since time immemorial. This one is really bad," I said and extended the tail of the already half-unwrapped medication to my traveling companion. "Like it? I won't be able to eat all of it myself."

"Well, then give me a piece." A smile appeared on his weather-beaten face. He extracted from his colorless cloak a folding knife with a wooden handle and snapped off the herring's tail. "Would you like some bread?"

"No thanks, I have to beat this enemy on an empty stomach." The herring's white eye glared at me ominously. My companion put the faded tail on a thick piece of rye bread and with gusto took a big bite. I began slowly chewing small piece after a small piece. It tasted as if it grew up in Soligalich's ancient salt mines. We were several minutes in the air when he said, "Maybe you had enough? Your face has turned blue."

His compassion didn't stop me.

When we landed in Soligalich, and the strong owner of the shotgun carried my feeble body, a displeased dog of a questionable breed greeted us deafeningly, but as I lay on the only bench on the edge of the green landing field he tried to make friends with me. An hour later, he was disappointed with an emergency vehicle when its driver was putting me in it. The vehicle—a barely alive gelding harnessed to a creaking dray *telega* with no springs—ignored my new buddy. My singular thought was—this magic herring ruined the evil plans of the First Kostroma Secretary. Stretched at full length in the straw, with a pain in my heart, I groaned and moaned on every rut and pothole of the road's petrified dirt. The driver kept turning his head back. He acted like a soccer fan eagerly expecting a long-awaited goal. Unlike the dog, there was not a grain of sympathy in his face. Irritated by his fascination with the impending end of my life, I ignored the pain and suggested he remove the off-white band with a faded red cross from his sleeve and instead paint crosses on both sides of his worn-out gelding. He took offense but stopped looking at me.

⟨ ⟨ ⟨

The entire hospital staff—two doctors, two nurses and a radiologist, all in white coats—attended a consultation held following my arrival. They were good and caring. After using their stethoscopes, the doctors gave me a large white pill called validolum. Almost without interrupting each other, they explained that this wonderful drug had a calming effect on the central nervous system and treated hysteria, neurosis, and airsickness. I had all the conditions they mentioned. The nurses put me on a stretcher again and carried me to the bathroom four yards away. Not letting me move a finger, they stripped me naked and laid me in a wooden tub of preheated water that the radiologist was bringing in tin buckets from somewhere on the ground floor. Armed with flax bast and brown laundry soap, the women ignored my deathbed plea to cool the water a little and scraped me zealously. Finally, they extracted my limp body from the bath and, with the help of the muscular radiologist, carried it to a room with a dozen sleeping patients. The challenging procedure made me think that I would be able to withstand severe trials of life. That was indeed a long, tough day.

In the morning, nearby shooting and rounds of applause awakened me; a gang of flies was busily roving across my face in search of fun and food. Several patients with fly swatters excitedly hunted careless flies. Swatters, old soles nailed to sticks, were producing the sounds of rifle fire. The radiologist entered the room and placed a similar murder weapon on the wooden windowsill by my bed. A chunky man with a husky voice and trembling hands asked, "Why are they all scurrying 'round you? Are'ye dying or something?"

"I don't know; my heart hurts. Can't even turn my head towards you."

He walked away saying under his breath, "Some boss, I suppose."

The doctor, he was the hospital's director, told me to stay outside, and a broad-hipped muscular nurse helped me to walk down to a bed in a tiny garden at the intersection of two mangled dirt roads. Each step caused pain. I lay motionless in the shadow of a thoroughly dusty birch when a hoarse voice from behind the bush confirmed the well-known fact: "These Jews will always find the best place for themselves."

When I managed to look into the bushes, he was already gone. The next day I felt a bit better and during the mealtime attempted to identify the man. I chose two lumberjacks with raspy voices. The grey-headed one, with trembling hands, was friendly and talkative. During the day, he abandoned me several times to approach the gate with the same love song, "Oh, bitch! Oh, whore! If she won't come today, I'll kill this fucking tart!" He wrapped this serenade in words related to various parts of the human body and their functions.

"You miss her," I said softly.

He looked at me intently as if checking if I were sneering at him.

The next day he said, "The nurse said you were a correspondent," and scraped the birch with his fingernail.

"Yes, I am."

"So now you can write about me. I'm Anton Baranov, boys call me Baran." He shook his gray curls and told me the story of his life. And what a life it was! His first arrest was for an armed robbery in Mytishchi, near Moscow, at the age of 13. I knew the scabby town. His mother did not come to the court; the judge said that the fault lay with her and sent the boy to an orphanage. The police had it in for her for some reason. Anton did not know what it was. He never saw his mother again. He didn't like her anyway.

"What weapon did you use?" I asked.

My new mate again looked anxiously at the wooden gate, sighed, and said, "A sharpened screwdriver." The sigh had nothing to do with that screwdriver. A year later, the 14-year-old was back in the dock for hooliganism. The orphanage director demanded a political verdict because he had painted a longer beard and side curls on the portrait of Felix Dzerzhinsky.

I giggled through pain and asked, "Why?"

"Because he was a Jew."

Through laughing and groaning, I squeezed out, "Anton, could you read then?"

"No offense," he said, "the literate boys told me that this Jew invented labor colonies for neglected children."

"Historians say that this Bolshevik was a descendant of Polish gentry."

"It's bullshit."

"Do you know who he was?"

"Lenin's crony."

I told my interlocutor that a year from now, in 1959, his sculpture would be installed on the Dzerzhinsky Square in front of the KGB headquarters.

"Whores!" muttered he and, with relish, spat into the dusty grass. "The judge returned me to the orphanage and said to the director, 'Your institution is like a prison, anyway.'"

Anton liked his appellation *Baran* (Ram), though he didn't realize that it fit him. A year later, he went to a juvenile camp in Siberia for seven years, this time for yet another robbery. At eighteen, Baran was transferred to a regular camp. After serving his term, this repeat offender had no right to live in his hometown and many other cities. He began jumping from one subject to another, his eyes now and then rested on the gate. I thought, "He's crazy."

"I could make a good soldier," Anton said and looked with disgust at his trembling hands.

"Why?"

"Because the Russian soldier is the best in the world. He can live in shit, eat shit, and use his piss pump as medication. Sometimes you land a blow with an ax on the leg, you piss on the wound, and after a week, it's as if nothing had happened."

"It's because you weren't given a choice."

"What choice? Between an electrical and a gasoline chainsaw? Both will shake the hell out of you. Both kick back right into you, choose any place—from the chest to the balls. The two-handed saw was better."

He reminded me of Ivan Kotov, only Rail was perfectly sane and dreamed of Siberia; Anton Baranov hated it and described the Siberian frosts in unflattering terms. "Arms get stiff, and you don't know how to warm up later." He believed that at the age of 22 he was the best lumberjack he had ever seen. "I could do many tricks with an ax and a crosscut saw," he recalled proudly. I thought of Rail's professional pride. Anton Ram didn't want to feed Siberian mosquitoes with his blood anymore, signed a contract, and came here, to Kostroma Region, to feed local gnats. By now he was used to them and did not suffer as much from their attention as in the first years of his logging career. After our prolonged conversation, the romantic Ram caught himself and went to the gate again to stare at the road and at the impenetrable wildwood surrounding it.

Once he boasted, "I knew guys who would kill just for the fun of it."

"How did you survive with them?"

"That's easy. Just learn quickly to eat shit."

"My boss will never allow me to write about you. Where have you ever read something like that?"

"Then you also eat shit," he said and returned to his favorite tune, with a sinking voice, "So, where's this whore?"

In the end, she arrived on a rattling cargo cart without boards, with a daughter he hadn't ever mentioned, and with goodies in a few bags.

"You look like your dad," I said.

Anton embraced them both. I never saw such happy faces. The wife put her hand on his trembling fingers on her hip.

"We live in a faraway plot," the girl said, "and were waiting for someone to bring us to Soligalich."

Her mother returned to the drayman and tried to put crumpled money into his hand. He jerked his hand away and asked, "When back?"

"Tomorrow morning," said Baran. "They will stay the night in the stable. The doctor promised me."

I advised Baran to ask the good doctor to help him find another job. "He treats all local bosses here," I said.

After four days of laying around and doing nothing, I could finally compete in the murder of innocent flies, though with ridiculous slowness. The hospital director looked at me reproachfully, "Sudden movements are contraindicated for you."

I promised to behave and asked him to discharge me. Earlier that day I had thrown my priceless validolum pill over the picket fence.

"Let's talk about it in a couple of days." He hesitated, then added, "Important people are interested in your health." The director scratched his disheveled head and asked how I awakened such a passionate interest in myself in the authorities. I didn't want to put him in an awkward position, did not tell him that the KGB was interested in the content of my conversations with the local loggers, and told him only about the feuilleton.

"I had to be rude to them," he said.

Baran, he followed me everywhere, said, "Whores."

Years later, a chiropractor in Richmond, British Columbia, told me that extended exposure to vibration leads to a circulatory disorder of the extremities. We were cutting down two trees in his vast garden with an electric chainsaw that was as light as a feather.

❖ ❖ ❖

The next day I had a guest. My old pal, the Soligalich *Komsomol* Secretary, visited me with a small wicker basket full of little wild strawberries he had gathered that morning. Ivan shook my hand. "Kostroma is looking for you; I've heard all sorts of speculation. They asked me to check if you're really ill."

I didn't burden him with the details of the war against me and said, "Ivan, I don't want to ruin your career. Loggers have complained that, despite the release from imprisonment, they had no right to leave the forest even now, in 1958. Five years after Stalin's death."

My wiry friend shifted from foot to foot, staring at the trees and the skies, chewed his fat lips, and finally said, "After you refused to talk with the big shots, somebody in the Regional Party Committee decided that you would talk only with me." When all of a sudden he asked me to go with him on a bear hunt, my heart stopped hurting. "Ivan, you're the best doctor!" I cried and slapped him on the shoulder.

"Don't tell anybody," he said shyly.

✦ ✦ ✦

The hospital staff was very good to me; they knew a lot about local medicinal herbs, but it is my professional duty as an objective reporter to stress that the hospital's x-ray equipment looked as if it had been made before the discovery of x-rays. The radiologist was in high demand. He kept sharpening medical needles, syringes, and repairing beds, kitchenware, chairs, shoes, the wooden fence, and the ambulance cart. His fly swatters served as the primary medical equipment and effective psychotherapeutic procedure. As a radiologist, this husband of the chief nurse was receiving better pay. Otherwise, it was a regular two-story hospital with two adjoining one-room wards, for males and females, and a treatment room on the same top floor. On the ground floor were utility rooms, the director's office, a large kitchen, next to it a drying room for firewood and an x-ray room with the plumbing, carpentry, and other tools.

The medical and technological advances of the 21st century did not bypass the hospital. In 2014, I found an internet posting inviting a gynecologist to work in Soligalich where "the countryside is so beautiful." When I was there, the hospital's director, just like the radiologist, also was a jack-of-all-trades—a gynecologist, an obstetrician, a surgeon, general practitioner, pediatrician, pathologist, and the medical examiner. He kept his word and three days later, discharged me after receiving my word not fly in the near future, not ride in jolting timber trucks on bumpy forest roads, and see him before leaving the town by bus. The 95 kilometer country road to Galich was still dry.

✦ ✦ ✦

In the evening, the Secretary took me for a health-improving stroll. We silently walked the petrified unpaved streets. That northern white July night my nervousness of recent months almost disappeared. The sleeping town looked more attractive than in winter, albeit a bit spooky under the dim moon. The white circle of age-old birch trees surrounding the pale ghost of the razed-to-the-ground monastery did not bother my friend. It did not belong to his world. Ivan loved his new world; he was a part of it and, with all his revolutionary convictions, he despised the ruins of the past. His life and his job were to look forward. The decent *Komsomol* leader trusted the predictions of a bright future for everyone, with no exception. He pointed at an old birch and broke our comfortable silence. "At night the branches hanging lower than at sunset."

I nodded at the whitish halo embracing five skeletal onions of the ruined church domes. "For every believer, any other religion is full of insoluble contradictions."

"Yes," Ivan said. "A good point."

"What an irony! We ruined all churches to worship this human."

"I cried when he died," my companion said.

"In 1953, millions cried. He was our God."

"Even after the exposure of his personality cult, in 1956, I couldn't get over it for a year."

"He used our ideology to cement his grip on the country. Some officials still miss him, even now, in 1958."

"Marxism isn't a faith, it's a science." Ivan sighed and shook his head.

"Some officials in Kostroma still miss him," I said.

"I turned thirty, and it's time to leave the *Komsomol*."

"What did the Party offer you? After all, you do belong to..."— I almost said, "its unsinkable bureaucracy," but checked myself in time—"...its *nomenklatura*, don't you?"

"A propaganda instructor of the District Committee or a collective farm's head, or Chief Forester. What do you think?"

"You aren't fit for bureaucratic hassles," I said. "Farms are dying; the forest is facing a better future. You know it inside out. Chief Forester is a beautiful job."

He said nothing. At my little hotel's door, Ivan asked, "Have you hunted before? Can you shoot?"

"In the summer military camp for university students. Fired a rifle, a machine-gun, and threw a training grenade at our sergeant."

Ivan laughed. "Half a mile from here, there is a large field of oats," he said. "Bears—we call them oat bears—come to the field at dawn to feast on the crop. I saw a couple of flattened areas."

"How will we drag him to your house?"

"I'll go home for a wheelbarrow."

"Maybe we better bring it with us?"

"No, it's bad luck."

"I'm amazed," I said, shaking my head. "This Marxist is superstitious."

He gave an embarrassed smile.

◈ ◈ ◈

The starless sky was the nightly pale blue when we were already on our way. I proudly tinkered with a shotgun belt on my shoulder and wondered whether I should prop its barrel against some fallen tree or rest my elbow against the ground.

"They smell the scent of man," Ivan said and took me around the bear's grazing land, along the forest edge; a couple of wind-fallen trees looked impassable even for a mammoth. "Maybe here?" I suggested.

"Speak softly," he whispered, "and best of all keep quiet. I've already chosen a good one."

I shut up and continued thinking of a fallen tree thick enough to stop a tank. Finally, Ivan said, "Here it is."

I couldn't believe my eyes. The sad tree stood apart from the others, and any angry animal could come to it from all sides. Six short steps made of young stumps were already nailed to the stem. At an altitude of three yards, a few branches dotted with leaves laid across two thick limbs.

"Climb up there!" he whispered. I did so with the enthusiasm of a man sentenced to die on this scaffold. Somewhere on the edge of the pale sky glowed the familiar morning star, whose name I couldn't recall. We peered into the field, scrutinized the silence, and heard only the breeze caressing the heads of oats. I caressed my shotgun endlessly; it probably couldn't stand me anymore and slipped out of my sweaty grasp. In horror, I watched its unpredictable flight through the branches until it hit the ground. A shot rang out. It was heard beyond the universe. A flock of small birds with a loud squeak rose high above the field.

Ivan looked at me with deep compassion and went down to the ground. Silently.

I followed him, smiling miserably. "You mean bears won't show up today?"

Two days later, before my bus departure, Ivan reddened when he asked, "Is it true that you're a Jew?"

"Yes."

"I'm proud to have a friend who appears in national newspapers."

He still shook my hand vigorously when I said, "You taught this Jew a lot. I will always remember that trees get stressed like people."

◈ ◈ ◈

Upon my return from Soligalich, I filed a notice of resignation and, by law, kept brushing up the writings of my colleagues for another two weeks. Editor-in-chief, hiding his eyes from me, said that the Regional Party Committee did not mind if I continued to work in the newspaper. It was sad. He knew I had to depart before they could deny me Party membership.

To say goodbye, Irina and I invited some good people to Kostroma

Restaurant. We went there before the agreed time to reserve a table in the party room. We passed the main dining room where two silent tramps were searching for remnants of food on the uncleared tables and plates and entered that small room. Inside it sat only one person—Nikitin, the leading figure of my satire, who froze, unable to pull a spoon out of his mouth. After the novelist managed to do so, he said, "Fifty rubles and you're dead. Gone for good."

"Alik, please, knock him out. For free," Irina said.

Nikitin did not finish the soup, swore obscenities and left.

Two hours later, at the beginning of our little party, Zoya Tikhonovna and the gravedigger had difficulties in figuring out what was going on. In anticipation of possible complications, I sat between them. My wife was tirelessly filling their glasses with vodka, but not mine. The old woman was in a restaurant for the first time in her life; even the shot glasses with a foot and a stem were new to her, but there was something more important in the air. She seemed to bend under her weightless white lace shawl; he straightened up like a dry stick. Both scowled askance at the couple in a strange dark uniform, at their insignia with a shield and two swords, and barely touched the food.

Uncle Peter whispered in my ear, "Why the sabers? I have never seen such a uniform."

I said aloud, so everybody would hear and learn, "That's because they sent you to build the White Sea Canal without a trial."

"It was a crime," said the pretty prosecutor.

The old man froze for a moment, his head recoiled, he unbuttoned the top button of his faded shirt, looked at me inquiringly, and began to laugh loudly. I have never seen him so uncontrollably laughing. His face flushed. When Uncle Peter stopped laughing, he rose from his chair, his Adam's apple clearly showing swallowing, and said in a choked voice, almost whispering, "It wasn't a crime, it was a murder. He killed people every day. Thank you, Arkady, I better go home."

I started yelling, "You people simply haven't understood each other! She called the construction of that canal a crime, not you, not why he sent you there! Don't get angry, Uncle Peter, this prosecutor is your friend. They saved me from the KGB handling!"

"Prosecutor?" Bewildered, he put his hand on my knee. "Two prosecutors?"

"Yes," the second prosecutor flinched as if under pain. "We came to Kostroma to fight crime, killers, and bandits."

"You know what?" Now I couldn't control my emotions. "It isn't that simple. Where I grew up, it wasn't a crime to steal from the state, but for many, it was a crime to steal from a neighbor. Once I stole a Russian dictionary from a neighbor and still remember it; he didn't need it anymore, he was killed in the war; we criminals, we were patriots, we worshiped Stalin." Why did you start talking devil knows what?—flashed through my inflamed brain. "How could we know that he kept shooting the dying at that canal in the back of their heads, thousands of them? It's difficult to understand what our laws are about."

"And for me," said Anna harshly, my only unreasonable colleague who dared to come here. She pulled out of a bag under the table two bottles of vodka, and set them firmly on the table, next to one almost empty one and a bottle of dry wine, almost full. "And, my dear Arkady, this is I who should be angry."

"We tried to help Arkady and failed," the man in uniform said. "We're trying to help our country get rid of lawlessness."

"Look at him, people!" Anna clapped her hands. "Another Jewish idealist with sad eyes trying to help humanity! How old are you?"

He muttered brokenly, "I'm 34."

"Is he a Jew?" The now shocked Zoya Tikhonovna whispered in my ear, "I never saw a Jew."

"My husband is a Jew," said Irina calmly.

The old woman looked at me almost in horror.

"Alas," I said and gave a hug to the drunken old lady.

"Even among the Jews there are some good people." My giggling wife tried to comfort Zoya Tikhonovna while pouring some more vodka for her, Uncle Peter, and not forgetting about herself. Now my pretty guardian angel began loudly laughing and said, "This vodka is perfect. It's better than Stoli."

She was walking to the old man to clink glasses with him when Anna said, "You should be sent to dig a new canal, right in your black uniform."

"Why me?" asked the smiling angel.

"Because you're drinking an illegal moonshine disguised as a bottle of vodka smuggled to this restaurant. But even if you apply to my body the Stalinist methods of interrogation, even on the rack, I'll never tell you who supplied me with this magic potion."

"I know where you got this poison," I smirked, "but I won't betray my friend."

Now we all laughed. The old man also laughed, seemingly relieved. Anna Galun got up, unsteadily walked around the table, stopped behind his chair, put her hands on Uncle Peter's broad shoulders and said, "These three Muscovites are cranks; they expect that something good can happen because Stalin isn't present in our national anthem anymore and the prosecutors abolished their shoulder straps. I rely only on vodka."

"Our new national anthem isn't present either," said my wife cheerfully.

"They are working on it," I said.

"For five years?" asked my wife.

"Stalin's heirs want to play it safe," I said. "They don't want to end up digging another canal."

"This is so true," said the old digger.

"It's a pity he didn't get a chance to turn the Siberian rivers back," I said. "In school, the geography teacher explained to us that to divert water from the Siberian rivers to Kazakhstan and Uzbekistan, the length of the new canals will exceed the length of the White Sea Canal tenfold."

The stubborn old man objected. "Where are they to get so many prisoners?"

"In China," my wife advised.

"It would guarantee the digging job for the entire Chinese population," I said.

"It's impossible to reverse even a little creek," said the old digger and undid another button.

Zoya Tikhonovna burst out laughing.

The conversation was getting too serious, and I described the recent funny scene with the novelist. Uncle Peter did not react to it, Zoya Tikhonovna gasped and straightened her shawl on her shoulders; my favorite prosecutors were not amused either. They grinned only when Anna said, "Our writers are really detached from the Soviet masses. A bottle of vodka is the normal price for such a humanitarian service."

When the old woman and the digger grew accustomed to this strange company, Irina surprised everyone by thanking Comrade Stalin for the New Year's gift.

"What?" asked Zoya Tikhonovna to my wife's delight.

"A warm sheepskin coat," explained Irina. "You saw it."

I had to clarify that my parents bought it in December of 1952, before the anticipated expulsion of Jews to Siberia.

"I love the Jews," said the pretty prosecutor and kissed her colleague on the cheek.

"This drunken woman," explained my wife, "wants to repeat my mistake and ruin her career."

The "drunken woman" pointed out, "Where else can you find a prosecutor who blushes and shakes with embarrassment when a beautiful woman kisses him?"

Zoya Tikhonovna shook her head disapprovingly, but smiled again, when the whole company heard, "Would you marry me?"

"These Jews lured us to this city." Now my wife was shaking her head disapprovingly. "With your waist, you should've worked in the Moscow House of Models."

"I don't like high heels," explained the failed model and cheekily put her hand on her colleague's knee.

The red-faced prosecutor put his hand on hers and suddenly changed the subject. "Your feuilleton was necessary for our country."

"Yes, that was the best thing Alik ever wrote." My wife supported him. "Thanks to this feuilleton, we are returning home."

"This is due to my ignorance and naiveté," I said. "How could I know that Florentyev decided to create a branch of the Writers' Union in Kostroma?"

At the end of our drunken orgy, Uncle Peter solemnly pronounced the only farewell toast, "Let the prosecutors not get angry at the old man, but I will say this: Arkady, don't look for the truth there in Moscow. As long as he lies next to Lenin in Mausoleum, you will not find the truth in Russia. While still young, be happy and live life to your joy."

"Thank you very much, Uncle Peter!" I said. "Moscow will always have bread."

◈ ◈ ◈

Two years later, in 1960, when, on the orders of Nikita Khrushchev, the embalmed Stalin was resettled in a nearby grave next to the Kremlin wall, I thought of Uncle Peter, Zoya Tikhonova, Rail, and Anna. They would certainly consider this relocation as a step in the right direction.

Index